THE ENIGMA OF
SISTER MARY LEO

THE ENIGMA OF
SISTER MARY LEO

*The story behind New Zealand's
most famous singing teacher*

MARGARET LOVELL-SMITH
with
LUISA SHANNAHAN

FOREWORD BY DAME MALVINA MAJOR, DBE

REED

The author was given access to the Sisters of Mercy Archives and interviewed Sisters who knew Sister Mary Leo. While the finished manuscript was submitted for comment to the Auckland Mercy Congregation, this work is not an official biography commissioned by that Congregation. The opinions in it are those of the author.

Published by Reed Books, a division of Reed Publishing (NZ) Ltd, 39 Rawene Rd, Birkenhead, Auckland. Associated companies, branches and representatives throughout the world.

This book is copyright. Except for the purpose of fair reviewing, no part of this publication may be reproduced or transmitted in any form or by any means, electronic or mechanical, including photocopying, recording, or any information storage and retrieval system, without permission in writing from the publisher. Infringers of copyright render themselves liable to prosecution.

Copyright © Margaret Lovell-Smith 1998
Front cover photograph © Anthony Henry
Back cover photograph © New Zealand Herald

The author asserts her moral rights in the work.

ISBN 0 7900 0652 9

First published 1998

Cover designed by Michele Stutton.
Text designed by Sunny H. Yang.
Front cover photograph by Anthony Henry.
Frontispiece: A studio portrait of Kathleen Niccol taken about 1921.
    (Joan Crompton née Harker.)

CONTENTS

Foreword by Dame Malvina Major, DBE	7
Preface	9
1. Kathleen Niccol 1895–1923	11
2. To the Convent 1923–1930	44
3. The Apprenticeship 1930–1950	65
4. The First Stars 1950–1960	85
5. The Emerging Celebrity 1956–1963	105
6. The Era of the Second Vatican Council 1964–1972	127
7. The Teacher	151
8. A National Icon 1973–1979	169
9. Fame and Frailty 1980–1989	188
Afterword — The Dame Sister Mary Leo Scholarship	203
Appendix	206
Acknowledgements	207
Notes	211
Select Bibliography	220
Index	225

Foreword by Dame Malvina Major, DBE

Dame Sister Mary Leo, mentor, psychologist, friend and teacher, was a woman whose vibrant personality and teaching methods influenced and guided me throughout my career.

I cannot claim that our association was smooth or without a clash of wills. She understood me superbly and dared, for example, to risk my performance in the Melbourne *Sun* Aria competition, when I was homesick and in low spirits. In order to make me angry and so perform better she reprimanded me on the pretext that I was an ungrateful student who didn't appreciate the effort she had made to be with me in Australia. The full story of this incident and its outcome is related in chapter six.

Sister Leo was a perfectionist and when she commanded, we obeyed. On several occasions I recall getting a speeding ticket en route to the music school to have a pre-concert warm-up. Sister always insisted we saw her before a concert, so she could give us last minute instructions and scrutinise our evening wear. One evening, one of the older, rather robust girls had wrapped a bandage of sorts around herself to conceal her ample bosom. Sister immediately spotted that something was different. 'What have you done to yourself?' she asked. Our colleague replied, 'Oh Sister, I'm so big!' Without a word Sister took the scissors from the drawer, unzipped the girl's dress and cut the bandage. 'Don't ever conceal what God has given you! I want to see that first when you walk on stage tonight.'

Sister always said that life's experiences, both good and bad, would add a dimension to our artistic capabilities. The actual timbre of the voice would develop, and our emotional capacity grow, enabling us to protray the heroines in opera with more understanding. We were encouraged to sing lieder, because these songs taught us how to tell a story.

Our personal problems and worries were dealt with by Sister before our lessons began. She believed one's mind and body had to be free of tension in order to learn.

I found this biography nostalgic reading, with an accurate account of Sister Mary Leo's teaching methods. This in turn reminded me of Sister Francis Xavier's piano accompaniments, and the comment by James Robertson — 'She plays like a full orchestra.'

The Enigma of Sister Mary Leo tells the story of a remarkable woman whose rare gift and colourful character are now woven into the fabric of New Zealand's cultural history.

I am honoured to have been given the opportunity to write the foreword, and I thank and congratulate everyone involved — especially Luisa Shannahan, who had the foresight to initiate the project, and Margaret Lovell-Smith, who brought the book to fruition.

Dame Malvina Major, DBE
July 1998

Preface

Ten years ago, while attending a lecture on New Zealand music at the University of Canterbury, I was startled to hear the lecturer state that the first professional musicians who came to New Zealand were male, secular, and settled in the urban areas. My immediate reaction was, what about the amazing female religious musicians who, since the mid-nineteenth century, lived and worked in rural and urban New Zealand?

This incident prompted my research into the music-teaching nuns who came to New Zealand from 1850 as missionaries, bringing with them western musical traditions, expertise in keyboard, strings and vocal teaching — not to mention the instruments with which to teach — and who set up music rooms and music schools the length and breadth of the country to earn income for the support of their communities.

Although over this period in our history there have been numerous teaching orders of nuns with many outstanding teachers of music, the four Congregations of the Sisters of Mercy have produced the largest numbers, with Dame Sister Mary Leo, of the Auckland Congregation, being the most famous of their members.

I felt qualified to undertake the research. I was raised in the practices and culture of the Catholic Church, I had personal experience of Sister Mary Leo as a teacher and friend, I knew the complexities of successfully teaching the accomplishments of the human voice, and I had both time and academic opportunities.

My entire education and musical training had been at the hands of the Sisters of Mercy in Greymouth, Blenheim and Wellington. As a 13-year-old I attended Mina Foley's Blenheim concert (part of her triumphant New Zealand tour) and was overwhelmed by the sheer beauty and elegance of her performance. I vividly recall being unable to sleep that night. Her singing triggered in me a deep artistic and spiritual response and became my inspiration to continue pursuing the vocal art. At age 16, I began singing lessons with Mina's teacher, Sister Mary Leo.

In 1976 I began teaching singing in Christchurch. Sister Mary Leo encouraged and mentored me in 1981 as I moved from being an amateur to a professional teacher. Like so many of her pupils, I felt I had a special relationship with her.

With the encouragement of the then Head of Music at Canterbury, David Sell, and with the approval of the Auckland Sisters of Mercy, I extended my research into Sister's life immediately after attending her funeral in May 1989. I began by devising a questionnaire and sending it out to her pupils who were known to have worked professionally as vocal performers or teachers. A total of 66 were sent. The number was extraordinary. When one considers this statistic, as well as the thousands of people Sister taught over her long career who have enjoyed their singing and music in their communities as amateurs, one can only marvel at the legacy she left.

My research was a labour of love. But another love intervened and took precedence: that of establishing the National Academy of Singing and Dramatic Art in Christchurch. I no longer had time to invest in the book. As the centenary of Sister's birth approached (and in true Catholic fashion), I began to feel guilty that the project had not been brought to completion in published form.

When Margaret Lovell-Smith approached me about completing the research and writing a biography, I was delighted and relieved. Margaret's qualities of thoroughness and professionalism as a historian and her dedication in completing the work have resulted in this publication. It has been my pleasure to collaborate and comment on drafts.

I sincerely thank and acknowledge the University of Canterbury and the Auckland Congregation of the Sisters of Mercy for initial research funding; as well as the generous support of Maree Williamson for her countless hours of typing and editing, my family, David Sell, Lyndsay Freer, Sister Joan Hopkinson RSM, Sister Eileen Burrell RSM, Sister Marcienne Kirk RSM, Maureen Smith, Rhys and John Bean, Mina Foley, Fr Paul Shannahan SM, Fr James Shannahan, Fr Michael O'Meaghan SM, Helen Clausen, Betty and Claude Carter, Jacqueline Driscoll, Elizabeth Steel, Margaret Shackel, Brigid and Dick Sullivan, and Sister's pupils who answered the questionnaire and gave interviews.

Luisa Shannahan
May 1998

CHAPTER ONE

KATHLEEN NICCOL

1895–1923

When Dame Sister Mary Leo died in May 1989, an obituary writer summed up her life with the headline, 'The Enigma of a Famous Nun'.[1] Behind the headline lay a question. How was it possible for a religious sister who had lived a life of poverty, chastity and obedience, largely behind convent walls, to become an internationally renowned teacher of singing?

Widespread recognition of Sister Mary Leo's ability as a singing teacher began in 1950, when her pupil Mina Foley became a New Zealand phenomenon and pushed her teacher's name into the limelight. Sister Mary Leo's prominence grew in the 1960s when her pupils won every Mobil Song Quest, and then crossed the Tasman to win the Melbourne *Sun* aria competition three years in a row. Two pupils in particular, Dame Kiri Te Kanawa and Dame Malvina Major, went on to become household names, known and loved throughout the opera world.

Sister Mary Leo's reputation as the best singing teacher in New Zealand was firmly established. Pupils flocked to learn from her, international stars visited her, and honours were bestowed on her: an MBE in 1963 and a DBE a decade later.

This biography seeks to explain the enigma of Dame Sister Mary Leo. How did this teaching sister become so successful, so well known and so widely loved? The answer is not to be found in any single factor. Rather, it is to be found in Sister Mary Leo's whole life story, beginning with the characteristics she inherited from her family — on her father's side the Niccols, on her mother's the Cannells. Answers are also found in the philosophy of the Sisters of Mercy, the religious order she joined as a mature 28-year-old, and the training and support she received from her religious community. Finally, one cannot overlook the individual spark of genius that made her such a great teacher.

To write the life story of a religious sister who denied self in order to devote herself to God's service, who saw her own past as negligible, who did not keep diaries or write self-revelatory letters, poses some challenges. The main source of information on the early part of Sister Mary Leo's life — or Kathleen Niccol, as she was then — is a series of interviews recorded with her younger sister Jessie many years later. By the time Jessie was interviewed, her elder sister was a nun of many years' standing and a famous singing teacher. It is perhaps not surprising, then, that many of Jessie's recollections illustrate Kathleen's deep devotion to the Catholic faith, her great musical ability, and her inherent love of teaching.

Listening to the recorded interviews it is clear that Jessie has a strong dramatic instinct and a gift for story-telling. Some caution is obviously necessary when relying on verbatim conversations from years gone by, yet there is a sincerity and frankness about Jessie's stories, and where photographs and written records exist they bear out her memories. The picture Jessie paints of Kathleen is a balanced one, in which the Sister Mary Leo of later years is already discernible. The older sister she describes is bossy, fussy, independent, uncompromising, pious, strikingly attractive, confident, intelligent and musically gifted.

But we can also learn much about the young Kathleen Niccol by looking into her family background, for she was descended from a family of some significance in the history of Auckland. Her paternal family was Presbyterian, her great-grandfather, Henry Niccol, a shipbuilder who arrived in Auckland in 1842, in the early days of European settlement. Together with his brother-in-law, Henry established a shipyard at Mechanics Bay which he later moved across the harbour to Devonport, on Auckland's North Shore. The business grew and prospered, and it was later said of Henry that he had 'created

Auckland's reputation as the shipbuilding centre of New Zealand'.[2] Henry Niccol's life was characterised by energy, enterprise and craftsmanship. He played an active part in the civic life of Devonport, bequeathing to his family a secure place in the history and development of Auckland.

Kathleen's grandfather Malcolm Niccol, Henry's second son, was born in 1844. Malcolm became a shipping agent and, like his father, entered public life, becoming the first mayor of Devonport, and for many years chairman of the Auckland Harbour Board. His extensive involvement in public life and sporting bodies led to his being dubbed 'the leading spirit in the town,'[3] who enjoyed 'the respect and friendship of all classes in the community'.[4] His name has been preserved in Devonport's Niccol Avenue.

In 1902, when Malcolm moved to Wellington as secretary of the Grand Lodge of New Zealand Freemasons, the *New Zealand Free Lance* described the man and his career in some detail, noting that he was:

> *a fluent, persuasive speaker, [who] owns the sunniest of tempers, and has never been known to take part in a scene. If you don't know him by sight, look out for a spruce, well-groomed, well-set-up figure on Lambton Quay, stepping along quite gaily oh, with a spring in his gait as if he wore one of those pneumatic soles, and a chastened smile upon his lips, and a genial 'How are you' look peeping out of his dancing eyes, and you may make up your mind you are face to face with Malcolm Niccol.*[5]

The fluent speaker, the spruce, well-groomed figure, the spring in the gait and the dancing eyes: there is much in this description that is reminiscent of Kathleen. Another of Malcolm's characteristics which was to become evident in his granddaughter was his 'kindliness of nature'. As Grand Master and later Grand Secretary of the Masonic Grand Lodge he was known as a master of diplomacy; conciliatory, courteous and kind, though firm in his rulings. His most lasting contribution was the establishment of the Widows and Orphans and Aged Masons' Fund.[6]

Henry Niccol, Kathleen's father, who was at one time a champion outdoor bowls player.

(Auckland Sisters of Mercy Archives)

Malcolm Niccol married four times, and was widowed three times. Henry Malcolm Niccol, Kathleen's father, was born in 1870, the eldest son of Malcolm's first wife, Annie Atkins. He too was a shipping agent and, like his father, enjoyed the outdoors. He was a keen race-goer, and at one time a champion bowls player. Unlike his father, however, he did not become involved in civic life or make an impact on the community, and there are few records of his activities. A small wiry man, he was described by Jessie as very gentle, affectionate and loving to his family. It is evident from Jessie's recollections that his wife Agnes was the stronger one in the partnership. Kathleen, it would seem, was more like her mother and paternal grandfather than her father.

From her mother's side of the family came two very significant influences in Kathleen's life; her musical ability and her devotion to the Catholic church. Her mother's ancestry was English, with a trace of Spanish further back. Kathleen's maternal grandmother, Mary Ann

Gorrod, was originally from Worthing, while her grandfather, William Thomas Cannell, was from Middlesex. With their six children they arrived in Auckland in June 1874 on the *Rooparell*. The Cannell family had considerable musical talent, and Kathleen's grandmother played the piano and sang until she was in her eighties. Kathleen's mother Agnes (who was born in England in 1869) was a lyric soprano who performed as a soloist with church choirs and the Auckland Choral Society. All of Agnes's five sisters — Alice Boylan, Frances Howard, Catherine Cunningham, Florence Cannell and Genevieve Cecilia (who became Sister Mary Wilfred of the Sisters of St Joseph) — were musical, playing the piano and organ and singing in choirs. Harmonising came naturally to them and five of the six were said to be music teachers. Alice Boylan produced operettas and pantomimes in Devonport, often composing her own music, and was organist at All Souls Catholic Church in Devonport for 25 years.

Kathleen Niccol's mother, Agnes Niccol née Cannell, taken in 1900 when Kathleen was five.

(Kathleen Karl)

Mary Cannell, Kathleen's grandmother, had converted to Roman Catholicism at the age of 12, and her husband followed her example in the early years of their marriage. They passed on to their family (in all eight children, six girls and two boys) a deep love of the church. It has frequently been observed that recent converts to Catholicism are often more zealous than those whose membership of the church is longstanding, and the Cannell family were no exception.

Given the Church's strict attitude towards sexual morality it is surprising to learn that Agnes Cannell's eldest daughter, Kathleen, was born in Devonport on 3 April 1895, just five months after Agnes and Henry Malcolm Niccol were married. Family recollections suggest that it was a happy and successful marriage, but the facts of Kathleen's birth are worth noting because they help to explain her later unwillingness to talk about her early life or to have her birth date known. Perhaps the circumstances of her birth also help to explain the tremendous compassion and understanding she showed for the personal difficulties of her pupils in later life.

Agnes gave birth to a son, John Henry (known as Jack) in 1896, and two further daughters, Jessie Sarita (known in the family as Bubby) in 1898, and Ysabel Alice (Belle) in 1901. Kathleen was known as Toots or Tootsie.

The family home in Devonport was a roomy wooden villa, with large bay windows, sharply pointed gables and borders of elaborate wooden lacework above a wide verandah. It was situated in Victoria Road, the major road leading from Victoria Wharf where passengers

The family home in Victoria Road, Devonport. Kathleen can just be seen in the garden.

(Auckland Sisters of Mercy Archives)

from Auckland city disembark from the ferries. Victoria Road skirts the lower slopes of Mt Victoria, one of the grassy volcanic hills that characterise the Auckland landscape. The Catholic Church of All Souls and St Francis de Sales is on the lower slopes of Mt Victoria, with the convent school of St Leo's directly opposite, on the other side of Victoria Road. It was here, in close proximity to church and school, that the Niccol family lived for the first eleven years of Kathleen's life. The Catholic church — at this time a small wooden building, originally the mortuary chapel of St Francis de Sales from the Symonds Street Cemetery — played a central part in the family's life.

To live anywhere in Devonport is to be always conscious of the sea. The young Kathleen Niccol lived within walking distance of beaches, harbours, wharves and headlands. A short walk from her home in a southerly direction brought her to Victoria Wharf and Devonport Beach. A walk in an easterly direction took her to Cheltenham Beach, a superb swimming beach with golden sand, which looked across to Rangitoto Island lying green and serene offshore. North-west of her home were the mangrove mudflats of Ngataringa Bay, while to the west lay the Naval Base and Stanley Bay wharf. From the top of Mt Victoria there are lovely vistas of open sea to the east and the harbour and seaside suburbs of Auckland in every other direction. It is no surprise, then, to learn that Kathleen grew up with a love of swimming and sailing.

People who knew Kathleen before she became a Sister of Mercy always remarked on her long wavy hair, a deep rich corn colour (inherited from her father's mother), which trailed down to the hem of her dress. Her mother Agnes and younger sister Jessie would each take a side to brush and plait it.

Jessie told how as children the three sisters would stand by the gate and wait for their father to come home from work. Passers-by would nudge each other and comment in admiration at Kathleen's long, beautiful tresses, and the little sisters would say:

'Did you hear what they said?'

'About what?' would be the cool reply.

'About your *hair!*'

'Oh keep quiet!'

Kathleen Niccol as the Fairy Queen, aged about six.

(Auckland Sisters of Mercy Archives)

This story contains the kernel of what became one of Sister Mary Leo's favourite maxims as a singing teacher. Her pupils were always told not to be proud of a beautiful voice, it was a gift from God. This attitude is very similar to that of her mother, Agnes, who would tell the younger sisters: 'Never tell her the remarks of passers-by. I don't want her to be proud. She is not conceited at the fact that God has given her such wonderful hair.'[7]

Kathleen's first school was St Leo's convent school, close to her home. The Sisters of Mercy, the religious order she was later to join, had established the school in 1896 when they bought a small cottage on the opposite side of the road from the church, and began teaching primary school pupils in both the cottage and the church. The school building in which Kathleen took her lessons was built in 1898. Here she attended a 'select school' or academy taught by the sisters. Pupils of select schools paid higher fees and were given extra tuition in arts and languages, their fees providing income for the sisters which they could then use to provide for the poor. In the schoolroom, however, these pupils were separated from those of the parish school only by a curtain, and they were taught by the same teachers.

At the age of about eight Kathleen began piano tuition from the Sisters of Mercy at St Leo's convent. A comment she made later in life, that 'it was all they could do to keep me from the piano',[8] illustrates her enthusiasm for these music lessons. According to Jessie, Kathleen was also an enthusiastic teacher. On Sunday afternoons, while the Niccol parents were resting and Jack was off playing cricket, Kathleen would instruct her younger sisters in the large washhouse. Perched on the edge of the copper, with Jessie and Belle squatting in front of her on the floor, Kathleen would instruct the younger girls in Bible stories, prayers and the catechism. She would take it all very seriously and her sisters were half afraid of her. In Jessie's words, Kathleen was a born teacher who 'had it in her always to control and teach'.

Later evidence suggests that Jessie was right: Kathleen was a born teacher and her inclination to instruct her younger sisters was more than just the natural tendencies of a bossy older sister. She also taught her sisters deportment and good manners. Before going out with them, Jessie said, she 'had a fussy way of priming our table manners':[9] showing them how to eat with the correct side of the soup spoon and not slobber or make a noise; how to manage their table napkins without either tucking them into their frocks or allowing them to slip to the floor, a terrible disgrace. Singing, dancing, walking with poise and grace, and recitations were also part of the curriculum.

Jessie's stories about Kathleen's piety show her to be uncompromising in her efforts to make her younger sisters take part in the religious observances which she herself practised. In Jessie's words, Kathleen had 'an overwhelming love of the Mother of God'.[10] She tells of the altar above the bed which Kathleen kept adorned with fresh flowers, and of Kathleen kneeling to recite the rosary every night at bedtime and making sure her sisters did the same. When she was older and living in Grey Lynn, Kathleen went to early mass almost every day in St Joseph's convent chapel, some one and a half miles away. Sometimes she would wake her sisters and ask them to accompany her to the 6.30 a.m. service. On one memorable occasion they all got up and set out in the dark and cold an hour too early, but when Jessie and Belle went back to bed Kathleen routed them out again, standing over them to make sure they went to mass. Kathleen's sisters also dreaded going to confession with her, because she spent so long in the confessional. People waiting outside would become impatient, while Belle and Jessie, knowing full well who was in there, would nudge each other, and later ask Kathleen, 'Couldn't you make it shorter?'

'Mind your own business,' would come the reply.[11]

Jessie's recollections also demonstrate Kathleen's early love of music. There is a story that as a small child she would stand by the canary's cage, listening intently, and trying to imitate the bird's trilling. When she was older she taught her sisters, from the age of four, to harmonise and to sing solos at 'penny' concerts put on for their parents. Musical evenings involving aunts and cousins were common, and Agnes and her three daughters often sang as a quartet. Some of their early performances were in pantomimes composed and directed by their aunt Alice Boylan, with practices held in Alice's large drawing room. Alice also gave Kathleen some help with her singing, and she and Agnes were probably Kathleen's first singing teachers.[12]

Although the family was a close and affectionate one, it does appear that Kathleen's musical talent and strong personality gave her a somewhat privileged position. Agnes went to great lengths to encourage her musical development, and when Kathleen was practising the younger children had to keep quiet: they could not even run the sweeper over the carpet. There is a story that Agnes would not let Kathleen wash the dishes, saying her hands were too precious and were to be used for better things. This special treatment may have set the pattern for favouritism which became apparent much later when as a singing teacher Sister Mary Leo would favour one pupil ahead of another. Her pupils had no choice but to accept the situation, just as her younger sisters had had to do.

Jessie had a quieter personality than Kathleen and generally accepted her leadership, though at times she found her sister's strength of character bruising. She recalled her mother warning her not to go into the bedroom that the two girls shared if she didn't want 'her head chopped off'.[13] If Jessie tried to arrange the bedroom in a way that she thought would please her older sister it simply didn't work. Jessie had to learn that if you wanted to please Kathleen you did it her way. But despite Kathleen's dominating personality her family were always considerate of her needs, and Jessie's loving support of her sister continued throughout her life.

In 1906, the Niccol family shifted to the city side of the harbour, living for a time in Middleton Road, at the Newmarket end of Remuera Road. Here the children attended St Michael's Church School, Remuera. By 1909 they had settled in Grey Lynn, living initially on the Great North Road, later at 10 Mennies Reserve, Arch Hill, and then from 1914 at 13 MacKelvie Street. There is no obvious reason to explain their move from Devonport, or why they should move several times within Grey Lynn. Jessie's explanation that they 'had to' move suggests that the family were living in rented houses. Taking this in addition to her statement that Henry's income was dependent on the number of ships in port, and that there were times

A striking portrait of Kathleen aged about 12, the long corn-coloured hair seen to advantage.

(Auckland Sisters of Mercy Archives)

when the family was short of money, it is clear that life was not always comfortable or easy for Agnes and Henry.[14]

In Grey Lynn the Niccol daughters attended St Joseph's Church School, also known as the Surrey Hills Convent School, while Jack attended his father's old school, Auckland Grammar. Jack had three years at high school, 1910–1912, but because the St Joseph's school records were destroyed by fire in 1921 it is not known exactly how long Kathleen was there. It is likely that she attended from at least 1909 until 1911, in the class of Sister Laurencia Smythe. In 1909 she gained her standard six proficiency certificate from St Joseph's, and she appears in a 1910 photo of the Surrey Hills Convent Drill Team. The marks she received for her proficiency test showed that she was a good scholar: twenty out of twenty for arithmetic; thirteen out of fifteen for composition; twelve out of fifteen for reading; eight out of ten for geography; seven out of ten for writing and spelling, and six out of ten for drawing. At that time the school did not offer an academic sec-

Kathleen's long hair stands out in this photograph of the Surrey Hills Convent Drill Team, taken in 1910. She is seated second from the right.

(St Joseph's School, Grey Lynn)

ondary education, but pupils could stay at school for a further two years after gaining their proficiency in standard six; two years (standards seven and eight) which were seen mainly as preparation for joining the workforce.

It seems likely that Kathleen stayed at school for these two years, while also giving considerable time and effort to her musical training. Her music teacher at this time was Sister Cecilia Cavalier, a notable music teacher in her day. Kathleen is said to have taught music with Sister Cecilia while she was still at school, and produced small concerts. Kathleen, whose mature voice was like her mother's, a lyric soprano, was often accompanied by Jessie when she sang, or else sang in harmony with her. According to Jessie, Kathleen's voice was so charming that when she was practising passers-by would often stand at the gate to listen.

Many pupils went straight from standard seven or eight into jobs as pupil-teachers. In 1912, the year she turned seventeen, Kathleen Niccol became a first-year pupil-teacher at Richmond Road School in Grey Lynn, earning an annual salary of £25. At that time Richmond Road School had a roll of 779 pupils, 13 teachers and 8 pupil-teachers, under the headmastership of Thomas Bull, BA.

Kathleen's decision to become a teacher was obviously one of the crucial decisions in her life, but there are few clues as to how or why she made this choice. Agnes, who placed great emphasis on girls behaving like young ladies and becoming gentlewomen, would probably have preferred her daughters not to work: Kathleen's decision may have been at least in part a response to the family's economic situation. What Kathleen did after her year at Richmond Road Primary School is not known. A likely destination at this stage in her career would have been Auckland Teachers' Training College, but her name does not appear among the list of students.[15] Nor does it appear among the list of teachers working in the Auckland area or those who sat examinations for their certification.[16] For two years she simply drops out of the records of the teaching service.

It is possible that Kathleen spent these two years at home helping her mother, having music tuition, and possibly teaching music from home. But another possibility also needs to be considered. During

Belle, Kathleen and Jessie, aged 12, 16 and 14.

(Kathleen Karl)

these years a tragic scenario was beginning to unfold in the Niccol home. In December 1915 Kathleen's younger brother Jack, now aged nineteen, was admitted to Auckland Public Hospital with pyaemia, a serious form of blood poisoning associated with internal abscesses. It was the first of many trips to hospital, cutting short a life that had looked full of promise. After eight months in hospital Jack was discharged, but after only two months at home he was readmitted with a typhoid spine, this time for a year.

Kathleen's disappearance from the teaching service records at this time, and her reappearance in mid 1915 as the assistant teacher at a two-teacher school at Onerahi, near Whangarei, may partly be explained by her brother's illness. By her own account, her health was not robust. Perhaps these two years included a period when she herself was not well. The decision to go and teach in a small country school in a 'healthy' seaside location may have been part of her recovery programme. Alternatively, her own health may have been good, but the family may have decided to remove her from a possible source of infection.

There are two other possible factors in her move to Onerahi. Friends there were told that she had been very much in love with a young man who unfortunately held different religious beliefs from her own. Neither was prepared to change their beliefs, and in consequence the friendship had been broken off. Kathleen's removal from Auckland may have been an attempt to recover from a broken heart. Another possible factor in the decision to move to Onerahi was that a fellow pupil-teacher at Richmond Road Primary School, Florence Ormiston, may have been a relative of Edward Ormiston, the head teacher at Onerahi.

There is some evidence that Kathleen spent the first part of 1915 teaching at the Grafton Road School in Auckland, but nothing further is known about this episode in her life. A large inner-city school with 18 teachers and an average attendance of 651 pupils, Grafton Road School was a marked contrast to the two-teacher school she was to join in Onerahi.

The township of Onerahi is situated on the Onerahi Peninsula, on the northern side of Whangarei Harbour. In 1915 it was a busy port serving mid-Northland. There was a 400-metre wharf, and up to a dozen vessels — both passenger and cargo — might be in the harbour at any one time.[17] A railway connected Onerahi and Whangarei, at one point traversing a causeway across the harbour, but there was no railway link between Auckland and Whangarei. Passengers from Auckland travelled instead on the regular passenger service provided by the Northern Steam Ship Company; Kathleen is most likely to have travelled on the 67-metre *Manaia*.

Kathleen did not live in Onerahi, but boarded in Whangarei with members of the Ormiston family, travelling to Onerahi School each day by train. A pupil, Betty Hawkes (later Betty Pullman), was appointed to meet her at Onerahi Station and carry her books up the hill to school. The village Kathleen walked through to get to school has all but disappeared. In her day there were guesthouses, shops, a post office and several churches. A large cement works on Limestone Island, just offshore from Onerahi Peninsula, employed some 250 men, many of whom lived in Onerahi and travelled across to the island each day.[18]

Kathleen Niccol was 20 when she arrived at Onerahi, on 10 August 1915; she was 24 when she left the district in 1919. These formative years in her life, when most young women are thinking of marriage and having a family, were for her dominated by the First World War, which cast its shadow even into this quiet rural backwater. Because Onerahi was the embarkation point for passengers leaving mid-Northland, the arrival of trainloads of men and their transfer to a passenger steamer bound for Trentham and service overseas was a frequent occurrence. The district's social life — dances and entertainments held in the Onerahi Town Hall — revolved around farewells or welcomes to young men who were leaving for or who had returned from the front. The speeches were patriotic, full of the glory of war and the importance of doing one's duty. At one such occasion attended by Kathleen Niccol in March 1916, Gunner Hirons, 'recently invalided from the front', told the assembled gathering that his four months on Gallipoli fighting the Turks was 'the time of his life. The young men who hung back did not know what they were missing. It was a glorious life, that of a soldier.'[19] Surrounded by such fervent patriotism Kathleen did her bit for the war effort by organising the school children into fundraising efforts, including an elaborate 'coronation ceremony' enacted at the school in December 1915 to raise money for the Wounded Soldiers' Fund. She also taught the children to sing the National Anthems of 'the three great Allies — Britain, France and Russia' for the Anzac Day celebration at the school. In November 1917 she organised a group of children to provide the entertainment when a war badge was presented to a member of the local Scout troop. The children sang choruses, staged a farce, a dance and a demonstration of Indian club swinging.

Kathleen Niccol was already becoming known for those things which would make her famous in later life: the training of young performers in song and dance, and the organisation and staging of concerts. Reports published in Whangarei's *Northern Advocate* newspaper note the excellence of the performers she trained and the discipline needed to achieve these results. The singing and recitations, both of the classes and of individual pupils, were described as 'really excellent' after the Onerahi School break-up in December 1915: 'There was ample evidence of careful tuition and of the willing application by the pupils that comes of perfect accord between teacher and scholars. Kindly discipline was perfect.'[20] A year later, the concert she produced in aid of the school fund received high praise:

> *To say that the performance was excellent is not saying too much. For the result attained, credit must be given unreservedly to Miss Niccol, the instructress, to whose unremitting attention and tuition the measure of success is due… Everything went with an exactitude of rhythm and harmony.*

While this reviewer thought that the high point of the programme had been three tableaux, the choruses and vocal solos were also 'excellently rendered' and the recitations were 'unmarked by pause or fault on the part of the young deliverers'. 'Miss Niccol' played the piano accompaniments throughout the performance, the full programme of which was published in the newspaper.[21] This highly successful concert was repeated in the Onerahi Town Hall a month later, to an audience of some 600 people. At the end of the concert Kathleen was presented with a 'lady's handsome handbag', and the chairman of the school committee spoke of the 'indefatigable energy and painstaking care displayed by that lady in bringing her pupils to such a height of perfection.'[22]

As the war continued a more sombre tone pervaded the local newspaper. In February 1916 the annual school picnic was cancelled, 'in view of the war and the attendant load of sorrow it has brought to many among us…' and the news from the Onerahi district that was published was increasingly the news received in letters from men serving overseas. Reports of school concerts disappear altogether during 1918, either because there was no space in view of the more pressing news of the war or perhaps because such frivolities had been abandoned.

When the war ended the flu epidemic followed hard on its heels. By the time news of Turkey's capitulation was received in Onerahi, early in November 1918, the school had already closed due to the flu epidemic. In the local paper the news that peace had been proclaimed joined stories of business in Onerahi township being practically at a standstill, with some 25 people affected by the flu. By the end of November, however, the news was that the epidemic had run its course and that Onerahi had been visited lightly, thanks to the township's 'splendid situation, its wide open spaces and cleanly sea breezes'.

In 1919, for the first time, Kathleen began the school year at Onerahi in a post-war atmosphere. The school picnic in February was reported in detail in the local newspaper and was pronounced to be the best ever, from the 8.30 a.m. embarkation on the *Lady Eva* to the return home at 7.30 p.m. The picnic was held at Marsden Point, at the entrance to the harbour, and the children played games on the sand, swam in the ocean beach, and had lunch under the gum trees of the Munro homestead. Miss Niccol, noted throughout her life for being quick on her feet, was the winner of the ladies' running race held during the afternoon's sports.

The same year there is also evidence for the first time of Kathleen taking her troupe of school children to perform away from Onerahi. In March 1919 they contributed to the St Patrick's Day concert in Whangarei, receiving a laudatory notice in the *Northern Advocate*:

> The histrionic talent of this excellent band of juvenile performers is more and more winning its way in the estimation of the public, and the unfailing appreciation of its efforts cannot fail of its gratification to all concerned.[23]

Throughout this period Onerahi School received good reports from the school inspectors. By 1918 there were 81 children at the school, 49 of them in Kathleen's care. Most of these (36 of the 49) were in primer two. The inspector's report dated September 1918 noted that the Lower School was doing music which was 'full of promise':

> On the whole good work is being done. All work is very neatly set out and a good tone prevails.
> In the Lower School some very interesting work is to be seen. The Handwork is very fine and the Experimental Work in Music is full of promise.

> *A unique and most commendable feature is the conversion by the little folk of their prize money into pretty pictures to adorn the walls of the schoolroom.*[24]

Cecilia Parkes, née Connelly, who was a pupil at Onerahi School at this time, recalls being taught to sing and dance — square dancing, Irish dancing, Scottish dancing — by Kathleen Niccol. The Connelly family, being Catholic and musical, had a lot in common with Kathleen and she became friends with Cecilia's older sisters. Cecilia remembers many school concerts in the Onerahi Hall, performances requiring elaborate costumes which were made up by Mrs Connelly. At Easter 1919 Kathleen took Cecilia Connelly, George Peterwood and George's mother to Auckland for a visit. They stayed with the Niccol family (Kathleen's parents seem to have been staying with relatives in Remuera Road at this point) and Cecilia has vivid memories of walking to church four times in one day. She and George Peterwood had been trained in song and dance and performed in the Auckland Town Hall on this visit, one of their items being 'O Where Are You Going To, My Pretty Maid?' Cecilia was dressed in a poke bonnet and carried a milking bucket and stool, while George, aged about nine, was resplendent in a top hat.

While to some extent Kathleen's work as a teacher can be traced in written records, it is more difficult to write about her personal life during this period. It is evident from sick leave she took in 1915 and 1916 that despite the bracing seaside environment her health was still not perfect. She had time off work in October 1915 with a 'relaxed throat', and further sick leave in December 1916. When school resumed in February 1917 it was reported that although she had been in 'indifferent health at the end of term' she was much benefited by the recess.[25] Her day-to-day life, with its round of school, the taking of dance and elocution classes after school, the organising of recitals and concerts, was probably happy enough. A photograph dating from Christmas 1916 shows her enjoying a picnic at Parua Bay with members of the Ormiston and Drummond families. Other photographs showing her relaxing with women friends — picnicking on hillsides, walking on beaches and in streambeds, or out on the harbour in a

A picnic at Parua Bay on the Whangarei Harbour, Christmas 1916, with members of the Drummond and Ormiston families. From left to right: Mrs Ormiston, Roy Drummond (in uniform), Kathleen Niccol, Alba Drummond, Florrie Armstrong (née Ormiston), Chris Ormiston, Mrs Drummond, Norman Drummond.

(Auckland Sisters of Mercy Archives)

small boat — also probably date from the four years she lived on the Whangarei Harbour. If she was so inclined, there were numerous opportunities to indulge her love of dancing at the frequent socials held in the Onerahi Town Hall.

Kathleen's farewell from Onerahi was held on 23 May 1919, and was reported in detail in the local newspaper. Well on 500 people crowded into the town hall for a typical country function — a dance interspersed with musical items. Predictably, one of the most memorable of these was the singing of a massed choir of 100 children, under the baton of the guest of honour. Special mention was also made of the solo performance of a very small girl, who had obviously been groomed to appear in public as Kathleen's young sisters had been trained years before.

A presentation was made to Miss Niccol by the chairman of the school committee. During the three years Miss Niccol had been among them, he said, she had endeared herself to all who had come into contact with her. Especially was this so in the case of the children. They loved her. She possessed to an extraordinary degree that human sympathy that never fails to win a child's heart. With it all, the discipline maintained in her classes was of the highest; but it was a discipline of love. While other teachers might be appointed, he was very sure it was few indeed who possessed the quality of winning the love and respect of the scholars commanded by Miss Niccol. As a teacher she was conscientious, painstaking and honourable, and he had never heard a complaint in connection with her. There was not one amongst them, the chairman concluded, who was not the better for her presence with them, and who would not feel her absence as a personal loss. Her teaching colleague, Edward Ormiston, speaking from his 30 years' experience as a schoolmaster, said that 'as a teacher she was remarkably gifted'. It had always been a pleasure to work with her.

The present given to Miss Niccol was an appropriate one, in view of the abundant corn-coloured hair which was still her great beauty: a silver toilet set of brush, comb and hand-mirror, inscribed with her initials in monogram. Rising to reply, Miss Niccol was cheered to the proverbial echo, as she assured the people of Onerahi that the warm memory of that night would remain with her for ever.

A speaker on behalf of the general public commented that her departure would cause a gap in the life of Onerahi that would be almost impossible to fill. For a young woman in her early twenties this was a remarkable tribute, and an indication that her career would always be exceptional. The qualities mentioned in this report — the human sympathy, the ready evocation of respect and affection, the discipline of love — are qualities which later marked the relationship between Sister Mary Leo and many of her pupils.

When Kathleen left Onerahi in June 1919 Jack was at home, but presumably his health was deteriorating because in September he was once again admitted to hospital. This time the letters 't.b.' appear in the hospital admission register, indicating that in addition to his other ailments Jack was also suffering from tuberculosis.

To understand what sort of impact this would have on the family we need to look more closely at the nature and incidence of tuberculosis at the time. The major cause of death in New Zealand in the nineteenth century, tuberculosis was greatly feared for the same reasons that cancer became the most feared disease of the late twentieth century: no-one fully understood why people got it, and there was no certain cure for it. The discovery of the tubercle bacillus in 1882 had shown that it was an infectious disease, but this discovery did not fully explain why some people contracted it while others did not. Environmental and hereditary factors also seemed to play a part in its incidence. The discovery of the infectious nature of the disease had the effect of turning patients into social outcasts; the social stigma against tuberculosis patients was strong, and families were reluctant to admit they had it in the family. The disease could kill quickly, but it could also disappear and reappear months or years later, or spontaneously disappear altogether. Fear that the disease could spread to other family members must have affected all decisions made at this time.

Jack's illness certainly affected Kathleen's younger sister Jessie who, like Kathleen, became a teacher. Jessie remained a pupil-teacher at the Grey Lynn Convent School for many years, accepting a low wage in return for flexibility of work hours. This gave her the freedom to visit Jack when he was in hospital, and to nurse him during the times when he was at home. It is possible that the fact that Kathleen lived away from home during this period, while Jessie and Ysabel remained at home, may be another example of the special treatment given to Kathleen.

When she left Onerahi, Kathleen made it known that she planned to enter the convent. Cecilia Parkes recalls that 'everyone cried, including me'. We do not know why Kathleen did not immediately do so, but she is next found working as governess to the family of Leslie and Eva Wilson at Waipukurau, in Central Hawke's Bay. It is possible that the presence of tuberculosis in the family may have delayed her entry into the convent, although this is only speculation. The Sisters of Mercy would have had good reason to be cautious about the disease; in the congregation's first thirteen years in Auckland ten sisters had died, most of tuberculosis.

Waipukurau had a reputation as a healthy situation for tuberculosis sufferers. Pukeora Hill, just south of Waipukurau township, was the site chosen by the New Zealand government for a sanitorium for TB patients from the armed forces after the First World War; reception of patients began in August 1919. If there were fears in the Niccol family about the possibility of Kathleen developing tuberculosis, what better place to send her than to a farm located in the same district as the newly opened sanitorium. Here she would enjoy the benefits of a good climate, fresh air and a healthy farm diet. At the same time she would be in a less stressful teaching position than in a school, and would not be shut in an enclosed space with her pupils.

Waipukurau was a farming service centre developed for European settlers as a 'model village' by H.R. Russell. Large sheep stations dominated the surrounding countryside until the early 1900s, when the stations were divided up into smaller blocks and many new farmers came to the district. The immediate post-war period was one of growth and development, especially evident in the local hospital and the school, which gained a secondary department in 1920. As well as the Catholic Church there were active Anglican and Presbyterian parishes, while the nearby town of Waipawa had traditionally been home to a lively musical and dramatic club, and an operatic society. The years that Kathleen lived in the Waipukurau district saw the introduction of the telephone; motor cars were beginning to be used more widely, and the advent of a modern drainage system and the provision of electric light was presaged in an announcement in the local paper in May 1922.

While it is not possible to say exactly when Kathleen arrived in Waipukurau, evidence suggests that she lived in the district for four years, from early in 1920 until the end of 1923. At Tangatupara, the Wilson family's farm, she lived in the house with the family and taught her charges at small desks on the homestead's wide verandahs. Set on rolling hills on Middleton Road, eight miles south of Waipukurau township, the homestead looked north over farmland and west to the Ruahine Ranges. Molly, the elder of the two girls, was about eleven when 'Nikki', as she was known to the Wilson girls, became their governess; her sister Nancy was one year younger. Molly

The Wilson family home, Tangatupara, Middleton Road, Waipukurau. It was on the homestead's wide verandahs that Kathleen taught Molly and Nancy Wilson.

(Molly Paterson née Wilson)

and Nancy were devoted to Nikki, whom they remembered fondly as the best governess they ever had and a teacher who definitely had some extra quality. Like everyone else who knew Kathleen at this time, they were impressed by the beauty of her hair, which was long enough for her to sit on, although she generally wore it in plaits around her head. She taught a good deal more than the three 'R's, including in the curriculum singing, tap-dancing, ballet dancing, Indian club swinging, and elocution. Recitations with actions were inflicted on all visitors to the Wilson home, a favourite being the dramatic and exciting 'Lasca', by L. Despriz. Other favourites, written out neatly by Nikki in a notebook for the girls to learn, were 'Grandpap's Spectacles' and 'Mrs Skinner's Visit'. Molly Wilson (later Mrs Molly Paterson) remembers this period of her childhood as a very vigorous time.

Tangatupara was a sheep and cattle farm of 3500 acres; it was a seven-mile ride to the back of the farm. Molly and Nancy had their own ponies, Pip and Bobby, and spent all their spare time riding, often helping with the farm work. The girls were intrigued to find that Nikki had never ridden a horse before, and Betty, a quiet old farm horse, was brought into service. Once Nikki learnt to ride she was able to go out riding with Molly and Nancy. Although the Wilsons were not Catholic, Leslie Wilson drove Kathleen the eight miles to Waipukurau every Sunday so that she could attend Catholic mass. While she was at church he would fill in the time at the men's club before driving her home again in the gig pulled by the white horse he called 'Caesar's ghost'.

At Waipukurau Kathleen taught a 'Dancing, Elocution and Singing Class', first advertised in June 1920 and again at the beginning of the third term in October. At the end of the year she presented a recital in the Waipukurau Town Hall. The rather long and ambitious programme included singing, dancing, recitations, a demonstration of Indian clubs, a play and pianoforte solos, all put on by just a dozen girls including Molly and Nancy Wilson, Eileen and Edna Whelch and

'The Seasons', one of the items performed at the recital put on by Kathleen Niccol's dance pupils in Waipukurau, Christmas 1920. 'Spring' was played by Molly Wilson (front left), 'Summer' by Gretchen von Dadelszen (front right), 'Autumn' by Nancy Wilson (back left), and 'Winter' by Eileen Whelch (back right).

(G. Shackelford/Auckland Sisters of Mercy Archives)

'little Joan Harker', aged only four. Photographs show that the costumes were elaborate, a tribute to the sewing skill of Eva Wilson.

In June 1921 Kathleen again advertised her song and dance class in the *Waipukurau Press*:

> Miss Kathlene [sic] Niccol (Auckland) is resuming lessons (class or private) in latest Plain and Fancy Dancing, also a few vacancies for pupils in Singing and Elocution. For terms etc., apply Tangatupara, Phone 1058 Waipukurau.[26]

The spelling 'Kathlene', rather than 'Kathleen', which was used in all the advertisements she inserted in the local paper while living in Waipukurau, is an intriguing affectation.

In September 1921 'Miss Niccol' appeared in a musical and dramatic entertainment held in aid of the St Mary's Choir Fund, one of the very few occasions for which there is evidence of Kathleen herself appearing on stage. The second half of the programme was a farce called 'My Turn Next' in which Kathleen played 'Cicely', alongside her employer Leslie Wilson, who played 'Taraxicum Twitters, a chemist'. A report of the concert, held in the Town Hall, described it as most successful, commenting that the seating accommodation was inadequate for the large attendance. 'The piece was well put on and the acting provoked hearthy [sic] applause'.[27]

At the end of the year 'Kathlene' Niccol once again presented a recital, extensively advertised in the *Waipukurau Press*. Her corps de ballet would perform beautiful ballets, with special lighting effects. There were to be humorous sketches and dances of every description. The public were invited to come and see 'the Children at the Cabaret Tinytown — as "Woodland Sprites", "Wonderful Widows" and again see them in the far Eastern Ballet'. A report of this concert provides further evidence of Kathleen's ability to train young performers. Attention to the details of costume, lighting and staging, so evident in her later work, is also noted. The concert was:

> *thoroughly enjoyed by the large audience present. The display was of all-round excellence, and the audience showed full appreciation by*

insistent demands for re-appearances and a lavish presentation of bouquets to the performers. The arrangements and staging effects, and the appropriate 'costuming' for the character dances, were excellent, being conspicuously enhanced by electric lighting under the supervision of Mr. W. Robinson. Miss Niccol played all the accompaniments and was kept busy in directing the arrangements. The exhibition was proof of her ability as an instructress and showed that the pupils have made rapid progress under her tuition.[28]

It was probably at the beginning of the 1922 school year that Kathleen Niccol moved to live with another Waipukurau family, Leslie and Eileen Harker. Leslie Harker was the district manager of the Hawke's Bay Farmers' Co-op. He and his wife Eileen, their daughters Joan and Marjory (always known as 'Bobs'), and baby son Peter lived in a large wooden villa, Woodbury, situated between Reservoir Road and Racecourse Road. Joan was five when Kathleen

Kathleen Niccol (at back) with Leslie Harker, Eileen Harker seated holding Peter, and their daughters Joan and Bobs, taken in Waipukurau about 1922.

(Joan Crompton née Harker)

joined them, Marjory two, and Peter probably less than a year. A maid also lived in. The house, which was surrounded by about two acres of garden and orchard, stood in a commanding position on the hill above Waipukurau township, looking across the Tukituki River flats to the Mt Vernon homestead on the other side of the valley. It was still standing in 1997, its verandahs, decorative bay windows and high roofs with finials clearly visible from the main road. Kathleen's room, the guest room, in the north-west corner of the house, had a bow window with a decorative circular ceiling.

While living with the Harkers, Kathleen taught a small school held in a cottage behind the home of Dr James Lewis Reed, medical superintendent of Waipukurau Hospital. Molly Paterson (née Wilson) remembers the cottage because it was built in a revolutionary new building material, asbestos board. The school was first advertised in the *Waipukurau Press* of 6 February 1922 as a private day school for girls, and boys up to the age of ten years. The first term commenced on 20 February 1922, and special attention was given to kindergarten work. The school was attended by about a dozen children, including Joan Harker (later Joan Crompton), Barbara Reed, and John and Cuthbert Raymond. According to Joan Crompton, Kathleen 'must have had a "flair" for teaching as the children all loved her'. Kathleen stayed with the Harkers for two years, continuing to run her dancing class in the St Mary's Anglican Church Hall and putting on regular recitals. She also advertised as a teacher of pianoforte, the theory of music, singing, voice production and elocution.

A 'breaking-up function' of Miss Niccol's dancing class was held in December 1922 at Dr Reed's residence, and fully reported in the local paper. Fourteen children (including two boys) presented a programme of dances, action songs, recitations, piano and violin solos. Supper was served and a small dance was held. The fact that Miss Niccol was presented with a clock by her pupils suggests that she was about to leave Waipukurau for good. Two days later came a report of the 'third annual Christmas concert given by the members of Miss Nicholl's [sic] children's dancing class' in the main ward of Waipukurau Hospital. According to the reviewer the most amusing and applauded item, 'irresistibly encored', was a duet in costume, 'When You're in Love', by

Bobs (Marjory) and Joan Harker. Both Joan and Marjory have memories of performing at the hospital, although the performance they remember was a song and dance called 'Little Mister Baggy-Britches I Love You'.

Another of Kathleen's activities at this time was training the choir for the local Catholic church. Leslie Harker was a staunch supporter of the church and Kathleen attended mass with the family. The Harkers, impressed by Kathleen's musical ability and personal charm, organised a musical evening to which they invited several eligible young men. But Kathleen was not to be tempted. When she left Napier (probably just before Christmas 1922), it was with the intention of entering the convent. Joan Harker, who had attended Kathleen's small school and her dancing class, was to miss her very much. As the steamer that was to take her to Auckland pulled away from Napier wharf, Kathleen stood in the stern and sang to Joan:

> *Look for the silver lining*
> *When e'er a cloud appears in the blue*
> *Remember somewhere the sun is shining*
> *So the right thing to do*
> *Is make it shine for you*
> *A heart full of joy and gladness*
> *Will always banish sadness and strife*
> *So always look for the silver lining*
> *And try to find the sunny side of life*

It is difficult to be precise about this period in Kathleen's life. Exactly how long she spent in Hawke's Bay, and how much time she spent in Auckland before and after going to Hawke's Bay, remain vague. Somehow during this period she became friendly with a Wellington girl, Jessie O'Sullivan, who wrote to her in January 1921 expressing regret that Kathleen did not spend Christmas with them, but saying she expected to see her for part of her holiday. A photo-portrait of Kathleen taken in a Wellington studio indicates that she did go there at some stage. At a later date this connection with the O'Sullivan family was to have far-reaching consequences.

Later in life Sister Mary Leo was inclined to make comments suggesting that at some period of her life she did some serious training as a singer and producer, and was a professional singer. For example in 1965, when she is reported as saying: 'I studied, trained and sang as a professional singer and producer,' or in 1981 when she said, 'I did a good bit of singing myself, public singing before I entered the convent'.[29] On another occasion she said that she 'had previously enjoyed great success as a singer in the professional field'.[30]

According to her sister Jessie, Kathleen learnt singing from some of Auckland's best teachers before entering the convent. This could have happened during the two years when Kathleen was eighteen and nineteen, a period of her life that we know nothing about; she also later told colleagues that she always attended courses of tuition in the school holidays. No doubt she also took part in amateur dramatic and theatrical productions: a photograph of the cast of *The Admirable Crichton* is evidence of at least one production in which she took part. But a question remains about the extent of Sister Mary Leo's experience as a singer and producer. It is worth noting that while she was teaching at Onerahi her name does not appear among the performers who sang at the many concerts and entertainments held in the Onerahi Town Hall, although she certainly achieved notable results as a trainer of young performers and a producer of concerts.

Jessie was confident that Kathleen went to Sydney at about this time in order to further her studies in singing, and also to have a look round and make up her mind about entering the convent. Another account of this trip describes how a friend invited Kathleen to go to Sydney with her, assuring her that if she did, she would never enter the convent. But after visiting Sydney her mind was unchanged, and she left all her evening dresses behind when she returned to New Zealand. Unfortunately nothing more definite is known about this trip; even the timing of it remains uncertain, although it is likely to have taken place between December 1922 and May 1923.

According to Jessie, Kathleen had an active social life in her school holidays. She enjoyed ballroom dancing, the theatre, films, glee-clubs, swimming and sailing, often with her cousins. Small balls were held at the Boylans' home, and she was much sought after as a partner. It was

Kathleen Niccol, fourth from right, as a member of the cast of The Admirable Crichton.

(Kathleen Karl)

probably also during the school holidays that she went shopping with her sisters. She liked clothes that were well-cut and neat, and was rather fastidious about shoes. Her younger sisters dreaded entering a shoe shop with her because of the way she would try on almost every pair of shoes in the shop and then, in a completely carefree manner, pick up her purse and say, 'I'm so sorry to give you so much trouble but I don't see anything there I really like.' By this time her sisters, in shame, had almost disappeared from view down Karangahape Road.

Jessie also relates that Kathleen received several offers of marriage, and her parents and family were puzzled as to why she did not accept one or other of the eligible young men they would have welcomed into the family: a doctor, for instance, a first engineer, a naval officer. But Kathleen had been thinking deeply about giving her life to God since the age of 13, and had made the decision to become a nun by the time she was 17. As a teenager, when her friends were getting 'buster cuts', Kathleen refused to cut her long hair, but wore it in a thick coil round her head or in a figure of eight. 'I'm keeping it to give to God,' she told Jessie. 'It's all I have to offer. I want it to be hacked off on the day I enter. It means nothing.'[31]

It would seem that Kathleen Niccol did fall in love, but as she commented much later in life, she used to 'always fall in love with the wrong people. They were either already married or atheists.' In the same interview she described how, 'I used to go to a lot of operas and dances in my youth. One night when I was going home I thought "it's all very shallow. I could do better with my life." So I gave my life to God.'[32]

Her reluctance to marry someone with different religious beliefs is an interesting comment on the church's attitude at that time to 'mixed marriages'. She had grown up in a family whose parents came from different religious backgrounds, but apparently did not want to repeat this situation.

That Kathleen Niccol, as a young teenager, should consider a religious vocation is not out of the ordinary. Middle-class Catholic girls were not expected to have careers, but were presented with two options: marriage or a religious vocation. At some stage in their lives all Catholic schoolgirls were expected to think seriously about whether or not they had a calling to religious life. But with Kathleen the feeling persisted.

There seem to have been two main factors involved in her decision. One was the ease with which she had already achieved some success in the world. She had been marked out from childhood as a talented musician, and later as a gifted and successful teacher. She is said to have had several proposals of marriage. She could easily have enjoyed a life like that of her aunt Alice Boylan: a mother of five children, prominent in the Auckland musical world, organist for her local church, greatly involved in charitable, community and parish activities. One gets the feeling that this was simply too easy for Kathleen Niccol. She could have done all this, and been a successful private music teacher as well, but still felt unsatisfied. She wanted a life with more challenge. Jessie's recollection of Kathleen saying: 'I want to serve someone more than just a man. I want to serve my maker,' sounds very authentic.[33]

But another probable factor in Kathleen's decision was the illness in her family. Watching her brother dying in pain and suffering, knowing that she herself may contract tuberculosis, and by this time possibly realising that her sister Ysabel was affected by the disease, may have played a major part in directing her thoughts in a religious direction. The presence of tuberculosis in her family may also have played a role in her decision not to marry. Perhaps a realisation that she did not have a future as an opera singer also influenced her decision.[34]

Kathleen also had the example of another aunt to look to. Her mother's sister, Genevieve Cecilia Cannell, had become Sister Mary Wilfred, a music teacher with the Sisters of St Joseph. If Sister Mary Leo did look to her aunts as role models, it was Genevieve whom she decided to follow.

Joining the Sisters of St Joseph would have been a logical choice. She had been educated by the Sisters of St Joseph at Grey Lynn, and her aunt was already a member of the order. But training to become a Sister of St Joseph meant going to live in Australia. With Jack now in the last stages of his illness Kathleen did not want to be so far away from her family. For the same reason she could not join the Little Sisters of the Poor, whose training required a trip to France. Other religious orders required their postulants to bring a dowry with them when they entered. This was something her family could not afford. The Sisters of Mercy, with their Mother House nearby in Ponsonby, thus became the chosen option. She also delayed her entry into the convent so as to support her family during Jack's last few months.[35] There is a story that one day when Sister Mary Peter [Burns] was visiting Jack in hospital he said to her:

'Sister, I'm sure Kathleen has a vocation. I know she's just waiting for God to take me... Take her now. Don't leave her another month and God will look after me.'[36]

Perhaps it was this conversation that finally persuaded Kathleen to enter the convent. It was on the third of May 1923, shortly after her twenty-eighth birthday, that she entered St Mary's Convent, Ponsonby, Auckland. Two weeks later Jack was discharged from Auckland Hospital, described in the hospital records as 'incurable'. He died seven months later on 1 December 1923.

CHAPTER TWO

To the convent

1923–1930

When Kathleen Niccol entered St Mary's Convent on 3 May 1923, she left her life as an individual behind. Henceforth her story is inextricably bound up with the life of the community that she joined. This poses a serious problem for the would-be biographer. The subject of the biography has slipped from view, gone into the convent and closed the doors. The attractive and eligible Miss Niccol who loved singing, dancing and swimming has gone forever.

At this stage in her life we can know her only through her corporate identity as a member of a religious community. As a religious sister she strives at self-denial and the renunciation of the world. Her personal aims and aspirations are submerged in the aims and objectives of her religious community.

The order she chose to enter, the Sisters of Mercy, was a relatively recent order which originated in Dublin in 1831. The founder, Catherine McAuley, was a single woman and heiress who decided to devote her life to works of charity and mercy. Her primary aims were the education and care of poor women and girls, visiting the sick and imprisoned, and helping those in need. Sister Mary Catherine, as she became known, was installed as the first Superior of the Sisters of Mercy in 1831. The order experienced phenomenal growth, quickly spreading to other parts of Ireland, and several other countries.

The Sisters of Mercy who arrived at Auckland in April 1850 had the distinction of being the first religious community of women in New Zealand. Mother Cecilia Maher, along with seven other sisters

An aerial view of St Mary's Convent and school which includes the three music rooms where Sister Mary Leo did most of her teaching. At first she taught in a room situated on the corridor that connected the convent building (back right in the picture) with the chapel, which can be identified by the spire just right of the photograph's centre. From 1929 Sister Mary Leo and Sister Mary Xaveria had teaching rooms on either side of the front door of the boarding school at the back of the picture opening on to the circular lawn. From 1949 they taught in 'Stella Maris', the two-storeyed wooden house on the road frontage at the extreme left of the picture.

(Auckland Sisters of Mercy Archives)

from Carlow, Ireland, came to Auckland as the result of a personal invitation from Bishop Jean Baptiste Pompallier, Bishop of Western Oceania since 1836. On a visit to Europe in 1848 he went to the convent at Carlow and asked for volunteers who could teach and instruct the Maori people.

On arrival in Auckland the sisters immediately began their work of visiting the sick, running a school and looking after orphans. They received a warm welcome from the Auckland settlers, many of whom were Irish Catholics. Concerns about possible attack by Maori had led to the recruitment of pensioners from the British Army and Navy who were given houses and land in the villages of Onehunga, Otahuhu, Panmure and Howick. In return they were to give their services to the New Zealand government in time of war. The 'Fencibles', as they were called, were mostly recruited in Ireland and about half of them were Catholic. By 1850 there were about 2000 European Catholics in the Auckland area and it was with them rather than the Maori that the Sisters of Mercy mostly worked. Their mission in Auckland grew rapidly, and in 1861 the foundations were laid on an 18-acre site at New Street, Ponsonby, for the Mother House of the Sisters of Mercy in Auckland.

By the time Kathleen Niccol joined the Auckland Sisters of Mercy in 1923 the order was responsible for two orphanages, some twenty schools, the high school for girls at St Mary's, Ponsonby, and the Mater Misericordiae Hospital in Mt Eden. The work was carried out by about 100 fully professed Sisters of Mercy, plus novices in training. Their Mother House in Ponsonby was a gracious three-storeyed wooden building, completed in 1863 and made of heart kauri. Of central importance to the community and school was the wooden chapel, built in 1865 on Gothic lines similar to the convent. A long corridor connected the chapel to the convent, and it was on this corridor that the convent's music rooms were situated. The daily routine of the convent and school was rigidly structured round a framework of regular prayer in the chapel.

At the time that Kathleen Niccol entered St Mary's the training to become a Religious Sister of Mercy took more than five years. For the first six months a new trainee was called a 'postulant', which meant she was a person seeking admission to religious life. Kathleen was one of an unusually large group of postulants. In 1922 Reverend Mother Mary Josephine Kenny, accompanied by Mother Mary Benignus Henson, had gone to Ireland seeking 'vocations', that is new enrolments for the Sisters of Mercy. They returned on 24 January 1923 with 19 postulants who were joined by 6 New Zealanders, making 25 in all.

Kathleen's decision to enter the convent was understood by her mother and sisters, who shared her religious beliefs. But to her father's

Sister Mary Leo as a postulant in 1923.

(Auckland Sisters of Mercy Archives)

family, who were not Catholic, it seemed quite inexplicable that she should 'shut herself in a nunnery'.[1] Her father is said to have followed her around for weeks telling her not to join. Many other friends and acquaintances were also puzzled and disappointed by her decision, because they saw her as stifling her talents and wasting her gifts. This was remarked on by Sister Mary Leo many years later when she said:

> *These kind well-wishers could have no idea of the wonderful joy I experienced at leaving all my worldly possessions, to try to follow in the footsteps of the divine Teacher, endeavouring to the best of my ability to bring the love of God into the hearts of others.*[2]

There were of course sacrifices to be made in leaving her family, and she soon learned that displays of affection towards them had to be kept in check. Her sister Jessie later recalled an incident that happened on the family's first Sunday visit to the convent, visits that were restricted to one a month. The family sat in the parlour awaiting the arrival of Toots. When the door opened she went straight up to her father. 'Hullo darling,' she said, and sat down on his knee. The Mistress of Novices, Mother Mary Benignus, who had accompanied Kathleen into the room, thought this show of affection unseemly.

'Would you stand up dear,' she said. 'You're crushing your habit.'

When the visit was over Mother Benignus took Henry Niccol aside and explained that Toots would have to break some of her affectionate habits. When he came to see her he should just shake hands with her, and sit beside her.

'Don't let her sit on your knee.'

Some time after this Jessie came home to find her father crying in the dining room, unable to concentrate on the paperwork spread before him. 'Will I break out of this silly nonsense in time?' he asked. Jessie reassured him that it was very natural for a father to want to express his feelings.

Indeed, it was only to be expected that all members of the family would experience some grief at the break-up of the family. A letter and poem written by Kathleen during her early years in the convent show how she sublimated her own feelings of grief. The sorrow she felt at leaving her family became a reminder of Christ's agony on the cross:

> *The joys of home which I forsake*
> *Must be, alas, my loss*
> *The sorrows of each step I take*
> *Reminds me of His cross.*

In contrast, the accompanying note to her mother expressed her natural affection:

'Good-bye — my own dear one — shall look forward to seeing you on the first Sunday.

'Give my fond love to dear Dad and the two girls — and accept my fond love and prayers ever, for your own self.
From
Your loving daughter
Toots (Sr. M. Leo)'[3]

Gradually Henry came to accept his daughter's chosen vocation, and indeed Jessie recalled an occasion when he found himself defending religious life in the company of a group of his friends who were speaking disrespectfully of nuns. 'You will all be very surprised to know,' he said quietly, 'that I am the proud father of a nun.' His family were delighted when he recounted this story to them. 'Good on you Dad!' they cried as they put their arms round him. But while the Niccol family accepted Kathleen's decision to become a religious sister, it was still a surprise to those who did not know the family so well. When Kathleen's grandfather Malcolm died in 1925, the Mistress of Novices, Mother Mary Benignus, and Sister Mary Leo were two of the first to arrive at the house, causing great astonishment to Malcolm Niccol's mason friends. When they knelt by the coffin and recited the De Profundis (a prayer for the dead, literally 'from the depths') the masons left the room, asking in astonishment, 'What are the nuns doing?' 'That's Malcolm's granddaughter,' someone said.

After six months as a postulant, if the trainee wanted to continue and the congregation thought she was suitable, the next stage was as a 'novice'. The 25 novices including Kathleen Niccol received their religious habit and white veil on 15 January 1924. It was a beautiful and romantic ceremony, known as a ceremony of reception. Because the novice was pledging herself to the Lord and to the religious life in vows similar to marriage vows, she dressed as a bride for the occasion. Indeed, novices often wore wedding dresses borrowed from their sisters or mothers.

Although there is no eye-witness account of the ceremony of reception Kathleen was a part of in 1924, the ceremony remained unchanged for many years. It began with a procession of the Sisters of Mercy into the convent chapel, the new novices in their bridal dresses with young girls, also dressed in white and referred to as 'angels', holding their trains. After a sermon from the Bishop, there was a public interrogation of the novices, to demonstrate they were there of their free will. The final question asked by the Bishop was: 'My child, have you a firm intention to persevere in Religion to the end of your life, and do you hope to have sufficient strength to carry constantly the sweet yoke of Our Lord Jesus Christ, solely for the love and fear of God?'

'Relying on the mercy of God, I hope to be able to do so,' came the reply.

When the interrogation was over the novices were taken to a side room where their hair was cropped short, to symbolise their renunciation of the world, and their religious habits were put on. Back in the church the Bishop gave them each a white veil, an emblem of purity. White cloaks were put around their shoulders, symbolising the stainless robe of immortality, and a leather belt or cincture was fastened round each novice by the Mother Superior as a token of obedience. Once clothed in their habits the novices proclaimed their renunciation of the world:

The kingdom of the world, and all earthly treasure have I despised, for the love of my Lord Jesus Christ, Whom I have seen, Whom I have loved, in Whom I have believed, Whom I have adored.

After the singing of the 'Quem Vidi' (literally 'whom I have seen'), came the 'Gloria Patri et Filio' ('Glory to God the Father and the Son'). The novices then prostrated themselves and lay motionless on the floor while the choir sang 'Veni Creator Spiritus' ('Come Creator Spirit'). The Bishop asperged the novices with holy water and prayed that they would be shielded from all worldly vanity and, by a faithful life in religion, merit being united eternally with the white-robed army of virgins who follow the Lamb wherever He goes. The novices were then led round the chapel to receive the embraces of the other Sisters of Mercy, their 'Sisters in Christ'.

It was at her reception that Kathleen received her religious name. The name Mary was given to all the Sisters of Mercy; the second part of the name was that of a saint. It is not known whether Kathleen chose the name of Saint Leo herself, or if it was assigned to her by the Reverend Mother of the convent, as sometimes happened. There are several possible reasons, however, why St Leo could have been chosen. The first Sisters of Mercy to arrive in Auckland had come from St Leo's Convent in Carlow, Ireland. Kathleen had also been taught at St Leo's parish school in Devonport. The story of St Leo, Leo the Great, an early pope known for his noble character and for his confrontation with Attila the Hun in 452, which she would have learned as a primary school child, may have come to have special meaning for her.

Kathleen Niccol, or Sister Mary Leo as she was now known, spent two years as a novice wearing the white veil: the first year, called 'canonical', was devoted to study of 'the rule' (the order's code of discipline), scripture, the vows, religious life and prayer. Perhaps the convent at Ponsonby had difficulty accommodating the 25 novices in her group, for it seems they spent part of their novitiate at the Onehunga convent. In their second year, from April 1925 until January 1926, Sister Mary Leo and her fellow novices lived at Monte Cecilia, a large Palladian-style house in Hillsborough. Monte Cecilia had been bought by the Sisters of Mercy with the intention of using it as a Mother House, but instead it was used as an orphanage until serving as a novitiate in 1925. After these few months at Monte Cecilia Sister Mary Leo was to live at St Mary's Convent, Ponsonby, for the next 60 years.

The habits that the novices received at the ceremony of reception were generally made by them when they were postulants. Indeed, they could be worn when they were still postulants, with only slight adaptations needed when they became novices. The habit was a full-length, long-sleeved dress made of black serge. A train at the back of the dress was usually hooked up, but was let down before they went into chapel. Wide sleeves, not usually worn in the classroom, were also buttoned onto the shoulder of the habit before they entered chapel. Rosary beads, which had a small cross with ivory inset on the end of them, were worn fastened to the stout leather belt. Also hooked over the belt was a larger crucifix. The cross, cincture and rosary beads were all presented to the novice at her reception.

A piece of starched white material, a 'coif', framed the sister's face and tied at the back of her head with tapes. Over her head she wore a small veil known as a domino, which protected her head from the outer veil, and vice versa. The outer veil — white for a novice and black for a professed sister — extended down the back. Around their shoulders the sisters wore a heavily starched black cape called a guimpe (pronounced gamp). This too was tied at the back with tapes. For special occasions like feast days, ceremonies of reception or profession, the sisters wore white woollen cloaks known as their Church Cloaks. On their feet they wore stout lace-up shoes and black woollen stockings.

The record number of 25 novices, including Sister Mary Leo, make their temporary profession of vows in the Church of the Assumption, Onehunga, January 1926.

(Crown Studios/Auckland Sisters of Mercy Archives)

After two years as a novice, if she still wished to continue and the congregation thought she was suitable, the trainee made her first, temporary, vows of poverty, chastity and obedience, and received the black veil. Sister Mary Leo made her 'temporary profession' in the Church of the Assumption, Onehunga, on 19 January 1926. Twenty-five was a record number of novices, and under the heading 'Record Profession', the Catholic magazine *The Month* described it as:

> an inspiring sight for the crowded congregation to see the white-veiled sisters kneeling around the sanctuary and making profession of their vows of poverty, chastity and obedience. There was many a moist eye even outside the family groups, but the hearts of all present rejoiced that the grand old Faith could still, even in this age of selfishness and worldly pleasure, inspire such a numerous band to surrender all for Christ.[4]

It is possible that the profession was held in the Onehunga Catholic Church because the chapel at St Mary's was not big enough to hold all who wanted to attend, but the Sisters of Mercy also believed in holding such ceremonies in parish churches as a witness to the wider church. A garden party was held at the Mother House of the Sisters of Mercy in Ponsonby in the afternoon.

To mark her temporary profession, Sister Mary Leo wrote an eight-verse poem which began:

It's come at last the happy day
For which I long have sighed
I am, ah! dare I say the word,
'Jesus', — I am Thy Bride.

The powers of hell may scoff and rage
Not all their might can sever
The ties, sweet Lord, which bind me now
To be Thy Spouse forever[5]

Members of religious orders traditionally make three vows: a vow of chastity, a vow of poverty, and a vow of obedience, based on the words and example of Jesus Christ as portrayed in the Gospels. While there is no record of how Sister Mary Leo saw the vows at the time of her profession, it is likely that her views did not alter significantly between then and a talk she gave many years later in which she explained that, contrary to popular belief, the vows did not warp or stunt the human personality, but helped 'its genuine development':

The vow of consecrated celibacy does not express an inferior opinion of married love and family life — far from it. But it frees the religious to offer pure and warm affection — a sort of spiritual motherhood, if you like — to all she serves, and even all she meets. The vow of poverty does not express a contempt for the good things of life. How could it, since God made them to contribute to man's happiness? But the vow restricts the religious — by her own mature choice — in her use and enjoyment of material things, to leave her free to follow Christ in his frugality of temporal possessions. The vow of obedience does not reduce the religious to a mindless automaton. By her free and mature choice she places the direction of her life at the disposal of Christ's Church for the good of others.[6]

After three years of wearing the black veil the trainee's final profession was made, and she received a silver ring as a sign that she had pledged herself to the Lord and to his service. Sister Mary Leo's final profession was made on 19 January 1929. Final professions were traditionally quiet affairs, private to the families of the sisters concerned. Sister Mary Leo's final profession took place in the St Mary's chapel, with Bishop J.M. Liston officiating. Her family turned out in force, including her non-Catholic father and his sister; 'It was a very sacred, precious moment,' recalled Jessie.

As a nun, Sister Mary Leo had very little personal freedom. The daily routine in the convent was rigorous and allowed for little free

A photograph taken when the 25 sisters made their final profession of vows in January 1929. Sister Mary Leo is standing, the second from the right.

(Auckland Sisters of Mercy Archives)

time. The sisters had to be up at 5.30 a.m. and in the chapel for meditation and the recitation of the morning 'office' (in Latin) by 5.50. At 7 a.m. a priest from a nearby parish would come and say mass. Each sister had a 'charge', that is a small part of the convent which it was her job to keep clean and tidy. Between mass and breakfast was a time in which they could make their beds and attend to their charge. A full day's work at the hospital, school or orphanage was followed at 5 p.m. by evening prayer in the chapel. There was a short break before the evening meal, study time between 6 and 7 p.m., then a recreational period followed by night prayers in the chapel at 9 p.m. Lights out was at 10 p.m., although if a sister was studying she could get an exemption to this rule. Sisters who were studying for exams could also study during the recreational period. At morning and evening office in the chapel the sisters would follow part of the 'Little Office of the Blessed Virgin Mary' which has been used by religious houses since the sixth or seventh centuries. Being an active order, the Sisters of Mercy did not say the whole office every day, but confined themselves to matins and lauds at morning office and vespers and compline at evening office.

During her 'canonical' year, her first year as a novice, Sister Mary Leo would have committed to memory the Sisters of Mercy *Constitution and Rules*, and would have carried a small edition of the rules in her pocket. She would also have kept devotional books such as *The Imitation of Christ* by Thomas à Kempis close at hand and made a daily study of them. The *Instructions before Reception and Profession* and the *Customs observed in the Order of Mercy*, handwritten by the founder of the Auckland Sisters of Mercy, Mother Cecilia Maher, would also have been part of her study as a novice.

Other guidebooks, now in the Auckland Sisters of Mercy Archives, detail the 'Customs in Use' learned by the sisters in training. These contain practical guidelines on all aspects of the sisters' life and behaviour in the convent, expressed in quaint language which harks back to the nineteenth century. There were rules about where the sisters could go in the convent and guidelines about how to move quietly, 'opening and shutting the doors with care'. There were rules about when they could speak and what they could speak about: strict silence was observed in the dormitory, and during meals in the refectory the silence was broken only by a sister reading in 'a distinct and audible voice' from a spiritual book.

When the sisters were permitted to speak their conversation was to be 'sweet, amiable and edifying'. Speaking about their 'interior' (their private thoughts or feelings) was forbidden except to the Reverend Mother or Mistress of Novices. There was also a list of 'forbidden subjects on which the Sisters do not converse' which included 'the pecuniary circumstances of the Convent' and 'criticisms on the manner of a Superior or any directions given'. They were not to show partiality for one sister more than another, not to walk with or sit near one sister more frequently than another. They had to undress and dress 'very modestly' and could not leave their cell unless they were entirely clothed and their cell was 'arranged in an orderly manner'. They were not to be idle, but to turn every moment of their precious time to good account.

There were also a lot of guidelines about the sisters' contact with the secular world. Before receiving visitors they had to pray in the chapel that God would preserve them from sin and give them 'grace to remember His Sacred presence' and to edify those with whom they may converse. They had to remember that they were 'not only Religious but gentle-women', and to be very particular as to their 'manner, gesture and conversation'. There should be no loud laughter or loud speaking: 'all are to be polite, gentle and moderate, sitting in a quiet, composed attitude, the feet neither crossed or too far forward'. They were not allowed to speak of the internal life of the convent, nor were they to speak of individuals in the convent. Similar guidelines covered the procedure to be followed when leaving the convent, which could only be done in the company of another sister. All letters written in the convent were to be 'edifying' and had to pass the scrutiny of the Mistress of Novices or, for a professed sister, the Mother Superior. The sisters made confession to a priest once a week and once a month confessed publicly to the other sisters in a ceremony known as the 'Chapter of Faults'. The faults to be acknowledged on these occasions included such things as lateness, untidiness, wasting time, speaking during times of silence, giving way to bad temper, or speaking about things they were not permitted to speak about.

This heavily regulated way of life would not have been considered an imposition by Sister Mary Leo. That was the way religious sisters lived in those days: it was the pattern of life she expected when she made her decision to join the Sisters of Mercy. If any trainee felt she was unsuited to the religious life she was free to leave at any time during her five years of training. But families must surely have been distressed by the apparent disappearance of their daughter behind a system of rules which did not permit her to speak about her life in the convent, and discouraged her from taking any interest in her family or the outside world. There are no hints that Sister Mary Leo ever regretted her decision to become a Sister of Mercy, but her old way of life, including her involvement with her family, had to be replaced by a focus on self-perfection and service. As the *Customs in Use* advised, 'All conversations on family matters should be banished as savourings of the world, forgetting the things that are passed, and stretching ourselves to what is before us.' That Sister Mary Leo did feel pain and sorrow at being separated from her family is apparent from the poem written at the time of her temporary profession in 1926. But she ascribed this pain to her 'weak nature', putting her confidence in Jesus to make the 'parting sweet' (the underlines are her own):

> *And though weak nature shun the thought*
> *I ne'er again may see*
> *The <u>parents, cherished, loved, revered,</u>*
> *<u>The friends so dear to me</u>*
>
> *I feel since Jesus bids me go,*
> *He'll make the <u>parting sweet</u>:*
> *And whisper to my wavering heart,*
> *In heaven we all shall meet.*
>
> *Then welcome to the parting hour,*
> *I ask for no delay.*
> *May Jesus <u>guard the friends I love</u>*
> *<u>When I am far away</u>.*[7]

A story later told by Jessie gives a poignant picture of the real distress Agnes Niccol felt at losing her daughter. When Agnes left the chapel after Kathleen's reception she saw her beautiful hair lying on the floor of the music room. Agnes grabbed the hair, took it home, plaited it, wrapped it in an old sheet and put it in the wardrobe.

'What on earth did you bring it home for?' asked Jessie.

'Because I love it. It's part of her.'

On many occasions Jessie came home in the afternoon to find her mother nursing the plait and crying her eyes out. In the end Belle and Jessie, with the heartlessness of youth and no doubt thinking it was time their mother 'got over' the loss of her daughter, took matters into their own hands and sold the plait of hair. Agnes tried to get it back but couldn't. But for both Kathleen and her family, sacrifice and suffering were seen as part of the religious way of life. The greater the suffering the closer they would feel to the experience of Jesus Christ. The ultimate comfort was that in heaven they would all meet again.

When Kathleen entered the convent Ysabel and Jessie were still living at home, both teaching and both serving as church organists. Ysabel, five years younger than Kathleen, entered Auckland Teachers' Training College in 1919 and taught at the Grey Lynn state primary school from 1921. Jessie was still teaching at St Joseph's convent school, also in Grey Lynn. At some time during the 1920s tragedy again struck the family when it became evident that Ysabel, like Jack, was suffering from tuberculosis. She finished teaching at Grey Lynn in 1927, and went to teach at a country school where she had a three-mile walk to work each day. Jessie, becoming concerned at Ysabel's deteriorating health, took over the teaching job so that she could go and recuperate at Cambridge, where it is probable that she stayed at Te Waikato, the first tuberculosis sanitorium to be opened in New Zealand by the Department of Public Health. Ysabel later moved to The Shelters, four-bedded, open-air wooden huts built on the Costley Home site, later to become Auckland's Green Lane Hospital. Here she received the standard treatment for tuberculosis patients: fresh air, good nutrition, and rest. Sister Mary Leo, along with another Sister of Mercy, Sister Mary Xaveria, who also had a sister who was dying of tuberculosis at The Shelters, was allowed to visit her every Saturday afternoon.

A letter Sister Mary Leo wrote to her mother in February 1928, one year before her final profession, shows the extent to which religious belief and language had become a part of her everyday expression. The letter also shows the importance in her thinking of an afterlife in heaven, where there would be no more 'pain and sorrow of partings'. With her mother having lost her only son and now facing the death of one of her daughters, the pain and sorrow of partings would have been uppermost in her mind. Ysabel was to die just two years later, on 3 February 1930.

> *My dearest,*
> *I enjoyed so much that last visit of yours, and, indeed, when your dear form had faded through the chapel door — after having paid your little visit — your spirit was still within my soul, warmly enveloped in the incense of my prayer. I trust to always carry that dear spirit in my heart, and each morning, at the Sacred Banquet to revive it with a tender caress, close to the Sacred Heart of my Spouse... Oh! how delightful when we all meet again — when all pain and sorrow of partings shall have faded with Time! — I feel sure, my dearest, that your place in heaven will be a very high one and your crown studded with the gems of noble and generous self-sacrifice.*[8]

Sister Mary Leo shared with other Catholics a central belief in eternal life. The idea that she and her sisters, parents and brother would all be together in the afterlife was very real to her. But she also believed that all children of God, whether still living or dead, could help each other through their prayers: 'I believe in the communion of saints, in the spiritual union of all the faithful of God, which links those who are still pilgrims here with those who have died...'[9]

There is a sense that in becoming a Sister of Mercy Sister Mary Leo saw herself as an intermediary between her suffering family and God; that in the face of the senseless suffering and death of two of her siblings the most helpful thing she could do was to become a religious and thus ensure that at least in the afterlife her family would be safe.

The religious side of Sister Mary Leo's life cannot be overemphasised. She was not a music teacher who happened to be a religious. She was a religious first and foremost, and her work as a teacher cannot be considered separately from her religious life. Her colleagues talk of her 'very deep spirit of prayer' and the many hours she spent alone in the chapel. They say that her daily round of mass, office and prayers were 'absolutely precious' to her. If her work as a teacher or choir leader ever prevented her from taking part in the daily prayers, she always made it up in the evening. To non-Catholics this extreme religiosity can be hard to comprehend. It can best be understood as a replacement for family relationships and the companionship of friends which are given up on becoming a nun or priest. In the absence of such social relationships religious women and men are encouraged to develop a personal relationship with Jesus. From the language used in her letters it is evident that Sister Mary Leo had done this, and the time she spent in prayer can thus be seen as a time of personal nourishment, refreshment and healing.

In becoming a Sister of Mercy Kathleen Niccol saw herself as consecrated by vow to the service of God and other people. In her own words she gave up marriage, home, family, control of her life and activity and free use of her possessions and property in order to be free to devote herself to God and his people, and to try to show what Christianity really means.[10] When she joined the Sisters of Mercy there were two career options open to her: nursing or teaching. Perhaps influenced by her recent experience of visiting Jack in hospital, Kathleen wanted to become a nurse when she entered the convent as an eager young postulant. But the Reverend Mother, Mother Mary Josephine Kenny, thought otherwise. Because Sister Mary Leo wasn't over robust the Reverend Mother, who was a remarkable teacher herself, is reported to have said: 'I think it would take you all your time to nurse yourself, my dear. I think you'd better keep to what you've been doing...'[11]

It would seem that initially Kathleen was destined to be a classroom teacher rather than a music teacher. According to Jessie it was only when one of the music teachers became sick that Sister Mary Leo was asked to take her place. But when Sister Mary Leo's talents as a music teacher became apparent, she was 'put to music', as the sisters expressed it. It is not known when these decisions were made, but it was probably when she was still a postulant. Nuns who were already trained teachers generally continued teaching in their year as postulants, stopping only for their canonical year. Jessie recalls Sister Mary Leo having music pupils when she was at Onehunga, and she was definitely teaching music in her second canonical year at Monte Cecilia. Despite reservations voiced by the school inspector who, remembering the great impact she had made as a classroom teacher, asked what the sisters were doing 'putting their very best teacher to music', Sister Mary Leo's musical education continued.

A belief in educating their own sisters was an inherent part of the Sisters of Mercy's philosophy which went back to the origins of the order. The sisters who arrived in Auckland in 1850 were mainly from upper-class Irish society. Many had received higher education in Europe, and one had been educated in America. They were schooled in English literature, economics, European languages, mathematics, arts and crafts, including painting, needlework and music. Proficiency at the keyboard, singing, string instruments and the harp were important in their education. The first Superior in Auckland, Mother Mary Cecilia Maher, placed importance on the convent having a piano so that music could be taught. The Sisters of Mercy believed that their own sisters should be proficient in their profession, and their gifts were to be developed.

As well as a philosophical belief in the importance of the arts and the development of personal talents, there was a very practical reason for the Sisters of Mercy to emphasise the teaching of music: it provided them with the income needed to run their other endeavours. In their early years when they had absolutely no other means of support they lived by teaching the arts; teaching the rich in order to reach out to the poor. In the early days they also took in parlour boarders; girls who had left school came to the convent as a sort of finishing school and were trained in the arts. One such parlour boarder was so impressed by the exquisite playing of Sister Mary Xaveria (on piano) and Sister Theresa (on violin) that she gave a Steinway grand piano to the convent. In fact, income received from teaching music remained essential to the Sisters of Mercy right up until State aid for Catholic schools was introduced in the 1970s.

From the time that Royal Schools and Trinity College examinations became accessible in the 1880s, the Sisters of Mercy music teachers had passed their exams. Novices were taught by the senior sisters, and in the Sisters of Mercy convents throughout New Zealand a tradition developed of music teachers passing their skills on to their junior colleagues. Under the guidance of teachers within the convent Sister Mary Leo learnt piano, violin and cello. It is not clear exactly who taught her, but she may well have had lessons from Mother Mary Genevieve O'Donnell. Later pupils of Sister Mary Leo may be interested to learn that their teacher failed the Art of Teaching paper for her Licentiate in Singing (LTCL) in 1923, the year she entered the convent, although she did pass with honours when she sat it again in 1927. She also passed her Licentiate of Trinity College London (LTCL) in practical piano in 1925.

It was also part of the Sisters of Mercy practice and tradition to seek tuition from outstanding musicians in the community for their more gifted members. It is indicative of Sister Mary Leo's promise and ability that she received lessons from at least three outside teachers. For piano she received tuition from Professor C. Moor Karoly, an Hungarian musician who settled in Auckland in 1922 and became one of the city's leading musical figures. As well as teaching music he conducted the choir at St Patrick's Cathedral for more than twenty years. The violin teacher chosen for Sister Mary Leo was the gifted Auckland violinist Ina Bosworth, recently returned from ten years studying and performing overseas. Ina Bosworth's successful overseas career had included numerous concerts for the New Zealand troops in France during the First World War. She too was a leading Auckland musician, who led the Auckland String Players in their formative years. Of most interest, however, given Sister Mary Leo's later career, was her singing teacher, the contralto Madame Irene Ainsley. Irene Ainsley was an old girl of St Mary's, who as Ivy Ainsley had been encouraged by Nellie Melba to go to London for further study. In London she studied with Madame Fischer and Nellie Melba, and in Paris she learnt from the German mezzo-soprano Mathilde Marchesi. Her London debut, under the patronage of Dame Nellie Melba, took place in 1906. After touring the world with the Carl Rosa Opera

Company Irene Ainsley returned to live in New Zealand in the 1920s, and was invited to train the novices at St Mary's. One of the songs she taught the novitiate was the 'Inflammatus' chorus from Rossini's *Stabat Mater*, for which Sister Mary Leo was trained to sing the soprano solo. There are few other records, however, of Sister Mary Leo singing as soloist. Sister Veronica Delaney heard her sing at a reception ceremony in the late 1920s and Jessie recalled her singing a duet at a profession of vows. But it would seem that Sister Mary Leo's singing career did not continue past her early years in the convent, and in later years her pupils found it hard to believe she had ever been a singer.

Sister Mary Vianney Park, who entered the convent in 1926, the year Sister Mary Leo made her first profession of vows, found her already firmly established as one of the music teachers who taught from the convent's three music rooms. Another was Sister Mary Xaveria McGarry, the daughter of a mine manager at Waihi, whose profession as a Sister of Mercy took place two years before Sister Mary Leo's. Sister Mary Xaveria taught mainly violin and piano. She was a brilliant pianist and accompanist, with a beautiful touch and an extremely good ear. She was also a very fast and very good sight reader. Before entering the convent she had been a pianist for the silent films.

Despite her extreme shyness, Sister Mary Xaveria had a real gift for teaching the technique of violin and piano, and for passing her teaching skills on to other teachers. She and Sister Mary Leo became close friends and colleagues, working together for the next 50 years, and Sister Mary Leo came to rely on Sister Mary Xaveria for her practical help and wise judgement. The two women had complementary skills: the other sisters referred to Sister Xaveria as 'the technician', while Sister Mary Leo was 'the interpreter'. Some pupils thought of them as 'the long and short of it': Sister Xaveria was short, while Sister Mary Leo was taller.

The reputation of St Mary's Convent music department as one of Auckland's musical and cultural centres had long been established. From 1864 the hall at St Mary's (created by opening up folding doors between the school's four classrooms) had been the venue for many

Sister Mary Leo (seated) with Sister Mary Xaveria McGarry, who in 1961 changed her name to Sister Francis Xavier. Their friendship and teaching partnership lasted more than 50 years.

(Belwood Studios/Auckland Sisters of Mercy Archives)

memorable entertainments. It became customary for the Governor of New Zealand to preside over the annual school prizegivings and concerts. Most of the notable names in Auckland's history can be found in the school's visitors' book, alongside that of a distinguished visitor to the city, Robert Louis Stevenson. Many musicians who visited Auckland paid a visit to St Mary's, and an autograph book in the Auckland Sisters of Mercy Archives includes a message from Nellie Melba (1903), an autograph in written musical notation from Paderewski (1904), the large, strong signature of Clara Butt-Rumford, and that of her husband R. Kennersley Rumford.

In 1930, the year after Sister Mary Leo's final profession of vows, she was put in charge of music at St Mary's. The following year she became a registered teacher of piano, singing and theory. For a newly professed sister to be so quickly placed in a position of leadership and responsibility is surely further evidence of her special qualities as a musician and teacher.

CHAPTER THREE

THE APPRENTICESHIP

1930–1950

The twenty years following Sister Mary Leo's appointment as head of music at St Mary's are largely unrecorded. We know that during this period she developed her expertise as a teacher, but in the absence of any personal records we can trace her career only through the achievements of the music school as a whole, the recollections of her pupils, and those of her colleagues.

In 1930 St Mary's was a small (just under 200 pupils) private school for young ladies. It had a good reputation for its academic training but was known even more for its long and proud history as a school where high quality instruction in music was given. This reputation went right back to the arrival in Auckland of the original Sisters of Mercy, who included two music teachers, Sister Mary Philomena Dwyer and Sister Mary Catherine Hughes. The Irish love of singing, music and performing, coupled with the regular round of liturgical music during the church year, meant that music was a significant part of the St Mary's way of life from the very beginning. Music was seen as vital to 'the formation of a gracious and cultured woman' and it was well known that pupils at St Mary's invariably obtained high passes in all vocal, instrumental and theory examinations.

By chance, Sister Mary Leo's first twenty years at St Mary's coincided with a period of growth and development for the whole school. An important first step was the opening of a handsome new building in 1929. This building, built of tawny coloured concrete, in Spanish Mission style, gave the school a distinctive profile on the Auckland landscape and enabled it to increase the number of pupils it took. In 1937 there were 227 girls on the roll, 60 of whom were boarders. By 1951 this number had almost doubled, reaching 410.

St Mary's prided itself on being a school whose 'young lady' pupils were always neatly turned out. The uniform was a long-sleeved dress with a Peter Pan collar and diagonally striped tie, later changing to a gym frock with a blouse and tie. Attention to dress is very evident in the photographs of the school's young musicians. Instrumentalists and members of the orchestra wore black velvet dresses with crochet or lace collars, while the singers generally wore neat white, long-sleeved dresses. The girls wore hats and gloves whenever they went out, they never spoke loudly in public, and they were taught to have impeccable manners.

The St Mary's school orchestra, 1943. Back row from left: Freda Hannaford, Betty Briggs, Carmel Hickey, Ailsa Dallow, Carmel Hall, June Waugh. Centre from left: Kathleen Reardon, Inness Lovett, Arthur Cole, Marie Alcock (pianist), John Herbert, Joan Negus, Maurice Hall. Front row from left: Noeline Davis, Maureen Hall, Patricia Hannaford, Antonia Braidwood, Patricia Price.

(Auckland Sisters of Mercy Archives)

Dancing and elocution, taught by Miss Daphne Knight, were part of the curriculum. Miss Knight was more than just a teacher of speech, dramatic art and physical education. She set great store by 'good deportment and correct speech', and became the guardian of what she saw as the St Mary's tradition. If she detected a 'flat accent' or the occasional lapse into current slang in the playground she would say, 'Not good enough for a St Mary's girl, my dear.'[1]

Boarders at St Mary's shared a rigorous lifestyle similar to that of the religious sisters. They had to be up by 6.30 a.m., and attended mass at 7 a.m. They had daily chores to perform, and the music students were expected to practise before and after school. Every minute of their day was accounted for; there was even a time put aside on Friday evenings for darning the black woollen stockings they wore summer and winter.

With the construction of the new building in 1929, Sister Mary Leo and Sister Mary Xaveria moved into two large music rooms, one on each side of the front door of the boarding house. As head of music Sister Mary Leo's responsibilities were wide-ranging. In addition to preparing individual music students — pianists, violinists, cellists and singers — for examinations or performances, she also took class music lessons, trained the school choir, the boarders' choir and the sisters' choir. She was also expected to provide music for a regular round of annual events.

Musical features of the St Mary's year included providing items for the St Patrick's night concert in March, a concert for the Old Girls' reunion in September, and a concert for the school break-up, usually held in the second week of December, and described as 'the musical event of the year'. The programme typically included items by the orchestra, choir, singing classes, and individual soloists. Then there were the special jubilees and celebrations, such as the centenary of the Catholic Church in New Zealand in 1938. Two hundred St Mary's girls were chosen to represent the angelic choir in the *Credo* play that was produced for the centenary; they also sang in the centenary concert in the town hall, and at the centenary mass in the domain.

The main feature of school performances was singing by the school choir, which varied considerably in size during this period. A photograph of the choir published in the 1944 school *Annual* shows 179 girls — at a time when there were only 254 girls in the whole school. In 1949 the choir which sang for the Auckland Music Festival was a more modest 78 girls, reflecting greater specialisation by this time.

As well as the school choir, Sister Mary Leo also trained the sisters' choir, which practised on a Sunday night. It provided regular sung masses for the convent and special music for the many religious celebrations held at the convent: ceremonies of reception or profession, or celebrations of the silver or golden anniversaries of the sisters. They would also sing for special masses held outside the convent, including the annual teachers' mass, held each year in January to invoke God's blessing upon Catholic teachers and their work. Jessie recalled listening to one such mass on the radio in Huntly and afterwards informing her sister that when the choir sang she could pick out her voice. Sister Mary Leo was *not* pleased: it is a basic rule of choral singing that individual voices should never be discernible. Under the leadership of the sisters' choir masses sung in Gregorian chant became a feature of St Mary's life. The pupils were also taught Gregorian chant, in response to Pope Pius X's wishes for the people to take a more active part in ecclesiastical functions.

Sister Mary Leo did not just train the sisters' choir to sing church music: on two memorable occasions, when there were large groups of Irish postulants at the convent (in 1938 and 1949), she directed performances of *The Mikado* (performed on two separate occasions) and *The Pirates of Penzance*. Colleagues recalling these performances marvel at the high standard of the productions.

No matter what the occasion, Sister Mary Leo always knew exactly what she wanted in a performance and moved heaven and earth to get it. She sometimes organised plays for special occasions too, and the rehearsals for these are remembered as being great fun. Two big tin trunks of dressing-up clothes, kept in a small windowless room known as 'the black cell', provided the costumes for these light-hearted dramatics.

During the 1930s it is possible to trace some developments at St Mary's which set the scene for the music school's more public success in the late 1940s. One important step came in 1934 with the formation of 'private singing classes'. These were classes held out of school time for which the girls (or their parents) paid extra fees. There were 27 girls in the two classes (junior and senior) in the first year, and it is likely that this extra tuition immediately helped to improve the overall standard of singing and musicianship in the school.

Another group which held extra practices was the boarders' choir, which sang mass in the chapel once a week. The boarders would also sometimes put on little concerts for the sisters on a Sunday night.

In 1936 the first recorded use of the term 'school of music' appears, along with an indication that some of Sister Mary Leo's students were choosing to continue their musical studies at St Mary's after leaving the school. In this way began the development of Sister Mary Leo's private teaching practice, which was eventually to take over all her teaching. Former pupils who continued their music studies at St Mary's included Doris White, Maureen Finlinson, Joan Negus, Maureen Fletcher, Inness Lovett and Mina Foley. Inness Lovett was also involved with the music school as conductor of the school choir: it was not done for a nun to be seen conducting in public, although Sister Mary Leo kept a close eye on performances, watching through a grill at the side of the stage in the Auckland Town Hall. The number of former pupils who were still associated with the music school at this time can be seen in the small choir of twelve 'extern singing pupils' which was formed in 1937.

Sister Mary Leo always oriented her teaching towards performance, and liked her pupils to be constantly working towards an examination or a concert. As she said: 'Appearing in front of an audience is very important. It's no good staying home and singing for yourself all the time.'[2] In 1936 she adopted the practice of holding impromptu concerts on the last Saturday of the month instead of choir practice, as a way of helping the girls overcome shyness and self-consciousness. From 1936 onwards St Mary's girls were heard regularly on radio 1YA, with the private singing class, individual singers, pianists and violinists taking part. Groups from St Mary's also contributed to Catholic radio programmes taken by Father Bennett and Dr Terry. In 1942, 26 girls were named in the school *Annual* as having given instrumental or vocal items on 1YA during the year. There are also fre-

The extern singing pupils choir, 1937. Standing, left to right: Margaret Simm, Kathleen Markham, Audrey James (conductor), Janet Drysdale, Marie Carroll, Beatrice Seagar, Betty Edwards. Sitting: Wynne Stone, Frances McKenzie, Doris White, Margaret Twohill, Mary Foley.

(Crichton d'Ora/Auckland Sisters of Mercy Archives)

quent reports of the school sending a choir or instrumentalists to provide music at old people's homes, the Blind Institute, Kingseat Hospital, fundraising events for the Mater Hospital, and at other charity events. The school put on patriotic fundraising concerts during the Second World War, took part in the Jubilee Mass for Pope Pius XII in 1942, and in the Military Mass held at Carlaw Park in 1944.

Sending pupils out to perform on such occasions was an important part of Sister Mary Leo's philosophy. She believed firmly that 'God's gifts' were not for 'selfish complacency', and urged her pupils not to spare themselves but to think of others: their voices were gifts that were to be shared. She also responded to a large number of requests for pupils to sing at weddings, funerals, family parties or meetings,

THE APPRENTICESHIP 71

leading one former pupil to describe her as a 'one-woman theatrical agency'.

Music competitions began in Hamilton in the August holidays of 1940, and were reactivated in Auckland in 1946, providing yet another opportunity for St Mary's girls to perform in public. Four students entered classes at Hamilton in 1940, and three (Patricia White, Zita Austin and Joan Negus) won first prizes. When the Auckland Musical Festival Society recommenced annual competitions in 1946, St Mary's girls immediately made their mark. Nine won instrumental classes in the competitions, and Mina Foley's singing won high praise from the judges. From this time on, preparing for the Auckland competitions became an integral part of studying at St Mary's School of Music, and it was in preparing pupils to compete at the competitions that Sister Mary Leo first began to train singers in operatic arias.

At the same time she was not neglecting the preparation of pupils for music exams. St Mary's record in winning medals, exhibitions and scholarships through gaining top marks in the Trinity College examinations had always been good (medals were awarded for gaining top marks in the local area; exhibitions for top marks in the North Island). In the 1930s and 40s the record became quite astonishing: in 1936 it was reported that since 1933 twenty medals had been won by St Mary's girls; in 1940 St Mary's girls won all the Trinity College music medals presented in Auckland. In 1941 they won nine out of ten of the Auckland music medals, and had won 27 of the 30 medals awarded in the previous three years.[3] In 1949 it was reported that all candidates from St Mary's had passed their exams, most had passed with distinction, three had won medals and one had won an exhibition.

It is important to look at how these results were achieved, as this is the period when Sister Mary Leo was building up the reputation of St Mary's music school. Later in her career the comment was sometimes made that Sister Mary Leo's pupils did well because she only accepted talented pupils for training. In later years there was some truth in this claim, but in the 1930s and 40s the pupils she taught were simply girls who had come to St Mary's as school pupils. They were no more handpicked than were pupils at any other high school in the country which had a long-established reputation in music. Certainly girls with musical ability were sent to such schools by parents keen to foster and develop their daughters' talent. But in this respect St Mary's was no different from many other Catholic girls' schools. The fact remains that something special developed at the St Mary's music school at this time.

One factor in its success must be the skill of its teachers, and it is not always possible to know which teachers taught which pupils. Some of the pupils already mentioned may have been taught by Sister Mary Xaveria or one of the other teachers who joined the school in the 1940s: Sister Mary Majella Patterson, Sister Patricia Graham (at that time known as Sister Mary Philomena), Sister Muriel Shallue (then known as Sister Mary Patrick) and Eileen Walker, née Tootill. Many of these teachers were trained by either Sister Mary Leo or Sister Mary Xaveria. Sister Muriel Shallue was one such; when she entered the convent in 1942 at the age of 18 she already had her ATCL, and during her novitiate was taught singing and piano by Sister Mary Leo, gaining her LTCL in the second year of her novitiate. It is illustrative of Sister Mary Leo's perfectionism that she told Sister Muriel she might not pass her LTCL but that they would give it a go. Sister Muriel later found she had got top marks in the Auckland area.

Eileen Walker, who was not a Sister of Mercy, came to St Mary's by an interesting route. During the war years she was manpowered and sent to work in a clothing factory. The Sisters of Mercy managed to arrange a dispensation for her so that she could continue her music studies while teaching at the Onehunga convent. When Mother Austin was moved from Onehunga, Eileen was given a teaching job at St Mary's. She later said that she adored every minute of the three years she was there.

When preparing for a performance the assistant teachers would train small groups of singers in readiness for later training of the whole group by Sister Mary Leo. The other teachers respected Sister Mary Leo's expertise and when preparing a pupil for an exam, or if they ran into particular difficulties, they would ask for her help and advice, sometimes with surprising results. Sister Muriel Shallue once asked for help with a singing pupil who was told by Sister Mary Leo to 'let those notes come from your armpits'. It seemed to work.

St Mary's pupils had frequent opportunities to hear top class visiting musicians: in 1934 they heard the Russian pianist Pouishnoff and an Australian boy pianist, Philip Hargrave; in 1935 and 1939 the Vienna Boys' Choir; in 1946 Lili Kraus, and in 1949 the Italian Opera Company, the Auckland String Players and the Sydney Musica Viva Ensemble. Visiting artists were often invited to give recitals at the school: names which recur frequently include the pianist Dorothy Davies, the Ina Bosworth quartet, the Dutch pianist Haagen Hollenberg, and the harpist Miss Winifred Carter. The National Symphony Orchestra also played at the school, occasions remarked on with pride in the school annual because by 1948 two former pupils, violinists Joan Negus and Zita Austin, had joined the orchestra.

Another factor in St Mary's success was the seriousness with which music practice was undertaken each day. Practice on the pianos in the boarding school began at six o'clock in the morning. From then on there would barely be any time during the day when the pianos were silent, leading one boarding pupil to ask, 'Is there no escape from sound?'

> *Sometimes I wonder if I have come to a Conservatorium, life seems one long musicale. Here in the boarding school, we make our beds to music — we sweep to Scherzos, we polish to Polanaises [sic], we study with piano productions pursuing us through the floor or echoing overhead. Songsters' notes find us everywhere and our very conversation is monologued by accompanying arpeggios from nearby practice haunts.*[4]

No one could dispute that the music pupils at St Mary's were expected to work hard and practise for long hours. The music teachers' high expectations in class music are also evident from such comments in the school magazine as: 'Failing memories result in an unusual number of lines at singing. The fine day dissolves in tears.'[5]

The development of St Mary's School of Music can be traced through the pages of the College *Annual*. It is more difficult to trace the changes and developments in the person of Sister Mary Leo, who at this stage in her career remained totally behind the scenes. Little information can be gleaned from family sources, as during this period she had little contact with her family: probably not much more than their monthly visits to the convent.

It was left to Jessie to be the carer in the family. She too had wanted to become a nun, and at one stage had her bag packed ready to go into the convent, but she gave it up in order to nurse Ysabel. A week before Ysabel died in February 1930 she asked Jessie to promise that she would take a holiday, and it is evident that there was some concern about Jessie's health at this time. Sister Mary Leo's friends the O'Sullivan family had by this time moved from Wellington to a farm at Huntly, and it was here that Jessie went for a holiday and met her future husband, James Bruce O'Sullivan. After a five-year courtship they married in 1935, and Jessie settled down to life as a farmer's wife and mother of three daughters: Margaret (born in 1936), Kathleen (1939), and Marie (1943). Jessie remained a devout Catholic all her life, and it was an event of tremendous significance to her when, seven years before his death, her father Henry converted to Catholicism. She recalled him saying to her, 'It has been the example of my dear Molly [Agnes] ... and of all my children that has made me really think and accept this Catholic faith.'[6]

After Henry's death in 1940 Agnes went to live with Jessie on the farm, and from this time Sister Mary Leo had no immediate family living in Auckland. Contact with her family in Huntly was maintained by an annual visitation, when Sister Mary Leo and Sister Mary Xaveria would be driven to Huntly for the day. Jessie's daughter Kathleen recalls the preparations for these visits; the house would be spring-cleaned, the silver polished, and a separate table set up in the sitting room so that the sisters would not have to eat with the family. When their car finally arrived grandmother Agnes, sitting by the window waiting for them, would call out in great excitement, 'Here they are! Here they are!'

Pupils like Maureen Gordon (née Fletcher) who came to know Sister Mary Leo well recall being part of such expeditions. Maureen also recalls Agnes Niccol having holidays at the Fletchers' bed and breakfast hotel in Auckland's Symonds Street. Agnes, Jessie and her daughters also spent summer holidays at the Boylan family home in Devonport, and Sister Mary Leo would visit them there.

Sister Mary Leo with her mother Agnes at Takapuna in 1952.

(Auckland Sisters of Mercy Archives)

Sister Mary Leo, meanwhile, lived a very different life in the convent at St Mary's. Compared with Jessie, and compared with a music teacher working in a private capacity, there were many things Sister Mary Leo did not have to turn her mind to: food-buying, meal planning, cooking, laundry, housework, running a car, home maintenance, rates, mortgages and household bills; all were taken care of through the communal organisation of the Sisters of Mercy. This meant that for the whole of her teaching day Sister Mary Leo was able to turn the full force of her creative intelligence to her teaching. She also received great benefits from living in a community with other teachers. There were always colleagues available with whom problems could be discussed, and burdens shared. In Sister Mary Xaveria she had a top class accompanist who was always on hand. Practical support and resources also came from her community. In the days before photocopying machines, she was able to call on the assistant music teachers and the novices to copy out music, or to transpose it into a different key, a job often done in school holidays. If she felt the need for new instruments or equipment, they would generally be provided for her.

In the 1930s and 40s students who Sister Mary Leo found to have musical talent were expected to make a total commitment to their music studies. Other aspects of their schoolwork were simply seen as less important, and some students spent a good deal of their school day in the music room. Sister Mary Leo could call them out of class at any time and always had first call on their time. If a question arose about whether a student should be studying for a music exam or some other external exam, the music exam always got priority. This led to a certain amount of friction between Sister Mary Leo and the other teachers at the school, but as far as the music pupils could see, Sister Mary Leo always won. Several music students of this period left school with no academic qualifications at all, but they did have their ATCL and LTCL.

One former pupil told of the friction that could develop over a small matter like ringing the bell to mark the end of study time at six o'clock. If the bell rang five minutes early Sister Mary Leo would come rushing over from the music room: 'Who rang the bell? They've got to practise until one minute to six.' But if the bell rang any later the sisters supervising study would demand to know why the bell was so late when the girls had to get down to angelus by six o'clock. Another pupil told how by the time she had been excused from her school class and changed her shoes in order to walk over to the music room she would always be late for her music lessons, and would get into trouble from Sister Mary Leo and Sister Mary Xaveria. But Sister Mary Leo had little regard for the time when the lesson was due to end, and would always send her pupils back to class late — an impossible, 'no win' situation for the students.

Sister Mary Leo was an authoritarian and demanding teacher, expecting complete obedience and extreme diligence from her students. In this she was no different from other Catholic teachers of the time. The Catholic Church was an authoritarian and hierarchical structure, with the Pope as its head. Below him were ranked cardinals, archbishops, bishops, monsignors, priests, religious and the laity.

While the women's religious orders had their own independent structure, they also had to fit into the overall Catholic structure. An order like the Sisters of Mercy could not operate without the support of their local bishop and clergy.

Sister Mary Leo was enmeshed in a system of authority and obedience. She worked under the immediate authority of the head of St Mary's College and the Reverend Mother of the Auckland Sisters of Mercy. At the same time she lived within the overall authority of the Catholic Church. Living a life where she was expected to obey her superiors without question, it is perhaps not surprising that she expected her subordinates and pupils to be equally obedient. Her motivation was spiritual: nothing was too good for God. As a religious she had to strive to do God's will in every waking moment, and to make every daily activity a prayer offered to God's honour and glory. This gave a total and uncompromising focus to everything she did. Not only was she striving for perfection in all her students' work, but for the glory of God and the Catholic Church she was also aiming for a continually growing and improving music department within the school. Any success in the Catholic schools was seen to enhance the cause of Catholic education and the Church itself.

The record of her early years as a teacher, however, show that Sister Mary Leo was already a perfectionist when she entered the convent, and that in many ways becoming a religious simply enabled her to develop her natural tendencies with the addition of a religious justification. Encouraging pupils to work hard and achieve their absolute best could be justified on the grounds that it was a sin not to recognise, develop and use God-given talents. She was by nature someone who liked to work hard, and she was a born leader and teacher. Her natural sociability was developed and maintained by her constant dealings with pupils and their families.

From her colleagues' accounts it is evident that Sister Mary Leo remained essentially herself, retaining her strong individuality. They describe her as a woman of boundless vitality who was always fully alive to the present moment. Fast on her feet, quick in all her physical movements, the speed of her mind was reflected in an extremely rapid-fire manner of speech. It was as if thoughts and ideas were continually jostling for position and then tumbling out. She seemed completely fearless to the other sisters: unafraid of staging major concerts in the Auckland Town Hall, but equally undaunted by the wetas which sometimes came into the convent dormitories on summer evenings. Often finishing a long day's teaching with a period of prayer alone in the convent chapel, she was quite at ease walking about the convent grounds in the dark.

Accounts of her teaching as recalled by former pupils present a more complex picture of a woman whose behaviour was individual to each pupil. On the one hand there are the pupils like Zita Austin (later Zita Outtrim), who felt she received special treatment from Sister Mary Leo. Zita came to St Mary's in 1938, her third form year, and passed her ATCL and LTCL while still at school, though she did not ever pass matriculation. The only pupil taking such an intensive music course at the time, Zita felt she was a favourite of Sister Mary Leo, who would bring her a scone, an apple or some other titbit from lunch, and tell Zita not to spend too much time on her daily 'charge' of cleaning the music room. She was also very sympathetic when she found Zita in tears one day over the difficulty of fitting in all her homework and music practice.

Sister Mary Leo provided Zita with the training and experience which launched her on a professional career as a violinist. She arranged auditions so that she began to play with the radio orchestra from the age of 15, and other engagements whose fees helped pay Zita's own fees at St Mary's.

Maureen Gordon, née Fletcher, who came to St Mary's in the 1940s as a ten-year-old boarder, was another who felt she was something of a favourite. Like Zita, Maureen's life revolved totally around Sister Mary Leo and the music school. Sister would call Maureen out of class at any time, and she was often chosen to go and sing at meetings of women's clubs or other entertainments. She recalls Sister Mary Leo as a very demanding teacher, but one who gave her pupils a lot of time. If Maureen was unsure about a passage in a song she was performing, she knew she could ring Sister and would always be given help, either over the phone or in an extra twenty-minute lesson fitted in somehow. Maureen's involvement with St Mary's continued after she left school, and she attended the music school every day until she was 21 and went overseas for further study.

Other pupils had a mixed experience at St Mary's. One who has few happy memories of her time at the school is Inness Anderson (née Lovett). For her the conflict between music, sport and school work made for a miserable life. Because Sister Mary Leo did not want her students to get 'swollen heads', it seemed to some of them that she never encouraged them and they heard only criticism, not a good foundation for professional work. Inness retains memories of an insistence on diction, deportment and everlasting breathing exercises. On one occasion when she was in hospital with an abscess on her arm she was visited by Sister, but felt she was more concerned about a coming violin exam than her pupil's arm. She told Inness's mother to bring the violin into the hospital so that practice could continue, and then, still talking in her usual rapid-fire manner, opened the wrong door and disappeared into a wardrobe. Mother and pupil, unable to get a word in, watched speechless.

Some pupils from this era are reluctant to talk about Sister Mary Leo for fear they will be misunderstood or simply not believed, so different are their recollections from those of pupils in later years. They recall intense pressure as they practised for exams, and a life that revolved so much around performance that they never had time to enjoy their music. There are memories of being in floods of tears before exams while Sister Mary Leo harangued them; of Sister Mary Leo listening at the door while exams were in progress, and if she detected a mistake later hitting the pupil on the arm. Like other religious music teachers of the time, Sister Mary Leo would sometimes use a ruler to discipline pianists on the hands and violinists on the arm.

If they passed their exams they might be sent to the chapel to say prayers of thanksgiving that God had closed the examiner's ears to their mistakes. If they failed at anything they could be sent off for prayers of contrition. Sister Mary Leo's focus on success at music was so intense that students felt she lost interest in them as soon as they decided there were other things in life they would like to do. One former pupil remembers an examination result not being published when she missed out on honours by one mark, and others recall a high-handed approach to pupils' families, including music or instruments being borrowed without asking.

One pupil of this era has described her group as 'Sister's experiments'. Yet it was the outstanding achievements of this group of students which led to Sister Mary Leo's increasingly high profile in the late 1940s. In view of her later reputation as a singing teacher it is interesting to note that in the 1930s there was a succession of outstanding pianists trained at St Mary's, including Margaret Simm, Maureen Finlinson and Valerie Harper. During the 1940s several violin students achieved outstanding results, including Zita Austin, Joan Negus and Inness Lovett. From the mid 1940s vocalists, such as Joan Negus, Maureen Fletcher, Mina Foley and Elisabeth Hellawell, also began to excel. During this period Sister Mary Leo made a gradual move away from teaching piano, violin and cello and began to concentrate on teaching singing. The reasons she later gave for this were that there were not many other singing teachers in the convent, and that she loved acting. A third reason must surely have been the outstanding results she achieved with her singing pupils.

The end of the Second World War led to an increasing number of opportunities for St Mary's girls to perform in public. In 1945 the first combined Catholic Secondary Schools Festival was held, and there was also a Combined Secondary Schools Orchestra by this time, for which St Mary's provided the leading violinist five years in a row. Two significant performance opportunities for the school's choir and orchestra arose in 1947 and 1948 when receptions for the visiting Cardinal Gilroy and Cardinal Spellman were held in the Auckland Town Hall. On both these occasions 'The Nuns' Chorus' from Strauss's *Casanova* was performed, with Elisabeth Hellawell as soloist. These performances led to the St Mary's choir being invited to perform at the opening concert of the Auckland Music Festival in 1949. By special request 'The Nuns' Chorus' was once again performed, with Elisabeth Hellawell as soloist, and it was so popular that it had to be repeated. This continued to be the signature piece of the St Mary's Choir for many years.

Throughout this period the music school continued to grow. Finding a practice time and place for all the girls became a major problem. Zita Austin, who learnt piano, violin and singing from Sister Mary Leo, practised her violin in a number of places: in the small lobby just inside the front door of the boarding school, in a room upstairs, and sometimes outside in the garden. Her piano practice mainly took place in the boarding school's reception room.

In 1949 St Mary's School of Music moved into a new home in the two-storeyed wooden house adjoining the convent grounds, known as 'Stella Maris' (literally 'Star of the Sea'). The memories of the pupils who came to learn from Sister Mary Leo during her heyday in the 1950s and 1960s are indelibly linked with the music room in Stella Maris (described in more detail in the next chapter).

The following year, the centenary year of the arrival in Auckland of the Sisters of Mercy, provided an ideal opportunity for St Mary's to hold major celebrations and make full use of its musical talent. The celebrations began with a 'Solemn Pontifical Mass of Thanksgiving' in St Patrick's Cathedral on 5 March. This was a month earlier than the centenary of the actual arrival of the Sisters of Mercy in April 1850, but was timed to coincide with the presence in New Zealand of the Most Reverend Paul Morella, the Apostolic Delegate (that is, the Pope's representative), who was visiting from Australia. Over two hundred Sisters of Mercy, community leaders, supporters and friends packed St Patrick's Cathedral for the sung mass, which was led by a choir of sisters trained and conducted by Sister Mary Leo. For the opening processional hymn the choir sang 'Ecce Sacerdos Magnus'; for the offertory they sang Moreno's 'Salve Regina'.

That afternoon a ceremony took place in the grounds of St Mary's in Ponsonby, during which the foundation stone of a new novitiate was blessed. The following day an open air mass was held in the grounds of St Mary's for all 1300 children at that time attending Sisters of Mercy schools in Auckland. The children sang the plain chant mass, 'Cum Jubilo', with Dom Moreno's 'Ave Maria' as an offertory, and finishing with a triumphant 'Jubilate'.

The climax of the celebrations, however, came that night when a Festival Concert was staged in the Auckland Town Hall. More than 3000 people attended, including the Apostolic Delegate, the Governor-General, Lord Freyberg, and Lady Freyberg. There were

The choir and orchestra performing at the concert held to mark the centenary of the arrival of the Sisters of Mercy in Auckland in 1850. The concert was held in the Auckland Town Hall on 6 March 1950.

(Zealandia Archives)

900 performers, all of them pupils from the Sisters of Mercy schools throughout Auckland. The programme included singing by the pupils of the combined schools, string music by the St Mary's College String Orchestra, songs by the St Mary's Senior Choir and the College Choir, a chorus by junior pupils and several solo items. Soloists were Elisabeth Hellawell, who sang 'Vissi d'Arte' from *Tosca*; Mina Foley, who sang Verdi's 'Ah Fors E Lui'; Patricia Price and Maureen Fletcher, who sang the Miserere Scene from *Il Trovatore*, and Shirley Hannaford, who sang with a chorus of junior pupils. Solo instrumentalists included violinists Antonia Braidwood and Colleen Doran, and pianist Winifrede Cooke. The concert finished with a tableau, 'A Century Under Mary's Banner', in which pupils from all the schools depicted Mary blessing the work of the Sisters of Mercy in Auckland.[7]

In describing the tableau the Catholic newspaper *Zealandia* paid tribute to the 'skilful direction' which had organised the event, which we know to have been that of Sister Mary Leo, helped of course by other sisters:

> *Choir on choir of angels flamed in the splendours of gold, blue and white about the throne of Mary. The children of earth, Maori and pakeha, mounted heavenwards protected by the blue-crossed shield of God's Mother, while the world beneath blazed even in its darkness with Mary's plea: MERCY.*
>
> *And the entire performance was achieved without stage effects, screens, or any of the paraphernalia of the modern theatre. Skilful direction made for a professional smoothness in the sequence of the items, and the perfect order in which all 900 children took their places for the tableau, to the organ accompaniment of the* Salve Mater Misericordiae *and the well-loved* Mother of Mercy, *was perhaps the final touch of excellence in an outstanding programme.*[8]

There is a story that 'Our Lady' — Mary the mother of Jesus — who stood at the pinnacle of the tableau, had twelve lights around her head; when the lights failed to come on at the appropriate moment Sister Mary Leo, always the perfectionist, crawled behind the lines of girls to set them right.

But this concert was not the end of Sister Mary Leo's contribution to the centenary celebrations. The following day a 'Solemn Pontifical Mass of Requiem' was held in St Mary's chapel, and a Gregorian Requiem was sung by the Sisters of Mercy choir. Following the service came the blessing of a new memorial to Mother Cecilia Maher and the sisters who had accompanied her to Auckland in 1850.

The 'Music Notes' published in the 1950 college *Annual* show just how far the music school had developed since Sister Mary Leo had taken charge. When the *Annual* began publication in 1931 the 'Music Notes' took up less than a page and consisted primarily of a list of girls who had distinguished themselves in Trinity College music exams during the year. Now, in 1950, three pages of the *Annual* were devoted to describing the 'grand centenary concert', the 'numerous opportunities of hearing noted artists', the first public performance of the

Auckland Junior Symphony Orchestra whose leader (Inness Lovett) and guest artist (Mina Foley) were both St Mary's girls, the success of many St Mary's girls in the Auckland Competitions, and charitable concerts where St Mary's pupils had performed. Photographs included the St Mary's College String Orchestra — 18 girls in long dresses; 8 instrumentalists who had won prizes in the Auckland Music Festival Competitions; the Singing Class (35 girls), and one of Antonia Braidwood who had won the Schubert violin scholarship.[9] Photographs of the centenary concert show the St Mary's Choir wearing full length pale-blue dresses with cerise and blue satin capes. The success of singing student Maureen Fletcher in a number of light opera roles was noted, but most startling of all were two additional pages devoted wholly to Mina Foley. The 'brilliant young coloratura soprano' had 'flashed this year like a meteor from comparative obscurity into a blaze of publicity'.[10]

These five pages in the college annual tell us much about Sister Mary Leo's development as a music teacher over a twenty-year period. It is obvious that she set high standards in both performance and appearance for her students, that she liked them to succeed, and that she liked their success to be acknowledged. Her confidence in staging major concerts and her willingness to promote her students is also apparent. But perhaps most significant is the two pages given wholly to news of the soprano Mina Foley. In future Sister Mary Leo would increasingly devote her energies to the training of solo female voices.

Chapter Four

The First Stars

1950–1960

Mina Foley was Sister Mary Leo's first star pupil, who more than any other brought her to public attention and made her known throughout New Zealand. Mina's outstanding success in the Auckland competitions began when she was 16. She came to prominence in 1950 when, at the age of 20, she won the Dawn Irwin Cup for Vocal Solo for Ladies 17 and under 21, the Ellen Tweddell Memorial Operatic Solo, and the John Court Memorial Aria Scholarship of £100 (singing the 'Bell Song' from Delibes' opera *Lakme*). This success led to an audition with the Italian tenor Tito Schipa, who described her voice as the most promising he had heard in more than forty auditions in Australia and New Zealand, and said she must go to Europe to continue her training as soon as possible.[1] When it became known later the same year that Mina Foley was going to Melbourne to compete in the prestigious Melbourne *Sun* Aria competition, she was described in the *Auckland Star* as 'Auckland's new singing star' and 'the greatest operatic find in New Zealand since Oscar Natzka'.[2]

In Melbourne Mina was placed second in the aria competition, just three points behind the winner. She 'dazzled' the audience in the Melbourne Town Hall at the final contest on 9 October 1950, and was described by the music critic of the *Melbourne Herald* as 'the outstanding singer of the night'.[3]

'I can honestly say that I have never heard a finer technique,' said the judge, comparing her singing to opera he had heard in Berlin, Budapest and Rome. Aucklanders in the audience were convinced that

Mina had won. Mina herself has said that she was asked whether she would mind giving up the first prize to an older singer. Sister Mary Leo later said she received a letter from one of the judges almost apologising for not giving the prize to Mina.

With the news of her second prize in Melbourne, the *Auckland Star* immediately announced the opening of a special 'Mina Foley Fund', with an initial contribution of £100, to help get her to Europe. Donations were recorded in detail in the newspaper. Among other gifts were £50 from the St Mary's College Old Girls' Association, and £65 from current pupils. The final tally was £1681.

For the two weeks that the fund was open for donations, the *Star* kept the Mina Foley fund and the Mina Foley story well to the fore, with a fresh angle on it each day. The judge of the John Court aria contest, Aucklanders who had been in the Melbourne audience, accompanists and local music teachers were all asked to give their views. One day it was the turn of Sister Mary Leo, 'music mistress at St Mary's College Ponsonby', probably the first occasion she had ever talked to a reporter. 'I think Mina was one of the shyest and most nervous people I have ever taught,' Sister Mary Leo was reported as saying:

> *She has a remarkable ear for pitch; I have never known her to sing off key… I have certainly nursed her voice carefully, realizing fully the responsibility of training such a rare gift of God.*[4]

Given the publicity that Sister Mary Leo enjoyed later in her career it is important to remember that at this stage she still led a very cloistered life, rarely being seen outside the convent. She apparently had no part in entering Mina in the Melbourne competition; it was said to have been a spur of the moment, last-minute decision, made the day entries closed by two friends assisted by Mr R. Barker, the secretary of the Auckland Competitions Society. One gets the feeling that at this stage in her career Sister Mary Leo was not quite ready to cope with such a phenomenally successful pupil. But even if she had wanted to play a more proactive role in taking Mina Foley to Melbourne she would not have been able to; convent rules were still strict.

When Mina returned from Australia by flying-boat a crowd of well-wishers was waiting to greet her. They included senior girls from St Mary's convent, members of the St Mary's old girls' association, and representatives of the Junior Symphony Orchestra. The *Star* covered her return in full detail, even including a photograph of the workers at the flying base who had stopped what they were doing in order to have a look at her.

Mina was a pupil at St Mary's throughout her school career and had learned the piano and cello from Sister Mary Leo. When she was older she continued her piano studies with Sister Mary Xaveria, while also playing the cello in the school orchestra, the secondary schools' orchestra, and the Junior Symphony Orchestra. In the junior choir Mina sang the alto part until one day Sister Mary Leo asked for a girl who could sing a soprano solo. Much to Sister's surprise, the other

Sister Mary Leo with her first star pupil, Mina Foley, about 1953.

(News Media: Auckland Star Collection)

girls all suggested Mina. After hearing Mina sing 'Lo Hear the Gentle Lark' (a song which, unbeknownst to Sister, she had been practising) she said to her, 'I've lost my alto but I've gained a very beautiful soprano,' and she asked Mina whether she could start private singing lessons. When Mina, who lived with her grandmother, replied that she would have to ask her permission, Sister Mary Leo went home with her one day and assured her grandmother that Mina would make her proud. Mina started lessons with Sister Mary Leo at the age of 14, and five years later passed her LTCL in singing.

Mina's success in Melbourne led to a Mina Foley phenomenon. Auckland audiences took her to their hearts; predictions were made about her being a second Patti, she was described as a 'girl in a million', her career was discussed in the Auckland newspapers. There was an assumption that she would shortly be leaving for Europe to continue her studies and that she would then go on to become an international opera star.

The day after she returned from Australia she sang in a Holy Year concert, thrilling the audience with her singing. The Mayor of Auckland, Sir John Allum, left a meeting in the council chamber in order to publicly congratulate her. A few weeks later there was a farewell concert for her in the town hall, sponsored by the Auckland Competitions Society, past and present pupils of St Mary's College, and the Auckland Junior Symphony Orchestra. She also sang at a concert with the National Orchestra. Reviews of these concerts, as of all concerts at which Mina sang in Auckland, are filled with hyperbolic praise of the beauty of her voice and her technique.

By the time she left for England in January 1951 the Mina Foley fund had risen to £1944; Mina had been granted a government bursary of £250 and, feeling that she had sufficient funds, she decided to give away the proceeds of her last concert to create two scholarships for other singers. One scholarship would be administered by the Auckland Competitions Society, the other would be for pupils of St Mary's College School of Music. More than 50 people went to the railway station to see Mina off when she left on the Limited Express for Wellington, where she was to embark on the *Rangitane* to sail for England.

One can imagine that others of Sister Mary Leo's pupils may have breathed a sigh of relief when Mina Foley left for England. Mina was not just one of Sister Mary Leo's 'favourites', she was the greatest favourite of all, holding a special place in Sister Mary Leo's affections which would never be supplanted. The main reason for this was that Mina had a unique and beautiful voice which Sister Mary Leo trained carefully and protectively. But Mina also received extra attention which could be a source of irritation to some of the other pupils. They recall her being given first choice of music, of lessons being postponed because Mina had a performance that night, of Mina being asked to sing on occasions when other girls would have liked the opportunity to do so. But there was nothing that could be done about it. They simply had to accept that Mina would always be Sister Mary Leo's underlying favourite.

Sister Mary Leo's emergence into the limelight as the teacher of Mina Foley came when her own career was well advanced. In 1951, the year she turned 56, Sister Mary Leo celebrated the twenty-fifth anniversary of her profession as a nun. As was usual, the occasion was celebrated with a 'Solemn High Mass of Thanksgiving' held in the St Mary's Chapel on 10 January, attended by 24 of the 25 nuns who had taken their vows at the same time. Bishop Liston, who had received the sisters' vows 25 years earlier, gave the sermon in which he offered congratulations and paid tribute to 'the generous service they had given to God so faithfully through the years of their profession, seeing and serving Christ in the persons of His sick, His poor and afflicted and His little children.'[5]

The sisters' choir sang the music of the mass, including the 'Veni Sponsa Christi' (Moreno) and 'Jubilate in Aeternum', and the jubilarians were presented with silver crosses to commemorate the occasion. More than 30 priests attended the mass and joined the Sisters of Mercy for a luncheon, numerous messages of congratulations were received, and a gathering of sisters took place at the convent in the afternoon.

A few months later news was received that Mina Foley had won an Italian government scholarship. Sister Mary Leo was quoted as saying that many critics in England had heard her star pupil and had given very good reports of her: 'They say no English teacher should touch her, and that she should go to Italy as soon as possible...'[6]

Public interest in Mina Foley was maintained with a double-page photographic feature in the *New Zealand Woman's Weekly* titled 'Mina Foley is Busy With Her Career', which included a photograph of Mina being farewelled as she left London for Italy in October 1951. In Italy she embarked on rigorous training under Toti dal Monte, who before the war had been the most famous coloratura in grand opera in Europe. It was later reported that after only a few months she was given the opportunity of making her operatic debut at La Scala opera house in Milan in the title role of *Lucia di Lammermoor*.

At this stage in Mina Foley's story comes the first hint of the tragedy which was to prematurely end her career. Mina had been only a few months in Italy before news was heard of a breakdown in her health, and in March 1952 she was reported to be leaving Rome to return to New Zealand. Exactly what was wrong with Mina was never fully disclosed, but after some time in Sydney where she received 'medical treatment' she finally arrived in Auckland in May 1952. She was then reported to be ill in hospital for several months. By September, however, she was well enough to sing privately before three judges in Auckland for the Competitions Society's festival. Donald Munro is reported as saying, 'I've never been so moved by any singing in my life,' while Gordon Short said, 'One of the voices of the century... She will be one of the great singers of our time.'[7] This comment appears to be the origin of the oft-quoted remark, one that Sister Mary Leo herself often repeated, that Mina Foley had '*the* voice of the century'.

In October 1952 Mina was the star attraction at a St Mary's School of Music concert put on to raise funds for the new novitiate. A review of the concert gave lavish praise to the choir, the 'exquisite' string orchestra, and to Mina Foley, whose voice was 'as enchanting as ever and very sure'.

The St Mary's College school of music gave last night the concert Auckland has wished for a long time to hear. Its choir was a sensation at the last two music festivals. Its solo singers and string players have become individually known in concerts and competitions. To have them gathered into one programme — with the school's exquisite string orchestra which has not appeared in public for two years — made an evening to remember, and a perfect setting for Mina Foley's return. The Town Hall was filled to every corner, and is booked out for tonight's repeat concert.

Where did the special beauty of St Mary's music come from? According to this reviewer it was 'the loving use of tone. From the singing of the large choir, to the flurrying passages of violins and coloraturas, there seemed to be a caress for every note.'[8]

Over the next few years Mina continued to enthral audiences and inspire the young singers who were coming along in her wake at St Mary's school of music. In 1953 she sang for the first time in Wellington, receiving outstanding reviews. One reviewer described how, when she finished singing, 'pandemonium broke loose. Insistent

Mina Foley as many people will remember her in performance, on stage at the Auckland Town Hall.

(J. Farrelly/Auckland Sisters of Mercy Archives)

clapping and cheering brought Miss Foley back once, twice, three times, four times, smiling now and making a full curtsey to each quarter of the packed hall.'[9] The headlines of other reviews also indicate the quality of her reception: 'Big Audience Spellbound by Mina Foley'; 'Auckland Soprano Destined To Be New Zealand Queen of Song'; 'Mina Foley Has Rousing Welcome'; 'Enthusiasm for Soprano Mina Foley'. Two years later she made a triumphal tour of New Zealand, singing to capacity crowds in Auckland, Christchurch, Dunedin, Invercargill, Timaru, Hastings, New Plymouth, Hamilton, Palmerston North, Wellington and Blenheim. When she sang in Auckland again after her tour, she was described as being: 'On the crest of a wave of popularity almost certainly greater than has ever before been won by a local singer.'[10]

In July 1955 Mina provided the final solos of the evening for a 'Classical Concert' put on by students of St Mary's to raise funds for a new swimming pool. A full-page photograph of Mina was included in the concert programme, a compliment which in the 1950 concert programme had been reserved for the Pope, bishops and the founding mothers of the Sisters of Mercy. In August 1956 Mina went to Los Angeles and New York where she studied with Madame Greta Stauber. She returned home in July 1957 to take the principal part of Violetta in the Auckland Light Opera Company's production of *La Traviata*, but another breakdown in health forced her to withdraw at the last minute, and she did not sing again in public until 1960.

Mary O'Brien, who was to share the lead role in *La Traviata*, found herself the principal performer. It was a successful debut for the young Aucklander, another pupil of Sister Mary Leo, who went on the following year to further success in the John Court Aria and as the 'bright and captivating star' of *The Barber of Seville*. The *Evening Post* reviewer commented on her glorious singing, vivacious acting and charm. 'Her diction was splendid and her top notes as glorious as a nightingale trilling happily at the height of summer; her acting too was a tonic.'[11] The following year Mary O'Brien played Norina in *Don Pasquale* at the Auckland Festival.

Increasingly during the 1950s the 'Music Notes' written for the college *Annual* devote more attention to the successes of individual

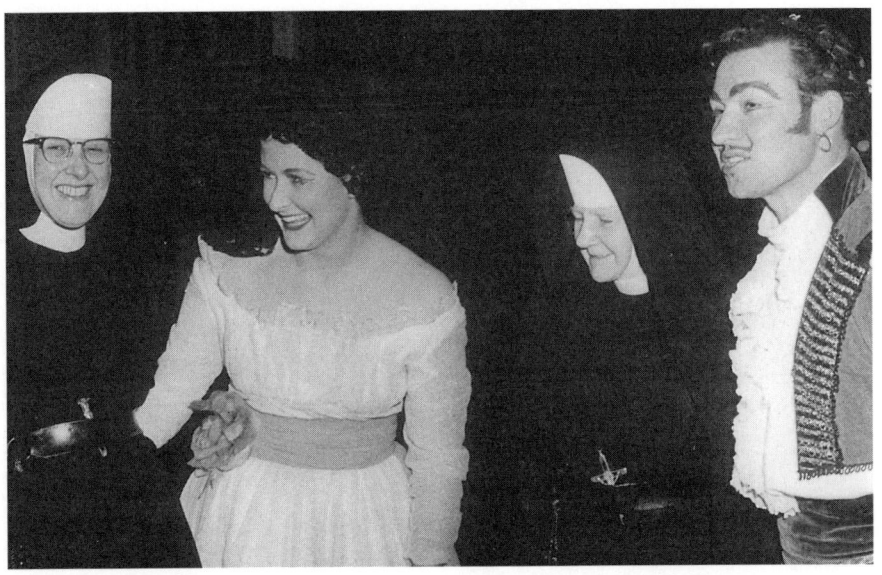

Sister Mary Leo and Sister Mary Xaveria congratulate Mary O'Brien on the occasion of her first professional engagement in New Zealand, as Rosina in The Barber of Seville, *1959. Also pictured is John Germain, who played the part of Figaro.*

(Mary O'Brien)

pupils. Pianists, violinists and singers continued to excel at examinations, but of greater importance were the successes that pupils and former pupils were having in the Auckland Competitions and local productions. Members of various societies — the Harmony Club, the Lyceum Club, the Travel Club, the Burns Club and the Clef Club — attended the competitions and took note of the winners. To win a prize at the competitions was often the first step in being invited to sing at other venues. The John Court Memorial Aria competition, reserved for women's voices for the first time in 1950, quickly became recognised as the 'blue ribbon' of women's singing events in New Zealand, and the 'major vocal test' at the Auckland Competitions. Sister Mary Leo's pupils dominated the competition throughout the 1950s, winning it every year except 1951 and 1956. Several of these

Kathleen Johnson, Beryl Dalley and Marie Robinson rehearse with Sister Mary Leo for their parts in The Marriage of Figaro, *1958.*

(Barbara Tipping/Auckland Sisters of Mercy Archives)

winners, including Maureen Fletcher, Elisabeth Hellawell, Marie Robinson, Beryl Dalley, Joan Cochrane and Angela Shaw, went on to study overseas. They also took leading roles in productions by the Auckland Light Opera Company and the New Zealand Opera Company, which was established in 1954.

Instrumentalists also continued to add to the glory of St Mary's School of Music, with students like Antonia Braidwood, Anthony Hollows, Colleen Doran, Anna Heald and Frances Wilson winning prizes and scholarships. The practice began of former pupils returning to give concerts. When Mina Foley sang for more than an hour in the St Mary's assembly hall on the first day of the third term in 1955, the college *Annual* commented:

> ...*we felt proud to think that, while people all over New Zealand queued to listen to Mina, we could hear her sing in our own school*

hall, on the stage where she first stood as a little girl some ten years ago, and sang Lo hear the gentle lark, in a small but exquisite voice...[12]

In 1957 it was Elisabeth Hellawell's turn to sing for the pupils of St Mary's while on a visit to New Zealand after three years' study and performance in London. 'Her voice has grown in maturity and artistry, but it is still the same beautiful instrument that has so long charmed New Zealanders,' was the comment in the *Annual*. Elisabeth returned to London in September the same year to play a leading role in Benjamin Britten's opera *Albert Herring*.

In 1956 came the announcement of a new voice competition which was to become a showcase for Sister Mary Leo's pupils. The Standard Vacuum Oil company decided to sponsor a vocal competition to be known as the Mobil Song Quest. Entrants were to be judged on the basis of the best voice for radio entertainment and were given a list of 280 ballads from which they had to choose two songs. From 1500 entries, 15 district finalists were chosen to sing in the Wellington

Elisabeth Hellawell photographed on a return trip to Auckland in 1957 after three years' study and performance in London, with Sister Mary Xaveria (seated), Sister Mary Leo, and Mina Foley (seated right).

(Elisabeth Hellawell)

Town Hall on 3 December 1956. Two St Mary's girls, Joan Cochrane and Judith Edwards, reached the finals, with Joan Cochrane coming third overall. St Mary's girls did not feature in the finals of the second Mobil Song Quest in 1957, but in 1959 Mary O'Brien won the competition, with Angela Shaw runner-up. This marked the beginning of a long string of successes for Sister Mary Leo, whose pupils were to win the Mobil Song Quest throughout the 1960s.

Until the 1950s Sister Mary Leo was still largely a school music teacher, whose pupils were those attending St Mary's College. But with the success of Mina Foley and so many other singers, a new type of pupil began to come to her; girls who were older, not necessarily Catholic, and who had not been brought up in a system of unquestioning obedience to nuns. Their experience of Sister Mary Leo as a teacher is obviously different from those who had first encountered her as a school music teacher. Heather Begg, for example, who began lessons with Sister Mary Leo in 1950 as a shy 17-year-old, always found her calm, positive and loving.

> ...I will always be grateful to Sister Mary Leo for giving me a safe and positive start and the early inspiration to press on to make a success of the talents I had... I was fortunate that our paths crossed at just the right time. She was at the peak of her teaching powers, untiring, dedicated, strict, ambitious for her 'girls' and for herself... She was considered absolutely the best singing teacher in New Zealand.[13]

Many other pupils will identify with Heather, whose recollections of Sister Mary Leo include the way she frequently tugged at her stiffly starched white headpiece and big collar:

> I can hear the swish of her long skirt and veil as she moved around the studio, the pleasant rattle of her rosary beads when she sat down at the keyboard, and her rapid, quiet way of speaking.

After only three years with Sister Mary Leo, Heather embarked on a professional singing career — with the National Opera of Australia in 1954, and J.C. Williamson's Italian Grand Opera Company in

1955. In the same year she won the Sydney aria competition. Despite the fact that Heather learnt from several other singing teachers during her career, Sister Mary Leo always regarded her as one of 'hers'.

Ann Stott is another non-Catholic pupil who began lessons with Sister Mary Leo in 1955 when she was 21, the year Sister herself turned 60. Ann maintains that she was never intimidated by Sister, who to her was 'kindness and patience and understanding'. Sister Mary Leo liked to think she was grumpy, Ann said, but underneath she was 'absolutely as soft as butter. She would try to be rougher and I would say "it doesn't mean a thing to me, Sister".' Ann stayed with Sister Mary Leo for sixteen years and their relationship become almost that of mother and daughter; so much so that when Ann married she brought her prospective husband to ask permission of Sister Mary Leo.

The religious music teachers had traditionally taught any pupil who came to them, regardless of their faith. Sister Mary Leo was no exception, saying 'I never ask a pupil about her religion. That is her own business and nothing to do with me. The voice is a gift of God.'[14] Obviously there was a practical rationale behind this attitude: the Sisters of Mercy needed the income provided by non-Catholic pupils. But the fact that her grandfather had been Presbyterian and Grand Secretary of the Masons, an organisation some Catholics believed conspired against them, may also have been a factor in her tolerant attitude. The degree of her broadmindedness was demonstrated when she agreed to be a witness at Ann Stott's wedding, where the toastmaster was Jewish and the bridegroom and officiating minister were both Presbyterian ministers.

In the 1950s Sister Mary Leo was still teaching a few boy sopranos, tenors and boy instrumentalists, although she later limited herself to teaching women's voices only. The memories of two boy pupils of the 1950s provide another example of her individual treatment of her pupils. Roy Bowden, a singing pupil from 1951 to 1955, recalls her as someone who could give criticism while also building confidence. 'Sister was able to challenge me and criticise me without damaging my ego, and then she would build my confidence being careful not to give false praise.' His memories differ from those of Anthony Hollows,

Sister Mary Leo as a witness at Ann Stott's wedding in 1974. Pictured from left to right are Len Stott, Sister Mary Leo, Ann Stott, her husband the Rev. John Cumming, and the Rev. Ernie Walsh.

(Ann Stott)

who began learning violin from Sister Mary Leo in 1950 at the age of 14, when he was a pupil at a Catholic school. Anthony recalls her as a teacher who never gave praise and who had no qualms about disciplining him by asking him to say acts of contrition and a decade of the rosary. The only boy learning from Sister for some time, Anthony was later told he had been her pet. This was not something he noticed at the time.

The private singing classes offered at St Mary's continued to flourish in the 1950s, with a senior group of 25 girls who had left school, their ages ranging from 16 to 25; an intermediate class of 12- to 15-year-olds, and a junior class aged 9 to 12. The senior group which met on Saturday mornings, attended mostly by university and training college students, was particularly popular. As well as vocal production the girls studied stagecraft and interpretation. Students had to audition to be accepted into a class and many saw it as a privilege to be learning from Sister Mary Leo. Leonie McRae, who had lessons with Sister while attending Teachers' Training College in 1952–53, spent most of each Saturday at St Mary's, and felt she was one of the 'privileged few'. Class members worked hard for Sister Mary Leo, who was 'blunt at times, forthright, but always encouraging… We had our "small group" lesson then were sent off to our individual or paired practice room to prepare for the next teaching session. And so Saturday went.'

Alana Cooke (née Bolton) who in 1958 joined a class of fifteen girls who met in the St Mary's hall every Monday afternoon, has written a vivid description of the singing class, including her audition when Sister Leo came over to her and poked her in the ribs as she was singing:

'Support, support,' she ordered.
Support what? I wondered, still singing. I didn't know what she was talking about. 'Feel firm around here,' she said, putting her hands around my ribs and holding me firmly. I felt the weight of her bony hands against me, but I still didn't know what she meant.[15]

By the end of the fifties Sister Mary Leo's reputation as the best singing teacher in New Zealand was firmly established, and the two pupils who were to become her greatest stars had joined the music school. The Te Kanawa family moved from Gisborne to Auckland so that Kiri could attend St Mary's College, starting when she was 14. For two years Kiri attended the school, receiving two singing lessons from Sister Mary Leo most weeks, and also singing in the school choir. After leaving school at the age of 16 Kiri continued her lessons with Sister Mary Leo.

Looking back thirty years later Dame Kiri Te Kanawa said that the training she received from Sister Mary Leo was essential to her singing, and a very solid start to her studies. The most important thing Sister Mary Leo taught her was 'the immense love of music, which she nurtured in me'.[16] Sister Mary Leo took care not to harm Kiri's voice by too much public performance, and in 1963 it was reported that

Kiri, despite 'many recent successes in competition work', was refusing most offers of engagements.[17]

Malvina Major began driving up from Te Kowhai (near Hamilton) for weekly lessons in 1960, remaining a pupil of Sister Mary Leo's until the end of 1964. Even Malvina, who had been singing and performing all her life, found that in her first year of tuition with Sister Mary Leo she had to give up singing in public. During that year she was taught:

> ...*how to stand, how to breathe, how to produce the sound, how to control it, how to pronounce your words and how to get the sound and the words — two separate things — blending together. She always likened it to a string of pearls: the music is the string and the pearls are the words and the two are married together.*[18]

As they waited for the year to be over, Malvina and her mother wondered if they had made the right decision in going to Sister Mary Leo, but Malvina later decided that the technique she learned then had sustained her voice ever since.

For many pupils the St Mary's School of Music became an all-absorbing way of life: a busy place where they spent long hours in lessons and practice. Every room in Stella Maris was dedicated to teaching or practice; some larger rooms had been divided up to create practice rooms that were just large enough for a piano and a piano stool. Pupils who learnt the cello were expected to practise in the (unused) bathroom, literally sitting on the side of the bath. Most of the practice rooms were at the top of the stairs. From her teaching room downstairs Sister Mary Leo listened to the practice going on above and around her, and if someone stopped practising she would bang on the wall or ceiling with a stick. If she suspected a pupil was not practising she would hold her rosary beads to stop them from rattling as she climbed the stairs, and surprise the pupil when she opened the door.

The seventeen teaching or practice rooms in Stella Maris — eleven upstairs and six downstairs — had no soundproofing and the building was constantly alive with music. For the younger pupils it was inspiring to hear the voices of the senior students practising. Many recall

'Stella Maris', the building which housed the St Mary's School of Music from 1949 to 1975. Sister Mary Leo's teaching room was behind the bow windows at the front of the building.

(Auckland Sisters of Mercy Archives)

listening in wonder and amazement — sometimes with their ears to the wall — to the beautiful voices coming from other rooms. There was an intensity about Stella Maris, recalls Vivienne Gordon (née Adams) which emanated from Sister Mary Leo. 'She was our inspiration. There was an emphasis on excellence. She expected excellence.'

One day, finding Stella Maris unexpectedly locked, Vivienne and a friend climbed in a window in order to do some practice. They were being reprimanded for this when Sister Mary Leo intervened, saying it was a feather in the girls' caps that they had wanted to practise.

In addition to the music teachers already mentioned, others who taught from St Mary's during the 1950s included Sister Mary Natalie

Byers, Sister Mary Fidelma Kearney, Sister Mary Dora Hotchin, and a former pupil, Judith Edwards. Yet while the other teachers were highly skilled, it was always considered a privilege to learn from Sister Leo, something that had to be earned. One pupil recalls the way she was instantly promoted to learning from Sister Mary Leo after winning a singing competition.

For longstanding pupils of Sister Mary Leo, her teaching room at Stella Maris became a second home, a 'holy of holies' which they all remember vividly. A large, L-shaped room, it had originally been two rooms, and was still divided by a semi-partition. Two large bow windows, with white venetian blinds, faced New Street. The walls were painted light green, with white skirting boards and window sills. The floor was of polished wood with rugs on it. In one corner, the focal point of the room, stood the grand piano, black and gleaming. With its coloured leadlights, a small glass-fronted cupboard, small dark red tiles in an inglenook at one end of the room, and a moulded plaster ceiling, the room had many artistic features. These were added to by Sister Mary Leo, mainly with gifts that were given to her by pupils. Pot plants, statues, busts of composers, china ornaments and photographs of her former pupils stood on every available shelf and ledge — of which there were many. Small brass busts of Schubert and Wagner stood on a window seat. Among the china ornaments were a set of Dresden china angels playing musical instruments, given to her by members of the St Mary's choir. There were low tables and flower arrangements, mirrors on every wall, and tidy heaps of sheet music on every available surface. Tucked away out of sight was a radiogram and a tape recorder. Heather Begg recalls the music room as having 'an old fashioned charm and a serene sort of elegance about it… There was never a speck of dust and the lovely smell of polish was ever present.'

The highly polished floor and furniture was the result of hard work on the part of the assistant music teachers and boarders who had the room assigned to them as their 'charge'. The boarders did the dusting, while the assistant teachers did the cleaning. Sister Mary Leo taught such long hours that it was difficult to find time when the room could be cleaned. Not only was it in use every weekday until about eight at night, but lessons continued on Saturday and there were always extra lessons arranged before examinations. Sister Mary Leo herself did not have a 'charge' by this stage in her life. Assistant music teacher Sister Muriel Shallue would often clean the room late at night after lessons had finished, while Sister Majella Patterson recalls the effort that was required to drag the large floor polisher from the convent to the music room.

Sister Mary Leo was known to have a 'special devotion' to Our Lady of Fatima, and a statue of her stood on prominent display in the music room. To those not versed in Catholic tradition this is a difficult concept to understand, but Catholics believe that Mary, the mother of Jesus, has come to earth on a number of occasions in different places. One such series of appearances occurred at Fatima, a remote village in Portugal, in 1917. Here Mary appeared to three poor young shepherd children and through them made various predictions, all of which were later believed to have come true. News of the apparitions travelled quickly and large numbers of pilgrims began to visit the site,

Sister Mary Leo giving a lesson to Anne Rasmussen, October 1965. 'Our Lady of Fatima', to whom Sister Mary Leo attributed her success, watches over the lesson. The 'hall of fame', photographs of successful pupils and former pupils, can be seen in the background.

(News Media: Auckland Star Collection)

believing that prayers made on the spot where Mary had appeared would find special favour with God. Today Fatima is a place of pilgrimage to many hundreds of thousands of people each year, and there have been many reported miracles of healing and personal renewal. Sister Mary Leo believed that her success as a teacher came in response to the prayers she offered to Our Lady, who intervened on her behalf. When she was congratulated on a pupil's success, her response was to say, 'Oh no, it wasn't me, it was Our Lady of Fatima.'

CHAPTER FIVE

THE EMERGING CELEBRITY

1956–1963

As the fifties progressed Sister Mary Leo became increasingly visible. An important first step came when she appeared in a photograph in the college *Annual* in 1956 with the world famous Spanish soprano Victoria de los Angeles and a group of her senior pupils.[1] Another notable step came in 1959 when, for the first time ever, Sister Mary Leo was thanked by name in the *Annual*. After mentioning various former pupils who had taken leading roles with the New Zealand Opera Company, the *Annual* commented:

> *We are very proud of all these performers who contribute so much to our national culture, and wish to congratulate and thank Sister M. Leo and the staff of the Music School for their devoted attention to our musical needs.*[2]

This process of giving an individual sister recognition and praise for her work was significant in a religious community which by its nature discouraged individual attention. The 'Customs in Use' which Sister Mary Leo studied as a novice included a section on humility:

> *…they shall not have the habit of speaking of themselves or of their concerns, deeming themselves beneath the notice of others and*

Victoria de los Angeles pays a visit to St Mary's in 1956. From left to right are Sr Mary Majella Patterson, Sr Gabrielle Mary Ladley, Sr Mary Xaveria, Victoria de los Angeles, Sr Mary Leo, Sr Mary Veronica Delany.

(Elisabeth Hellawell)

unworthy to occupy attention. They shall speak thus: – 'We do so.' 'It is ours', or 'for our use' etc. Two sisters are frequently engaged in the same work, it is not our custom to say which Sister in the Community has painted, printed, transcribed, illuminated, worked, played, or sung etc. All are executed by the Community, no mention of individuals.[3]

It is unlikely that the community as a whole had made a decision to change its attitude towards individual recognition for achievements; it is more likely that the acknowledgement just happened, without any particular decisions being made.

Another significant development was an illustrated feature article which appeared in the *Auckland Star* in November 1959. Under the heading 'Sister Leo's "girls" have a special quality in their voices', the article discussed Sister Mary Leo's teaching in some detail; it also included two photographs of Sister Mary Leo, one with Mina Foley and the other with singers and officers from the New Zealand Opera Company. Ultimately the decision to talk to the reporter would have been made by Sister Mary Leo herself.

The photographs of Sister Mary Leo that were published at this time were often taken during the visits of celebrated singers, who increasingly made their way to her music school. The first visit by Victoria de los Angeles came about when Angela Shaw and Marie Robinson were invited to sing at a reception for the Spanish soprano, who asked if she could meet their teacher. A few years later the *Annual* included a photograph of Sister Mary Leo and pupils with Lili Kraus. The celebrated pianist, on her second visit to St Mary's, had 'talked to Sisters and girls as an old friend'.

When Sister Mary Leo was asked, 'Why does nearly every visiting woman singer of any note visit the school?' her reply was simple: 'We invite them.' Her reason for doing so, she explained, was that, 'The girls profit from meeting the successful. And such is my interest in physiology of the throat that I like to look down their throats.'[4] Several pupils and colleagues remembered the occasion when Sister Mary Leo asked Victoria de los Angeles to stand by the window and open her mouth, and then invited some of her senior pupils to peer down the great singer's throat in order to study her physiology. Sister Mary Leo's own account of this occasion was:

> *When I asked Victoria de los Angeles to sing softly while I looked down her throat she humbly did so — while I watched what she did with her soft palate.*
>
> *Negro singer Ella Lee did the same for me last year. I study the shape and size of the throat and the fascinating action of the soft palate.*[5]

It was obviously an honour to be chosen to sing for famous visitors to the music school. Mary O'Brien met two of her greatest supporters, Gerard Souzay and Lili Kraus, in this way. French baritone Gerard Souzay was so impressed by Mary's singing that he assumed she must have been trained overseas.

'What part of Italy did you train in, Mary?' he asked. 'Did you train overseas?'

'I've never been out of New Zealand,' she replied. 'My teacher's in the room.'

Other visitors included Elizabeth Schwarzkopf, Rita Streich, Mattiwilda Dobbs and Guiseppe di Stefano. These occasions obviously meant a lot to the visitors as well as the students. After Ella Lee visited the music school in 1964 she wrote saying she still thought about the time she had spent there:

> ...*it was one of the delights of my trip... How are the girls, please give them my regards and tell them it was so wonderful to see and hear them, and if I get a chance to return one of these days, I hope to hear that they have progressed.*[6]

As well as becoming more visible in the media, Sister Mary Leo was also beginning to go out in public. Ann Gordon (later Alexandra Gordon), who began learning from Sister Mary Leo in 1959, recalls that Sister always supported her pupils by attending competitions with them, something that would have been impossible in her earlier days as a teacher. Such excursions could be justified on the grounds that it helped her teaching to know how her pupils were performing in public: 'I can find out better what they are doing in performance if I hear for myself.'[7]

Some pupils may have preferred her not to come to the competitions. The long string of last minute instructions given to the girls in her rapid-fire voice often did nothing to help, but only made them more nervous. Even more disconcerting was to get up on stage and hear a clickety-click coming from the front row where Sister Mary Leo sat praying over her rosary beads. One pupil recalls that when she performed Sister Mary Leo would sit in the audience mouthing the words with exaggerated facial expressions.

Sister Mary Leo's attitude towards the competitions is full of contradictions. On the one hand she is quoted as saying that she hated 'that competitive spirit', instead instructing her pupils to: 'Go into the competition, not with the intention of winning, but with the hope of gaining experience,' and telling them that if they were defeated they should take it well and show a friendly spirit towards all other contestants.[8] Yet former pupils and colleagues agree that she liked to win. 'Every post a winning post,' is a comment which according to one former colleague was frequently made about her.

In 1960, the year Sister Mary Leo turned 65, her mother Agnes Niccol died in her 91st year. Several of Sister Mary Leo's former pupils attended the funeral and Mina Foley sang at the graveside. A year or two before her death Agnes had recorded a song, 'My Task', accompanied by Sister Mary Leo. The song has a high tessitura, and although she had some difficulty with the high notes at the age of 89, they were notes that she had sung easily in the past. Sister Mary Leo later recalled that her mother was 'one of my pet pupils'. 'I was telling her not to make so much noise over the breathing and she said, "Remember my dear, I'm not 80 any longer. I'm 89 so make allowance for that."'[9]

Agnes had always been exceedingly proud of her eldest daughter, and had photos of Sister Mary Leo's pupils pinned up on her bedroom wall. When Sister Mary Leo began to become known as the teacher of Mina Foley and other successful singers Agnes would hasten to tell visitors to the O'Sullivan home, '…and I'm her mother you know.' Agnes was never to know just how famous her daughter would become in the years ahead.

Later in 1960 Sister Mary Leo was one of thirteen New Zealanders selected to talk about their lives on the radio, as part of the programme 'This is New Zealand'. There were only two women among the thirteen participants, all of whom had excelled in their particular calling; the other was the dancer Rowena Jackson. It was this sort of publicity which made Sister Mary Leo a household name throughout New Zealand.

The college *Annual* quoted some of the appreciative tributes that were written after the programme went to air:

If Arthur Lydiard can claim to be the best known athletic coach in New Zealand of late, there is hardly another person to match a similar claim in the field of music than Sister Mary Leo… For some years now there has been hardly a major contest winner or an accomplished woman singer who has not studied at one time or another under her...

The *Annual* then added a comment about Sister Mary Xaveria:

In addition, we at St Mary's know very well that the indispensable complement to Sister Mary Leo's work is provided by Sister Mary Xaveria, our incomparable accompanist of the exquisite touch...

These two remarkable teachers have never sought the limelight, and will not wish us to direct it on them here. But we must train the spotlight of these lines on them long enough to say: 'We are proud of you, and we thank you from our hearts.'[10]

Sister Mary Xaveria's skill as an accompanist is rarely mentioned in other articles. While Sister Mary Leo increasingly became a public figure, Sister Mary Xaveria (who in 1961 changed her name to Sister Francis Xavier) managed to stay out of the spotlight. Temperamentally they were very different. Sister Mary Leo, who always did things quickly, would become more and more excitable at times of stress, when preparing for a concert, competition or examination. The students knew that Sister Francis Xavier could be relied on to stay even-tempered, like a mother who could be turned to for comfort. 'It's all right dear,' she would say to a tearful, overwrought pupil. Always kind and sympathetic, she would have morning tea with the junior teachers and pupils in the kitchen of Stella Maris on a Saturday morning, in contrast to Sister Mary Leo who rarely took a break.

Former pupils often comment on the close relationship between Sister Francis Xavier and Sister Mary Leo, because they so often became aware of a tension between them. This would arise when Sister Mary Leo called Sister Francis Xavier out of her teaching room — regardless of who Sister Francis Xavier might be teaching at the time — in order to accompany Sister Mary Leo's pupil. Sister Francis Xavier would express her displeasure with a grimace, by rolling her eyes or muttering under her breath. One pupil recalls her trying to remonstrate with Sister Mary Leo, saying that she had something else to attend to, and Sister responding, 'I think the Good Lord will forgive you, now play.' Yet it was also evident that this sparring was only superficial. At a deeper level the two sisters were very attached to each other, each respected the other's artistry, and they had a very real and lasting friendship. While other music teachers were often moved from one convent to another, Sister Mary Leo and Sister Francis Xavier stayed at St Mary's, forming an enduring partnership. There is a story that one year in the early 1960s Sister Francis Xavier was sent to Epsom, but had to be recalled: Sister Mary Leo could not cope without her.

Many former St Mary's girls recall the quality of Sister Francis Xavier's accompanying, a quality that she herself would always deny. But visitors to the convent would ask in wonder, 'Who is that playing the piano?' One pupil taking a violin examination was asked, to her dismay, to play a particular piece again. Her relief was great when the examiner explained that the first time round he had been listening to the violin, this time he wanted to enjoy the accompaniment.

The Diamond Jubilee Concert for the Mater Hospital, 11 December 1960.

(Selwyn Rogers)

The achievements of St Mary's music school were becoming more widely known. Harold Rutland, who had been in New Zealand in 1960 as the examiner for Trinity College, London, wrote in the English magazine *Music in Education:*

> *The devoted musical work of the nuns in the many convents I visited was shown in its most magnificent form at a concert in Auckland Town Hall, when a choir of two hundred girls and a number of talented solo singers, including Mina Foley, Elisabeth Hellawell and Lynne Cantlon, provided shining evidence of the vocal training abilities of Sister M. Leo and her assistants at St Mary's College.*[11]

This concert, held in the town hall on 11 December to mark the Diamond Jubilee of Mater Hospital, was the major event for the music school in 1960. One of the soloists was Mina Foley, who had recently returned to the stage, but less than a year later she tragically suffered a major breakdown in health which forced her to give up singing for many years.

It was to be eighteen years before Mina Foley sang in public again. Throughout this period Sister Mary Leo remained a loyal friend, visiting Mina, giving her singing lessons and, when asked by reporters, continuing to name Mina as her most gifted pupil. Mina was one of many pupils who later described her relationship with Sister Mary Leo as that of mother and daughter.

While Mina's career was tragically foreshortened, the Mina Foley legend lived on. Those who heard her sing at the height of her career in the early 1950s still marvel at the purity and beauty of her voice. Sister Veronica Delany would not be alone in her view that hearing Mina sing was 'a spiritual experience of the greatest intensity… I have never listened to any singer that gave me the spiritual experience that Mina did.'

In 1962 another successful concert was put on in the town hall as the grand finale to the St Mary's Queen Carnival campaign, held to raise money for a new science block. The *New Zealand Herald* music critic, 'LCMS' (Lin Saunders), was lavish in his praise:

The singing of the choir of St Mary's College and its School of Music is one of those luxuries of elegant sound that always satisfy a critical listener...

Discipline was the keynote of the evening's success. It was evident in the stage deportment of each of the several hundred performers and in their music. This and expert musical training produced a programme of uniformly high standard.[12]

The senior choir, the massed choir and the soloists (Mary O'Brien, Hannah Tatana, Lynne Cantlon, Patricia Price, Hazel Millar, Pettine-Ann Croul and Anne Rasmussen) all received mention.

Sister Mary Leo with soloists who performed in the St Mary's College concert in the Auckland Town Hall in July 1962. The concert was in aid of the new science block at the college. Left to right, the singers are: Pettine-Ann Croul, Hazel Millar, Mary O'Brien, Lynne Cantlon, Lois Shannahan, Patricia Price and Hannah Tatana. Following the concert a critic described the choir's singing as 'one of those luxuries of elegant sound'.

(Barbara Tipping)

Sister Mary Leo was at the peak of her career, and when she was awarded the MBE in the 1963 New Year's Honours List a flood of congratulatory letters poured into St Mary's from people all over the country, including the Prime Minister, Keith Holyoake, and the Leader of the Opposition, Walter Nash. Some of the writers were known to Sister Mary Leo, but many others began their letters: 'Dear Sister — You do not know me, and I am not of your Faith, but I felt I must tell you how glad I am…'

As a result of the honour Sister Mary Leo became a nationally recognised public figure. The college *Annual* described the glittering evening in Wellington when the Queen herself presented the award. It is evident from this description that Sister Mary Leo was one of the most popular recipients of honours that night:

The appearance of Sister M. Leo, her dark habit contrasting strongly with the elaborate colours and jewels all around her, arrested the

Sister Mary Leo on the stage of the Wellington Town Hall, about to receive her MBE from the Queen. The investiture took place on 12 February 1963.

(St Mary's College Annual)

attention of the onlookers. 'Perhaps the most dramatic figure of the evening,' wrote an Auckland Star *reporter, 'sombre in her black habit, was Sister Mary Leo, beloved of all in the north, irrespective of creed.' 'Her Majesty had a few words of conversation with each recipient,' commented a Wellington daily, 'speaking perhaps for a longer time with Sister Mary Leo of St Mary's Convent, Auckland, who has trained many of New Zealand's top singers.'*[13]

Sister Mary Leo later revealed that she had wanted to greet the Duke of Edinburgh on this occasion, but it was not protocol to do so. They had got on well during the Duke's visit to New Zealand in 1959, when Sister Mary Leo's student string sextet played at a luncheon attended by the Duke, and she would have liked to acknowledge him. The Queen had recently seen Mary O'Brien and Lynne Cantlon playing lead roles in David Farquhar's *A Unicorn For Christmas*, and questioned Sister Mary Leo about her students and teaching. Her Majesty is reported to have described the New Zealand-composed opera as 'a very lovely work'.[14]

At this stage in her life, in the mid 1960s, several interviewers tried to find out the reasons behind Sister Mary Leo's great success as a teacher. These interviews break through the silence that surrounded her life after she entered the convent. They present for the first time written accounts of Sister Mary Leo's speech, and in the absence of any more personal records they are important sources of information about her. It is evident that, while she was always willing to talk about her pupils, she resisted attempts to make her talk about herself. At the same time she was naturally garrulous; at times she may have said things she later regretted, and it would seem that she agreed to some of the interviews in order to correct something that had been reported, or misreported, in a previous article. This was particularly apparent in two articles which appeared in the *New Zealand Herald* in September and October 1964. In the first she was quoted as saying, 'I teach my girls deportment and dress sense before I even let them sing their first note,' while in the second she is reported as saying it was 'definitely not true' that she did not allow a pupil to open her mouth until she had learned dress sense.[15]

One reporter wrote that she was as easy to talk to as Tom Pearce (at the time chairman of the Rugby Union), while another quoted her as saying she would not talk about her past because since taking her final vows her past was negligible. The effect of this apparent reluctance to talk about herself was to add to her mystique, a mystique enhanced when she described herself as 'a rebel music teacher' and 'quite unorthodox'. One interviewer who asked her why she was so successful received the reply, 'I often wonder why... It's just one of those things.'[16]

Yet in these interviews Sister Mary Leo did in fact reveal a lot about her teaching methods. She emphasised the psychological element in her teaching, saying that she treated each pupil individually and had no hard and fast rules. She was friend and confidante to her pupils, and tried to develop their personality as well as their voice. She urged her pupils to think of others and to see their voices as gifts from God to be shared with others. She believed in encouragement but not flattery. An article headed 'Clue to Nun's Success as Music Teacher' came to the conclusion that it was the psychological aspect that was all-important. Sister Mary Leo had found that she needed to be 'psychologist, friend and confidant' to her pupils. The 'clue' to her success lay in the fact that she could recall each of her singers as an individual. In fact, while Sister Mary Leo appeared not to be giving away the 'secret' behind her success as a teacher, this psychological approach and the individual treatment of her pupils was probably the most significant factor in her success. (Sister Mary Leo's teaching methods are discussed in more detail in chapter 7.)

Only one reporter attempted a description of Sister Mary Leo's physical appearance at this time, describing her as:

> ...*a slight, wiry woman with eyes that twinkle with good humour behind her glasses and a face warmed by a lovely smile. Anyone meeting her is impressed not only by her matter-of-fact sincerity but also by her down-to-earth common sense.*[17]

A former pupil remembers Sister Mary Leo as by now already round-shouldered, slightly stooped and generally holding her head on one side. This may have come from long hours spent sitting at the piano with her legs crossed, while looking over her shoulder at her pupils. A 'lazy' muscle in one eyelid meant that it was permanently half closed, giving her a slightly quizzical look. She still spoke 'presto' and, rather surprisingly for a singing teacher, she had not taken care of her voice which was gravelly and unsupported. Her voice problems were in fact typical of someone who habitually talks too fast.

One way of assessing personal fulfilment is by using the 'hierarchy of needs' concept developed by the psychologist Maslow,[18] which says that the highest need in the hierarchy, self-actualisation, can only be realised after other more basic needs have been met. Looking at Sister Mary Leo's life in the 1960s in the light of this 'hierarchy of needs', it is evident that this was the case, and she had attained a high degree of self-actualisation, or self-fulfilment. The community life of the Sisters of Mercy provided her with the ultimate in psychological, physical and emotional security. Her physical needs — housing, food, clothing, personal care if she was ill — were met without her ever having to cook or wash up the dishes; her emotional needs were met by the friendship and affection of the other sisters. She had a totally stable living environment which also, of course, met all her spiritual needs. She had a strong sense of belonging, and knew that she was both needed and accepted in her community.

In addition she had been given the freedom to develop her own particular gifts as a teacher for the honour and glory of God, while at the same time knowing that she was providing essential income for the community. She had gained and enjoyed widespread approval and recognition far beyond that gained by most people. She had been able to fully pursue her desire for knowledge and understanding, had built up an extensive library and had not been denied access to lectures or information. Her aesthetic needs were met by the great beauty in the liturgies of the church and in the musical performances she attended or directed.

Sister Mary Leo was a highly developed individual with a lifestyle which reflected her extraordinary vigour and capability. During the 1950s her workload increased until she was teaching a twelve-hour day: from 8.30 in the morning until after 8 p.m. at night. Colleagues say she spared little time for meals and was often the last person to leave the chapel late at night.

When former pupils and colleagues are asked about their recollections of Sister Mary Leo a number of themes emerge. She is remembered as a woman who always got what she wanted, often acting in an autocratic or dictatorial fashion. Yet in speaking of this, there is remarkably little resentment. This is due partly to the brilliance and charisma (some say genius) of her personality, and partly to the fact that she never wanted things for selfish reasons.

'She was brilliant, unique, but kindly with it. She would move heaven and earth to get what she wanted the way she wanted it, but she was never nasty with it,' said a music teaching colleague, Sister Patricia Graham. Sister Mary Leo was following a wider vision, and was not self-seeking. All agree that she had a remarkable ability to achieve goals that seemed impossible — whether they were goals for the music school or for an individual pupil, though no one can quite explain how or why she was able to do this. 'It was a quality in her character. There was just something about her.'

Sister Joan Hopkinson recalls finding herself playing the cello or double bass on one occasion. 'Even though she couldn't do a thing herself she could make you do it. It was extraordinary really.' Colleagues recall rehearsals in the town hall when she placed demands on everyone around her, leading one disgruntled electrician to comment, 'It's not an electrician you want, it's a magician.' During one dress rehearsal she called for male volunteers to shift the piano on the stage. When none of the parents sitting in the auditorium stirred she accosted one of them: 'You're a man aren't you?'

Sister Mary Leo would stand up to anyone if it were in the interests of her pupils or the music school. Anthony Hollows recalls the year he sat Grade 7 violin. For some reason they had been unable to obtain the music and so Anthony played the previous year's syllabus. The examiner began to object to this, at which point the door was flung open and Sister Mary Leo entered, her robes flying. There was a short altercation, Sister Mary Leo, as usual, having her way.

In a perceptive interview published in the *New Zealand Woman's Weekly*, Elizabeth Dunn described Sister Mary Leo as 'a woman of curious contrasts — at once worldly, and yet innocent'. Her music room, she went on to say:

> ...is strongly evocative of Sister Mary Leo's music — tranquil and flooded with sunshine, it retains a holiness that is much a part of her music; yet ... behind the tranquillity, lies an iron determination that the voice in song be perfection, that talents be shared, and that song shall help to free souls.[19]

Worldliness and innocence; humility and an enjoyment of recognition; competitiveness and community life; spirituality and celebrity status; these are some of the contrasts and contradictions that make up the personality of Sister Mary Leo. Her 'iron determination' also

Sister Mary Leo with her senior choir in November 1963. Among the choir members can be seen Malvina Major, Kiri Te Kanawa, Ann Gordon, Patricia Price, Raewyn Blade, Elizabeth Loomb, Gillian Redstone, Laurette Gibb, Hannah Tatana, Janice Lunn, Lynne Cantlon, Catherine Harrop, Marie O'Leary, Alana Bolton, Sally Rush, Hazel Millar, Adrienne Davis, Pauline Chambers, Diane Winterburn, Rae Chapman, Lyndsay Kearns, Jackie Chapman, and accompanist Frances Wilson.

(Brash Studio/Auckland Sisters of Mercy Archives)

needs to be seen alongside the warmth and compassion she showed for her pupils. By this time Sister Mary Leo was a more relaxed, affectionate and amiable teacher. Because she was less involved with school music and almost wholly occupied with her private teaching practice, the tension that had existed between her and the academic teaching nuns, when she took pupils out of class for their singing lessons, was less evident. Her pupils were mainly mature young women who were keen to learn. Several of her more talented pupils spent a year or more as full-time students at the music school after leaving school, while others who were performing with the New Zealand Opera Company or other companies would call in for lessons when they were in Auckland.

Singing pupils of the fifties and sixties generally have very warm and happy memories of St Mary's and Sister Mary Leo. A 'busy, motivating, wonderful place' is how Kathleen Johnson, a singing pupil from 1953–69, described it. 'A sort of paradise where everyone was good, but at the same time great fun,' said Rita Geraghty, a pupil from 1955–60. Collene Roche (née Dawe), who was a pupil from 1959 to 1962, described the 'friendly, welcoming atmosphere'.

An indication of the warmth of feeling Sister Mary Leo inspired at this time is the way 23 pupils and former pupils gathered at Christmas 1962 to present her with a stereogram and a collection of classical records. Yet while she may have been a more amiable teacher, Sister Mary Leo was still a strict disciplinarian who didn't stand any nonsense or time-wasting. Pupils still found her a stern critic who could be very blunt in her comments, and she was still very sparing in her praise. As part of her psychological approach to teaching she would praise one singer to another, but rarely would she praise them directly. If she did, the praise was valued very highly. One of the greatest compliments she ever gave her pupils was to say that their singing had moved her.

Some pupils always retained great awe and respect for Sister Mary Leo; others developed a closer friendship with her, especially if they continued to learn from her for many years. 'She was my friend, we loved each other…' said Hazel Millar Boyd, who was a pupil for twelve years.

Sister Mary Leo and Sister Francis Xavier with the stereogram presented to Sister Leo by her pupils in December 1962. Among those making the presentation are Fiona Wright, Monique Palmai, Ann Gordon, Margaret Hempleman, Patricia Price, Kiri Te Kanawa, Colleen Dawe, Leah Wilbraham, Lynne Cantlon, Mary O'Brien, Adrienne Davis, Daphne Payne, Elizabeth Loomb, Hannah Tatana, Gillian Redstone, Val Isbister, Elisabeth Hellawell, Janice Smith, Marie O'Leary and Lyndsay Freer.

(New Zealand Herald)

A common theme among students who learnt from Sister Mary Leo in the late 1950s and 60s is the great concern she showed for their personal lives. 'She was involved with the whole person,' said Marie Morris (née O'Leary), a pupil from 1959–68. 'She ... gave wise counselling in times of personal difficulty. I often told people she was like a concerned, loving aunt.'

Malvina Major has said that Sister Mary Leo was more than just a singing teacher; she was also a friend to all her pupils:

She was a counsellor and I think she understood us girls better than we understood ourselves. And she always was able to pick up if you were not feeling well or if you had a problem in life ... that side of her was something that nobody else saw, only we as her students ... I can't speak more highly of her from that point of view.[20]

Several former students have described their relationship with Sister Mary Leo as a mother-daughter relationship. Julianne Adamo (née Picot) has said that she and her sister Mary were like daughters to Sister Mary Leo: 'When my mother was very ill Sister used to check out all our clothes, what we were doing and she wanted to meet any boyfriends. She was absolutely delighted when I married a Catholic...' She also approved of Patricia-Anne Shaw's fiancé, the Australian tenor Ken Cornish. On his first visit to Auckland Patricia-Anne took him to visit Sister Mary Leo, who commented in a very loud stage whisper, 'I think he'll be very nice for you dear.' Louise Malloy recalls her asking questions like, 'Does your fiancé approve of music?' 'Will he allow you to continue singing once you're married?' and giving advice like 'Don't have too many babies too quickly because it won't do your career any good.'[21]

Sister Mary Leo herself said she felt like a mother to 'her girls', telling a television interviewer in 1981:

...I feel more of a mother to them. I feel like the old woman who lived in the shoe who had so many children she didn't know what to do... they feel they've got a home here and they'd always come and discuss things with me. They don't keep anything secret...[22]

Lyndsay Freer (née Kearns) said the friendship that developed between her and Sister Mary Leo became one of the closest relationships in her life:

I loved her dearly, almost as a kind of substitute mother, and I found that she was extremely affectionate and extremely loving and a very tactile person, who loved to hold your hand and put her arm round you, and sit you beside her on the stool... If you had a problem or a difficulty to talk over ... she was very sympathetic, always a very good listener, never judgemental.

The compassion and understanding that Sister Mary Leo showed for her pupils at this stage in her life may well have had its roots in the feelings she had for her own mother's situation. She was understanding if her pupils had a young baby and couldn't find a babysitter, telling them to bring the baby too.

'This place is like a nursery sometimes,' she said in 1972, going on to relate how the previous day she had asked a pupil to put her baby out in the corridor. 'I couldn't hear her singing. When the mother took the high notes the baby took them at the same time.'[23]

Sometimes Sister Mary Leo would ask her pupils about one of the other students: 'What do you think is happening with so and so. Do you think she's happy?' and a whole lesson might be spent discussing someone else's personal problems. But lessons lost in this way would always be made up.

There were many practical ways in which Sister Mary Leo helped her students, ranging from producing a piece of fruit or a muffin from her pocket to stave off hunger pangs during or after a lesson, to organising professional engagements for them, benefit concerts when it came time for them to leave her, or helping them find suitable placements overseas.

Someone who gave Sister Mary Leo a great deal of practical help with her pupils, and was probably her closest friend outside the convent, was Robina Reardon, for many years president of the Auckland Grand Opera Society. An extremely generous person who belonged to several service organisations, Robina not only organised professional engagements for students but also provided dresses or other accessories when they were needed. She remained a very significant friend of Sister Mary Leo's to the very end.

Some former students talk of Sister Mary Leo wanting to control their private lives, but once again there is remarkably little resentment of this. They realised that for Sister Mary Leo music was everything and that it never occurred to her that anything else could be as important to them. Marianne Mackie (née Bowden), who was a pupil from 1952–61, recalls her mother receiving two calls from a distressed or angry Sister Mary Leo. The first was when Marianne was accepted into the Greenlane Hospital School of Nursing. Sister Mary Leo had wanted her to train at Mater Hospital and take time off to continue with her singing. The second call came on the morning of Marianne's wedding: 'What a waste!' said Sister Mary Leo. 'My one singer with soul.'

So completely did Sister Mary Leo immerse herself in her teaching that other aspects of life were simply forgotten. As a result she was continually running late and always losing things. Her glasses, pens, appointment books and pieces of music were always going missing, and any senior pupil who happened to be at the music school would be called on to look for them. Lynne Cantlon, who spent long hours practising at the music school in the years after she left school, recalls eternally rummaging through the music stools looking for tiny pieces of music that had somehow got mislaid. She also became well acquainted with the cry that would go up whenever Sister Mary Leo lost her glasses: 'Lynne, Lynne, have you seen my specs anywhere. Where are my specs darling? Will you look for my specs?' With two pairs of glasses, one for reading music and one for doing other things, the unused pair was always going missing. Because Lynne had a car she was also frequently asked to go and pick up something, or drop someone off. And the requests were always urgent. Sister Mary Leo seemed to lack a sense of the passing of time, so that she would forget that something had to be done until it was already ten minutes late and then there would be a panic.[24]

The impractical side of her character also became evident in her problems with the tape recorder. Ann Stott remembers that an hour or two before she was due at her lesson there would often be a ring on the phone. 'Do you think you could come in a few minutes earlier? I've had a bit of trouble with the tape recorder.' She would arrive to find tape all over the floor. Sister Mary Leo, always alive to the present moment, could just as quickly become immersed in something else. One day Patricia-Anne Shaw was in the middle of a breathing exercise which involved lying on her back with the piano stool and reel-to-reel tape recorder placed on her stomach when a ring on the front door bell summoned Sister Mary Leo to talk to the Monsignor from the Bishop's house. Totally forgetting Patricia-Anne, who was unable to move, Sister Mary Leo proceeded to have a long conversation with the Monsignor; Patricia-Anne was finally rescued by a surprised Sister Francis Xavier, who asked, 'What are you doing there dear?'

There was an innocent, child-like side of Sister Mary Leo which is apparent in the many stories about her great love of cats. On one occasion when she was conducting a school choir, a small kitten's face was seen by the delighted girls to emerge from the sleeve of her habit. Other pupils recall the ongoing battle between her and Sister Francis Xavier over the cats that Sister Mary Leo would entice into the music room. Sister Francis Xavier always put the cats outside again. 'I wish I could have one. I'd have a cat in every place but my confreres don't like the idea,' Sister Mary Leo once told a reporter.[25]

This side of her character also came to the fore when she was on holiday. The Auckland Sisters of Mercy owned a holiday house on Waiheke Island and it was here that Sister Mary Leo went every year for a twelve-day rest. The holiday house, known as St Mary's Convent, was situated back from the road on a cliff high above Oneroa Bay, with commanding views on both sides. The sisters went swimming, often two or three times a day, walked, read books, and took turns to prepare meals for each other.

Colleagues agree that Sister Mary Leo was great fun on holiday. She relaxed completely, forgot all about her work and enjoyed herself. She went swimming and walking, read, listened to the radio, sat and talked, and joined in any fun that the sisters were having. She couldn't cook but she would offer to help by peeling the vegetables. Every Christmas Robina Reardon made two Christmas cakes, one for Sister Mary Leo and one for Sister Francis Xavier, and these were always brought to Waiheke Island for the sisters to share.

Many former students clearly remember their first meeting with Sister Mary Leo. For some the greatest surprise of the interview came when they were leaving and Sister told them not to step on 'the brass' (doorstep). Patricia-Anne Shaw, who did stand on the brass step, was asked what she was doing, and told she was 'a bold creature'.

Patricia Wright has particularly vivid memories of her first lesson with Sister Mary Leo because she was asked to go and sing on the verandah so that Sister could hear her from a distance. Not knowing which door to go through, Patricia went through the first door she came to and found herself in a room where a violin lesson was in progress. Hastily excusing herself, she went through another door to find a choir practising. Excusing herself again, she went through a third door to find a piano student. Finally she found herself on the verandah where she sang her little piece and then returned the way she had come, excusing herself through all three rooms once again.

'Patricia, where have you been? I couldn't hear a thing,' said Sister when she finally reappeared. 'You stupid girl, I meant you to go out *this* door onto the verandah.'

By this time, with former pupils scattered throughout the world, Sister Mary Leo spent a great deal of time writing letters. Many of her 'girls' stayed in touch with her until the end of her life, and treasured the letters and cards she sent them which always contained a personal message. When Heather Begg first left New Zealand in 1954, her mother gave her a leather-bound Bible, in which she still keeps some of the inspirational messages Sister Mary Leo sent her from time to time. Many of Sister Mary Leo's former students responded with gratitude for her prayers and concern: 'Thank you for your prayers and good wishes, they are a great consolation far from home and friends,' one wrote from Europe in 1961.

The latest letters were always carried round in the pockets of Sister Mary Leo's habit and produced during lessons. The younger pupils would be shown postcards and told titbits of information passed on from the older, successful singers they were trying to emulate. A tradition developed of pupils and former pupils sending a photograph to Sister to mark a major achievement in performance or examinations. The alcove in the music room where these photographs were displayed soon became known as the 'hall of fame'. Reporter Jo Noble, who interviewed Sister Mary Leo in 1965, described the photographs as a 'Who's Who in New Zealand Music'. 'We saw Mina Foley, Elisabeth Hellawell, Heather Begg, Angela Shaw, Hannah Tatana, Pettine-Ann Croul, Malvina Major, Mary O'Brien — far too many to mention them all by name, but each has achieved outstanding success in her particular musical field.'[26]

Chapter Six

The Era of the Second Vatican Council

1964–1972

In 1964 Sister Mary Leo travelled to Australia to prepare three pupils for the Sydney and Melbourne *Sun* Aria competitions. This was her first trip away from New Zealand since entering the convent in 1923, and was evidently a last-minute decision. The college *Annual* described how 'special arrangements were hurriedly made' for Sister M. Leo to fly to Australia after three of her pupils (Hannah Tatana, Pettine-Ann Croul and Malvina Major) were among the seven finalists chosen from 128 entrants to be in the Sydney *Sun* Aria contest. Sister Mary Leo flew to Australia on the Thursday night, spent most of Friday working with her pupils, 'polishing their work for the final', and attended the final, held as part of the Sydney Eisteddfod competitions, on Saturday night. While in Sydney she stayed with the Sisters of the Good Shepherd in Ashfield, who always gave her a warm welcome.

Her readiness to fly to Sydney on this occasion can perhaps be explained by the events of the previous year, when Pettine-Ann Croul had been eliminated in the semi-finals of the Sydney *Sun* Aria contest.

It was an unpopular decision and loud booing greeted the judges' announcement of the finalists. Sydney musician, singing teacher and adjudicator Max Aronsten, stunned by Pettine-Ann's elimination from the finals, queried the decision — to be told that she was 'too young' — and later made contact with both Pettine-Ann and Sister Mary Leo. Out of this correspondence a close friendship developed between Sister Mary Leo and Max and Joan Aronsten, who generously gave their hospitality to many of Sister Mary Leo's pupils in the years to come.

But in 1964, with Sister Mary Leo in the audience, there was to be a different outcome. When the results were announced Pettine-Ann Croul had won the Sydney *Sun* Aria, with Malvina Major second and Hannah Tatana in seventh place. When interviewed in Sydney, Sister Mary Leo was quoted as saying, 'Oh, yes, I am very proud of my girls,' allowing herself a contented smile.[1]

This was not the only success for the trio in Australia: Pettine-Ann Croul also won the Dame Nellie Melba memorial aria cup, the Marjory Conley memorial award for the most outstanding singing of a Mozart aria, and the French song section. Hannah and Malvina then travelled to Ballarat to compete for places in the Melbourne Aria contest. Sister Mary Leo kept up the pressure, putting the girls through a rigorous training schedule. At one stage Malvina expressed the thought that it would be nice to go home for a day or a weekend. 'Our present home is Ballarat and our future home is heaven, so let's get on with it,' replied Sister Mary Leo.[2]

At Ballarat Malvina was the first place-getter, thus winning the right to compete at Melbourne. There were two weeks to go and Sister Mary Leo, using her 'psychological' approach to teaching, put heavy demands on Malvina.

> *I was homesick and in low spirits, and in order to make me angry and so perform better she reprimanded me on the pretext that I was an ungrateful student who didn't appreciate the effort she had made to be with me in Australia. (Ostensibly she had travelled to Australia to make sure her New Zealand pupils were being judged fairly in the competitions.)*

Sister continued to berate me while we were stuck in a lift that had broken down in the Melbourne Town Hall, and continued in the taxi home until she had me in tears. Hannah Tatana and I decided she was not the humble religious nun we knew back at the convent and we vowed we would not have another lesson from her.

The lesson, of course, was in my reaction — I became aggressive and angry. My extreme homesickness and 'sorry for myself' attitude vanished, and my performance in the [Melbourne] Sun *Aria competition won me first place. Sister was quickly in the wings after the announcement and put her arms around me saying, 'I'm sorry, dear, that I had to treat you like that, but it paid off.'*[3]

When Sister Mary Leo returned from Melbourne on 19 October, there were friends and pupils waiting to greet her with flowers at the airport. Boarders from St Mary's stood outside the school to cheer and wave to her as she drove to the convent. Sister Mary Leo, taken by surprise by the welcome, said she was overwhelmed by the warmth and sincerity of those who greeted her.

Sister Mary Leo was no longer the invisible, behind-the-scenes teacher, but was becoming a celebrity in her own right. No fewer than

Kiri Te Kanawa, who had recently won aria competitions in Auckland, Tauranga and Hamilton, during a lesson in 1965.

(New Zealand Magazines Archive)

three photographs of her were published in the *St Mary's College Annual* of 1964: one showed her with her triumphant pupils Malvina Major and Pettine-Ann Croul; a second was with Elizabeth Schwarzkopf and a group of pupils at St Mary's Music School, while the third showed her with the American soprano Ella Lee. By this time, with several photographs having appeared in the *New Zealand Herald*, she was also well-known to the general public. The exposure continued in 1965 with a double-page photographic feature and accompanying article in the *New Zealand Woman's Weekly*, and a cover photograph and accompanying article in the *New Zealand Weekly News*.

One senses that Sister Mary Leo actually enjoyed this media attention, which could be justified on the grounds of gaining publicity for her pupils and the music school, and bringing honour and glory to St Mary's and the cause of Catholic education. This view is shared by former pupil Heather Begg:

> *For a nun, I think she really quite enjoyed being in the limelight, and seemed to welcome any opportunities for publicity — maybe not always for her own glory and praise, but to bring attention to the success of her best pupils and the profession in general. She was certainly not shy in this area.*

By the time the *Weekly News* article appeared Sister Mary Leo had made another flying visit to Australia, this time to support Pettine-Ann Croul, Lynne Cantlon, Joan Kennaway and Kiri Te Kanawa as they entered the 1965 Australian competitions. Hospitality was once again provided by the Sisters of the Good Shepherd at Ashfield, and the Sisters of Mercy at Ballarat. All the girls did well. Pettine-Ann Croul won the £1000 Shell Aria prize in Canberra. Lynne Cantlon sang in the semi-finals of the Sydney and finals of the Melbourne *Sun Arias*, won the French art song event in Sydney, the ladies' championship and, with Kiri Te Kanawa, the Grand Opera duet in Ballarat. Joan Kennaway, who shortly before going to Australia had won the John Court Aria Competition, won the Champion of Champions award in Sydney, the coloratura aria and the song by an Australasian composer.

But it was Kiri Te Kanawa who made the greatest impact in 1965. Sydney critics gave high praise to her performance after she came second in the Sydney *Sun* Aria competition. Moving on to Melbourne, she repeated Malvina Major's achievement of the previous year by winning the coveted first prize, the most valuable vocal award in Australasia. Kiri's voice had been developing steadily since 1960 when, at the age of 16, she was named as the most promising new voice in the Auckland Competitions. In 1963, the night after coming second in the Mobil Song Quest, she won the John Court Aria Competition in Auckland, with another of Sister Mary Leo's pupils, Ann (later Alexandra) Gordon, coming second. In 1964 Kiri won the Hamilton Aria competition.

In mid 1965 Sister Mary Leo wrote a long letter to the director of the London Opera Centre, James Robertson, outlining Kiri's abilities and achievements and asking him to advise her regarding her career and a suitable coach. She explained that Kiri was much sought after in New Zealand, and that the New Zealand Opera Company had been most anxious for her to join them, but that she had not consented to this as she considered 'her voice has too much potential to allow her to accept a touring contract and be without tuition for six months or more'.[4] James Robertson, who in 1963 had been the principal judge of the New Zealand Mobil Song Quest, replied that he remembered Kiri Te Kanawa very vividly, and that she would be accepted at the Opera Centre without audition.

In later years people often asked whether Sister Mary Leo could predict which of her pupils were going to achieve greatness. Did she know that Kiri Te Kanawa and Malvina Major were to become her two most successful pupils and did they accordingly receive special attention from her? The answer would seem to be that yes, she did realise they had great potential, and if they received special attention it was only because more was expected of them. Asked in 1981 if she had seen Kiri's potential greatness back in the 1960s, Sister Mary Leo replied with a cautious, 'Yes and no,' adding that in her days at St Mary's Kiri had preferred netball to singing practice and was at the stage of having to decide between being an opera star or a singer of light music. Yet the fact that Kiri and Malvina were described as 'the two "Golden" girls' in the school *Annual* of 1966 is a good indication that they were perceived to have outstanding potential.

At the same time Sister Mary Leo did not ever predict the future for her pupils, being only too aware of the things that could go wrong in a musical career. As she often said to her pupils, their voice was a gift from God which could be taken away from them tomorrow. Among her students were several who did not achieve their full potential for a variety of reasons. Mina Foley's breakdown in health has already been mentioned. Two other promising pupils or former pupils died tragically young: Kathleen Reardon in 1960, and Diane Winterburn in 1966. In the late 1960s another pupil with a great deal

An impressive array of talent is present in this photograph of Sister Mary Leo with pupils and past pupils who were soloists at the 'Popular Operatic Recital' given by St Mary's School of Music in December 1964. From left to right are: Pettine-Ann Croul, Hannah Tatana, Patricia Price, Heather Begg, Elisabeth Hellawell, Kiri Te Kanawa (front), Lynne Cantlon, Malvina Major, Beryl Dalley.

(New Zealand Herald)

of promise, Donna Awatere, gave up her singing career when her father was imprisoned on a murder charge.

Sister Mary Leo's choir and soloists continued to delight Auckland audiences. At the end of 1964 'Pupils Past and Present' put on a 'Popular Operatic Recital'. The line-up of talent was formidable: in addition to Malvina Major, Pettine-Ann Croul and Kiri Te Kanawa, the soloists included Hannah Tatana, Elisabeth Hellawell, Heather Begg and Lynne Cantlon.

In 1966 Lynne Cantlon gained second place in the Sydney *Sun* aria competition and went on to win the Melbourne contest; the third year in a row that one of Sister Mary Leo's pupils had achieved this double success. Following the Melbourne win Lynne's singing career continued with several years of engagements in Canada and a contract as resident principal soprano with the Hamburg State Opera from 1972 to 1975. Gillian Redstone also did well in Australia in 1966, winning the Dame Nellie Melba Cup and coming fifth in the Sydney aria competition.

This period in the mid sixties marks the climax of Sister Mary Leo's teaching career, as her pupils achieved a breathtaking series of successes. Many went on to study or win contracts overseas. Malvina Major went to London in 1965 to study at the London Opera Centre, to be joined there in 1966 by Kiri Te Kanawa and Ann (Alexandra) Gordon. Pettine-Ann Croul, whose win in the Sydney Aria in 1964 gave her a scholarship for study overseas, went to America in 1966, making her operatic debut in New York in *The Magic Flute*. In 1967 Gillian Redstone became the first New Zealander to study at the Juilliard School of Music in New York.

By 1966 the *St Mary's College Annual* was opening its music pages with a paragraph of praise for Sister Mary Leo, describing her as:

> *one of the greatest musicians and teachers of Australasia… Her impact on music in New Zealand is one that it would be impossible to overestimate. No small measure of her success is due to that pianist and instrumentalist of incomparable skill, Sister Francis Xavier…*

The same magazine included a photograph of Sister Mary Leo with a group of pupils and another international star who had come to visit her at the music school — Rita Streich. It is interesting to note that when this photograph was originally published the caption began 'Visit to famous teacher...', the implication being that Sister Mary Leo was just as famous as her visitor, possibly even more so.[5]

Throughout the 1960s Sister Mary Leo's pupils continued to dominate the John Court Memorial Aria competition, winning it every year from 1962 to 1967 and again in 1969. They also won every Mobil Song Quest from 1961 to 1970. In 1961 Patricia Price was the winner, with Hannah Tatana in second place. Patricia had been a pupil of Sister Mary Leo's since 1946, learning violin and piano as well as singing while she was at school. She also conducted the school choir for many years. The Mobil Song Quest was held every two years: in 1963, when the final was held in Hamilton, it was Malvina Major who won, with Kiri Te Kanawa runner-up. Illustrative of Sister Mary Leo's wry sense of humour is the story that after the results were announced Malvina and Kiri were handed a note which said simply, 'Congratulations. Back to work, both of you, Tuesday.'[6] Kiri's turn to win came at the final in Dunedin in 1965, while another of Sister Mary Leo's pupils, Anne Rasmussen, was the winner in 1967. Anne had been learning singing from Sister Mary Leo since arriving in New Zealand from Denmark at the age of eight. She won many talent quests and competitions, made her first record at the age of 15, and was not quite 18 when she won the Mobil contest.

In 1970 Patricia House won the Mobil Song Quest, the sixth consecutive win for Sister Mary Leo, and another student, Louise Malloy, was also a finalist. But this was to be the end of Sister Mary Leo's domination of the competition. When Christopher Doig won the Mobil contest in 1972, it marked the beginning of a series of successes for male singers.

Sister Mary Leo's greater freedom to attend her pupils' performances, and to be photographed, interviewed and praised for her achievements has already been noted. To a large extent these decisions seem to have been made by Sister Mary Leo herself, although there may have been some behind-the-scenes activity by parents of pupils or other 'secular' friends. A colleague has commented that Sister Mary Leo would not have pushed herself forward or sought publicity, and

A photograph taken at Auckland International Airport in August 1969 when Sister Mary Leo met up with three of her former pupils. Anne Rasmussen, on the left, was leaving for further study in Austria; Malvina Major, centre, holding her son Andrew, had just arrived home from a singing contract in Salzburg, and Gillian Redstone, on the right of the picture, was home for a holiday from her study at the Juilliard School of Music in New York.

(Selwyn Rogers)

that she was a stickler for seeking permission for absences or anything unusual. Yet it is evident that someone must have telephoned the newspapers to ask them to send a photographer to St Mary's on appropriate days.

Decisions to travel to Australia to support her pupils in the competitions, however, were a little different because they involved spending community money. These decisions must ultimately have been made by the Mother Superior, although in approving such trips she was not necessarily giving Sister Mary Leo special favours. The Sisters of Mercy had always had a policy of recognising superior talents among their members, and various Sisters of Mercy had travelled overseas in order to pursue higher education or training. By the 1960s several of the Auckland sisters were studying for degrees at Auckland University. But Sister Mary Leo, because of her lifestyle, her travel and her regular contact with members of the Auckland music world, can be seen to have been in the vanguard of the changes which were to affect religious communities throughout the world during these years.

The catalyst for many of these changes was the Second Vatican Council, which opened in October 1962 with the aim of reviewing those aspects of the Catholic Church's life and teaching which were out of step with the modern world. Among the sixteen documents issued by the Council was 'Perfectae Caritatis', or the 'Decree on the Appropriate Renewal of the Religious Life', published in 1965. This document called on religious communities to examine their structures and rules in the light of modern life, and make any changes that seemed appropriate. The Auckland Sisters of Mercy responded with weekly discussion groups (in which Sister Mary Leo took part) and lectures on the decree. Study commissions were set up to look at various aspects of religious life — the vows, community life, apostolates — and these reported back to the chapter meetings in 1969 and 1970. Changes and decisions made as a result of these discussions tended to be gradual and consultative. Thus the sisters were given options to do things in a new way, but were not obliged to take up the new alternatives. Eventually they were given the freedom to choose how and when they made their meditations and daily devotions, and the choice of whether to use Latin or English for their private prayer. Convent life was no longer strictly regulated by the sounding of bells, and the sisters gained the ability to stay outside the convent when it was necessary to meet family needs. The changes were not made as a simplistic desire to gain greater personal freedom, but were the result of much thought, prayer and discussion as part of an effort to better equip the sisters to live and work in the modern world.

The Decree also commented on religious habits; they were to be 'simple and modest, at once poor and becoming. They should meet the requirements of health and be suited to the circumstances of time and place as well as to the services required by those who wear them.'[7]

There had already been a significant, though not very noticeable, change to the sisters' clothing in 1953. The skirt of the habit was shortened slightly, the coif was no longer heavily starched but made of a soft material, and the under veil (the domino) was done away with. The only item still starched after this time was the dimity, the white band that went across the forehead. Later a lighter material was introduced for the summer habit, there was a reduction in the number of pleats in the dress and bodice, and the skirt train and oversleeves were removed. Now, in 1968, the Auckland Sisters of Mercy made a dramatic change to the coif and the habit. Instead of the floor-length habit of black serge, the sisters could choose to wear a significantly shorter, commercially made black dress known as 'the American habit'. The coif was replaced by a less imposing veil made in a softer material, which allowed some of the sisters' hair to be seen. A photograph published in May 1968 shows that Sister Mary Leo had by then adopted the new style of habit, with a soft collar and veil and her hair showing.

The greater personal freedom enabled Sister Mary Leo to become increasingly involved in the public life of the city. In November 1963 she joined a committee which aimed to assist young musicians. One of the committee's projects was organising an annual concert in the Auckland City Art Gallery, the result of their belief that if competitions were the only opportunities young musicians had to perform, then a 'wrong attitude toward art' would result.

A few years later, in 1967, Sister Mary Leo was invited to form the choir at St Patrick's Cathedral and developed a system whereby two choirs alternated in singing the mass on Sundays. The first choir was made up entirely of girls from her School of Music; the second was a mixed-voice choir of former St Patrick's choir members, augmented by girls from the music school. Sister Mary Leo was conducting the choir on Kiri Te Kanawa's wedding day in August 1967, but had difficulty getting inside through the enormous crowds that had gathered to see Kiri. An overzealous door attendant tried to stop her entering, thinking she was a gatecrasher. Sister Mary Leo later described how in the evening after the wedding Kiri brought Desmond to see her, saying, 'Thank God to sit down for a while in the quiet of the Convent.'

In August 1967 comes the first report of Sister Mary Leo conducting in public, at a recital in St Mary's Cathedral, Parnell, in aid of the centenary appeal of the Royal College of Organists, London. Sister Mary Leo took her St Patrick's Cathedral Girls' Choir to the recital, the first time a choir from the Catholic Cathedral had sung in the Anglican Cathedral. Later the same year, at a formal civic farewell to the Governor-General, Sir Bernard Fergusson, and Lady Fergusson, Sister Mary Leo (now aged 72) conducted for the first time at the Auckland Town Hall. For this occasion she had selected a small choir of 30 voices. The girls, in their long white gowns, white gloves and coloured capes, made a great impression on their audience, not just for their beautiful singing, but also for their appearance and deportment. Sir Bernard (who was seated in a central position on the stage) was so moved by the choir's singing of 'Ye Banks and Braes' that he shook Sister Mary Leo's hand as soon as it was over.

In May 1968 Sister Mary Leo agreed to conduct a concert in the Auckland Town Hall as the opening attraction in a week of activities planned to raise money for the Laura Fergusson Trust, with proceeds also going to the St Mary's building fund. The music school put on many fundraising events for St Mary's, where a major rebuilding programme between 1964 and 1971 resulted in a new accommodation block, community and administration block, and chapel.

'I'm not usually keen on public appearances,' Sister Mary Leo is quoted as saying in 1968, 'but because it's for such a worthwhile purpose I'm happy to do it.'[8] This concert attracted publicity as the first occasion when Sister Mary Leo, 'internationally known as a singing teacher', would conduct at a fully public performance. An advertisement headed 'In Person! Sister Mary Leo makes her first public appearance as conductor', and featuring a photograph of Sister Mary Leo, appeared in the *New Zealand Herald*. A few days later the *Herald* published a photograph of Sister Mary Leo conducting at a rehearsal for the concert. *Herald* music critic L.C.M. (Lin) Saunders, who had so often praised performances by Sister Mary Leo's pupils, also gave high praise to this concert, saying that 'cultured and beautiful singing was the order of the evening'. He went on to note that the excellence of teaching at St Mary's was stronger than ever:

The audience was a capacity one, the programme of more than generous length, and its presentation smooth and extremely well disciplined.

The excellence of the teaching at St Mary's is no new thing but its impact does not diminish. It was in fact stronger than ever as one listened to the Junior Choral Group of nearly fifty young singers, whose tone quality, word enunciation and deportment were alike exemplary.

In their ranks there is an assured supply of well-trained voices for the future such as already exists in the senior choir.

Sister Mary Leo with her junior choir in 1968. Front row, from left: G. O'Leary, S. Beren, P. Wright, P. Eddleston. Second row (seated): L. Marryat, T. Turnock, H. Fryer, J. Farry. Third row: K. Ockelford, C. Alderson, I. Meima, L. Bender, R. Tamihere, S. Brodeur, A. Jackson, L. Pearson. Fourth row: S. Ding, K. Weber, Sister Mary Leo, L. Rowe, S. McLeod. Fifth row: A. Hoko, A. Stanfield, L. Dunn, M. Battersby, J. Appleby, M. Churchill, J. Thurlow, D. Black, L. Rogers, L. Shewan, M. Menehira. Sixth row: T. Marinovich, R. Stead, B. Lynch.

(Auckland Sisters of Mercy Archives)

> *This group, with its customary beauty and unerringly good pitch, sang motets, traditional songs (among them a Welsh lullaby that was exquisite) and operatic choruses concluding with the 'Nuns' Chorus' which for sentimental rather than musical reasons has, along with Mascagni's 'Easter Hymn', virtually become a signature tune for this choir.*[9]

Sister Mary Leo's successes with solo female voices had not in any way prevented her from continuing to train magnificent choirs from whatever raw material she had among the school pupils. Back in 1959 she had said that she was able to produce a very good singer from any girl who was not actually tone-deaf. The reviews of concerts put on by her choirs throughout her career show that she never lost this magic, her choirs always being noted for their vibrant, resonant tone and rich operatic timbre.

Sister Mary Leo acknowledges the audience with a wave after a concert in the Auckland Town Hall in October 1971.

(Zealandia Archives)

Now that Sister Mary Leo was wearing the shorter habit it became evident that she still had a fondness for smart shoes. She walked with a tripping, ballet-like gait, her narrow feet slightly turned out and supported by tiny ankles. Even in the days before she conducted her choirs in public she had come out at the end of a performance to take a bow, always to great acclaim from the audience. Obviously enjoying the applause, she would raise her fingers in a rather royal wave and sparkle at the audience. She also loved to go to orchestral concerts and now had the freedom to do so, commenting freely on the performances to whichever pupil accompanied her.

Former pupil Christine Hallett (née Treseder) often took her to New Zealand Symphony Orchestra or choral concerts in her old Anglia car. Max Cryer, who first became acquainted with Sister Mary Leo as a teenage pianist who accompanied many of her pupils, has suggested that he may be the only man to have had a date with Sister Mary Leo. While working as a television producer he and Sister became 'friendly colleagues' and he once asked her to accompany him to a concert by Cleo Laine. Despite some nervousness on her part at the possibility that she might be going to see a pop singer who would embarrass her in some way, she agreed to go and was most impressed by Laine's beautifully trained voice. Heather Begg was grateful for the way Sister Mary Leo showed her continuing loyalty and interest by always attending her Auckland concerts, though it was a *little* disconcerting, she said, to see Sister conspicuously scrutinising her through small binoculars.

By October 1969, when Sister Mary Leo 'consented to appear in person as conductor of her famous choir' for the final concert in the Manukau Festival of the Arts, her name was given more prominence in the pre-concert publicity than the soloists:

> *The Manukau Festival of the Arts has drawn big crowds to its widely varied attractions, but the biggest crowd of all is expected to be drawn to Manurewa High School on Saturday night for the final concert, featuring Sister Mary Leo in person conducting the St Mary's school of music choir, with Malvina Major and supporting soloists.*[10]

Sister Mary Leo with some of her students who took part in a concert in Huntly in 1966. Standing, from left to right, are: Susan Smith (accompanist), Louise Malloy, Patricia-Anne Shaw, Patricia Price, Jackie Chapman. Seated are Laurette Gibb and Ann Hodgetts with Lyndsay Freer in front.

(Lyndsay Freer)

On the programme she was described as 'undoubtedly the greatest teacher of singing in the Southern Hemisphere'. The following month a concert was organised by the Rotary Club of Otahuhu to raise funds for a milk biscuit scheme for children in Ceylon (and the St Mary's Convent Building Fund) which was titled the 'Sister Mary Leo Concert'. Despite the two and a half hour programme being 'too long', *Herald* critic H.P.V. still gave lavish praise to the singers, who 'displayed the highest standards of artistry and taste, as well as the quality of tone production that is their teacher's trademark'.[11]

By this time Sister Mary Leo and her choir were also travelling to other centres to perform. As early as 1966 they had performed in Huntly and New Plymouth, and in 1970 they appeared with Kiri Te Kanawa in the Bowl of Brooklands 'Festival of the Pines' at New

Plymouth, at a concert in the Dargaville Town Hall (held to raise funds for a new church) and at a concert for the Taupo Community Arts Centre. The following year they 'captivated' an audience of 300 in the central North Island town of Taumarunui. Early in 1972 they were among supporting artists who sang with tenor John Boulter of the 'Black and White Minstrel Show' in Auckland, Hamilton, Thames and New Plymouth. A review of the Hamilton concert said Sister Mary Leo's choral group had almost stolen the show from right under Boulter's crescendo.

A letter Sister Mary Leo wrote to her Mother Superior from New Plymouth described how the Mayor of New Plymouth had met the choir at the airport and driven Sister Mary Leo to the Westown Motor Hotel. The fact that they had also been met at the airport by 'numerous other interested folk, including, of course, a reporter and the usual camera men' shows how dealing with the media had become a familiar occurrence. The detail included in this letter displays a simple delight in the unaccustomed experience of staying in a 'very elaborate hotel'. It had taken Sister Mary Leo some time to get accustomed to all the gadgets in her self-contained flat, she reported. She had eaten dinner at the very aristocratic hour of 9.30 p.m. and the following day a luncheon of '<u>immense proportions</u>' went on until 3.10 p.m. She also asked 'mother' to remember a little prayer for the continuation of the beautiful weather they were enjoying in New Plymouth.[12]

Carrying on the St Mary's tradition of involvement in the civic affairs of Auckland, the St Mary's Choral Group was invited to sing on many significant occasions, including a function in the Auckland YMCA for Prince Charles and Princess Anne in 1970 and, in April 1971, the official opening of the Municipal Association Conference in the Auckland Town Hall. Later the same year the St Mary's College and School of Music put on a concert in honour of the centennial of the city of Auckland. Items by the School Choir, third form pupils, fourth form pupils, the Senior Choral Group, the Junior Choral Group and combined choral groups were interspersed with solo items. The following day the *New Zealand Herald* described the concert as a tribute to Sister Mary Leo:

> *If ever a tribute could be paid to a woman who has inspired hundreds of young voices and old hearts, then Sister Mary Leo received hers last night.*
>
> *The choirs of St Mary's College and School of Music sang with true excellence under the baton of Sister Mary Leo at a concert in the Town Hall in honour of the Auckland City Centennial.*[13]

Another newspaper report quoted the Mayor of Auckland, Sir Dove-Myer Robinson, who described the concert as a fitting finale to the city's celebrations and a tribute to the city. 'We have not had anything like this for years. The discipline of the girls was marvellous.'[14]

The fact that this concert was described as both a tribute to Sister Mary Leo and a tribute to the city reflects the unique position which she held in Auckland at that time. For more than 40 years her pupils and choirs had been enthralling the city's audiences. As a Sister of Mercy she was a continuing link in the order's long tradition of musical culture in Auckland, widely known and loved even by people who did not know her.

By the 1970s Sister Mary Leo belonged to a church which had undergone a revolution. The mass was now said in English rather than Latin by priests who stood facing the people, new hymns and prayers — often with an indigenous flavour — had been introduced, confession was replaced by a voluntary face-to-face encounter called reconciliation. The ghetto mentality of earlier years was replaced by a willingness to take part in ecumenical initiatives, as was evident when Sister Mary Leo addressed an ecumenical gathering at the Baptist Tabernacle in 1974. The old authoritarian structure became less rigid; a greater freedom of opinion was allowed, and the clear divisions between clergy and laity became less marked.

Sister Mary Leo appears to have adapted to the new developments in the church with remarkable ease. There is a sense in which she was already so totally at home with herself as a teacher and religious sister that changes in the church around her seem to have had little impact. As a colleague has commented, '…she lived under the "old" regime and accepted the new with equal fervour and peacefulness — because she was always centred on God and was not easily disturbed by externals'. Now, the experiences of her late seventies show how thoroughly at home she was in the wider world. At no time was this more obvious than during a three-month world tour in 1972.

The trip was financed partly by a $500 grant from the Queen Elizabeth II Arts Council, made in recognition of Sister Mary Leo's outstanding contribution to music and singing, and was also supported by the Auckland Grand Opera Society and other friends and admirers. A farewell concert to raise funds towards the trip, held in August, was attended by more than 500 people. Sister Mary Leo's travelling companion was to have been a friend from the Grand Opera Society, but ten days before they were due to leave the friend was told she had a heart murmur and shouldn't go. Sister Mary de Porres (who later reverted to her baptismal name of Sister Margaret Browne), the Matron of the Sisters of Mercy Hospital at Onerahi, had called in to St Mary's Convent on her way to Onerahi when, like a bolt out of the blue, the Mother Superior asked her if she would consider going overseas with Sister Mary Leo. It was a wonderfully exciting offer and Margaret was happy to accept.

Their departure on 15 September 1972 was marked by a special eucharist for travellers, said in the St Mary's Chapel, followed by a meal to which members of their families were invited. At the airport they received a moving farewell from about twenty former pupils of Sister Mary Leo who formed a circle around the travellers and raised their well-trained voices in 'Now Is the Hour' and 'Auld Lang Syne'.

There were many facets to this three-month trip. It was a chance for Sister Mary Leo to visit former pupils and hear them sing in leading operatic roles. It was an opportunity for her to experience opera in the great opera houses of the world, meet with some of the leading voice teachers, pick up new ideas and new music. It was also partly a holiday, a religious pilgrimage and a chance to sightsee. But above all it became a means by which she would receive recognition for all that she had done to enhance New Zealand's musical reputation. Wherever she went she was recognised as the teacher of her famous pupils and acclaimed for her work.

A trip diary which Sister Mary Leo kept is the only extant diary she is known to have written. But rather than providing revelations into what Sister Mary Leo thought or how she saw things, it tantalises by saying very little. In London the diary stops altogether, reflecting how busy she was, while in the great cities of Europe she recorded little more than the famous sights seen. But it is on this trip — the only significant holiday in her long teaching career — that we see Sister Mary Leo simply being herself. The different facets of her character which have become apparent earlier in her story can all be seen.

The recognition which had by now become customary began early on when 'a man in uniform' 'very respectfully' requested her autograph on the flight to Los Angeles. It continued with the warm welcome given her by Joan Sutherland at the San Francisco Opera House. The great diva made a fuss of Sister Mary Leo, saying she had wanted to meet her for a long time because she admired so many of her pupils. Sister Mary Leo's pride in the achievement of her students can be seen when she proudly records that Kiri Te Kanawa was the only singer who received a standing ovation and loud bravos after her (San Francisco) debut performance as the Countess in *The Marriage of Figaro*.

In the stories of after-show parties that the two sisters attended we see again the young Kathleen Niccol who loved to socialise. In San Francisco they attended a first-night party on the 52nd floor of the Bank of America building until the early hours of the morning. Similarly, in New York they attended an after-show party which went on until 3 a.m. Sister Mary Leo's legendary stamina and determination to make the most of every opportunity is evident in the way she managed to pack five operas into her two-week stay in New York.

In London Sister Mary Leo saw more of her pupils perform: Kiri Te Kanawa and Heather Begg in *Figaro* at Covent Garden; Heather Begg and Marie Robinson in *Patience* at Sadlers Wells; Marie Robinson in Honegger's *Peace and War* (a marathon four and a half hour performance), and Raewyn Blade in the West End musical *I and Albert*.

She demonstrated her support for her students by visiting the London Opera Centre, where Marie-Thérèse Laurijssen, a pupil for ten years, and Sherry Demyan were studying, and attended the Stella Memorial competition for young New Zealand musicians under the age of 30, organised by the Royal Overseas League. Marie-Thérèse

Laurijssen was the winner, and was naturally thrilled to have her former teacher in the audience. Former pupils were by now in many parts of Europe. In Paris the two sisters visited Marie Robinson and in Hamburg they saw Lynne Cantlon in *The Magic Flute*. They heard Anne Rasmussen sing in *The Fireworks* in the Bern Opera House in Switzerland, while in Naples they stayed with former pupil Rita Geraghty.

Sister Mary Leo's unceasing quest for knowledge took her to discussions at the operatic school of the Royal College of Music and in search of new music in the London music shops. In Vienna she visited the opera centre and had discussions with Professor Robert Schollum and Professor Losser-Scholssinger. Even her love of cats was not left at home. In Washington she took a great fancy to the New Zealand ambassador's pedigree cat and insisted on holding it when a photograph was taken.

Her aristocratic tendencies were also alive and well in Washington, becoming apparent when the ambassador's chauffeur asked her where she wanted to go. 'To the White House,' she replied in a very grand voice, and on arrival was swept to the front of the queue. In their hotel rooms Sister Margaret was on the receiving end of these imperious inclinations in the mornings, when she would be woken by Sister Mary Leo's voice saying regally, 'Room Service please. Room 515. One fruit compote and one cereal please.' Then in less grand tones, 'Quick, quick, get up, the man's coming up with breakfast.'

The religious dimension of Sister Mary Leo's life is ever-present in stories from this trip. When she had difficulty sleeping on the plane to Los Angeles, she walked the floor and said her morning prayers. In Washington she met Sisters of Mercy from all over the United States at a workshop that was being held by the Washington Sisters of Mercy. In France the two sisters made a pilgrimage to Lourdes, where they had four days of rest and spiritual renewal. In Rome, on 6 December, they had an audience with Pope Paul VI, obtaining seats in the second row of the audience hall. For Sister Mary Leo the papal audience was the highlight of the trip.

The trip was not without some elements of adventure. Arriving in London to find that their hotel booking had been cancelled was one

Sister Margaret Browne and Sister Mary Leo await the papal audience at the Vatican, 1972.

(Auckland Sisters of Mercy Archives)

adventure they could have done without. On this occasion the sisters were helped by a mysterious note left on the airport message board, telling them to phone Monsignor Bruce Kent. The Monsignor, despite being totally mystified as to how his name had appeared on the noticeboard, helpfully rallied round and found them rooms in the Ivanhoe Hotel in Bloomsbury, where they stayed for two weeks. (It later transpired that the note had been left by Kiri Te Kanawa's husband, Desmond Park.) Finding themselves in a sleeping compartment with four French soldiers on the train from Paris to Lourdes was another such experience. After they had trailed the conductor up and down the station platform for some time, an alternative compartment was finally found for them. Once in the train they found there were two switches: one turned off the light, while the other stopped the train. Not sure which switch did which, Sister Mary Leo decided she would not risk turning off the light, and slept with her umbrella up instead.

In Hamburg Sister Margaret had the unhappy experience of being arrested for using fake American money. As she was marched by a German officer down a long, dark tunnel she had visions of being thrown into some terrible dungeon, but realised later the tunnel was simply the easiest way to get to the police station. Two hours later, after a visit from the Criminal Detection Officer, she was relieved to regain her freedom having helped the German police in their inquiry by recalling that the fake American dollars had come from a travellers' cheque cashed at the cafeteria at Orly Airport in Paris.

But the day that Sister Margaret will never forget was the day on which the two sisters travelled from Rome to Naples. Finding their train very full, Sister Margaret left Sister Mary Leo in a crowded carriage while she searched for two free seats together. Not finding any, she eventually settled in another carriage, assuming that she would meet up with Sister Mary Leo again on arrival in Naples. Unfortunately, she had not taken account of Sister Mary Leo's independent spirit. Unbeknown to her, Sister Mary Leo got out of the train, upgraded her ticket and took a faster express train to Naples, arriving there first. For Sister Margaret the rest of the day was a nightmare, as she sat in the missing person's office while the officer in charge phoned every railway station between Rome and Naples, and the convent in Rome, asking for possible sightings of a missing New Zealand nun. When the office closed at 9 p.m. Sister Margaret, worn out with exhaustion and worry about her missing charge, had to find her way to where they were staying by train and taxi cab. The last straw came when the taxi stopped in a narrow back alley and the gesticulating driver motioned her to get out. Sister Margaret wondered if her last hour had come. She finally realised that her cab had broken down and the driver was trying to get her to transfer to another cab.

Sister Mary Leo, who had left the railway station in order to find out about a dress rehearsal at the opera house, and had spent the rest of the day sitting in a hotel lobby in Naples, phoned soon after Sister Margaret's arrival and the two were finally reunited. From that day on Sister Mary Leo was a less independent, more compliant travelling companion, who was more willing to recognise the importance of sticking to previously made arrangements.

On 12 December Sister Mary Leo and Sister Margaret left Rome for Hong Kong, on a long flight which went via Damascus, Kuwait, Bahrein, Dubai and Rangoon. After a stopover in Hong Kong Sister Mary Leo also spent time in Australia, seeing former pupils Else Welesten in Brisbane and Adrienne Davis in Sydney. The two sisters eventually arrived back in Auckland on 24 December.

Sister Mary Leo's world trip was a source of great enjoyment, a vivid demonstration of her achievements, and it enriched her with a wealth of musical experiences to bring back to her pupils. On her return she said it would enable her to give worthwhile advice to pupils who wanted to study overseas. (Her main advice was that singers should get all the experience they could in New Zealand before they thought of going overseas.) Yet while the trip was sometimes described as a 'study tour' on which Sister Mary Leo had studied 'modern teaching methods',[15] it can perhaps be seen more as a richly deserved reward for long service. It can also be seen as an encapsulation of many of the significant features of Sister Mary Leo's life: her success as a teacher; her religious devotion; her love of music; her sociability and ability to relate naturally to people from all walks of life, from the barrowmen in the streets to the ambassador; her independence, and her love of adventure.

Chapter Seven

The Teacher

The style of singing for which Sister Mary Leo became famous is generally described as 'bel canto', which literally means 'beautiful singing'. A modern definition of bel canto is a tone of voice in singing that is free from tension, has pure vowels and a ringing quality. The voice is flexible and agile and has a consistent vibrato. Bel canto also means that these qualities are carried through the whole range of the singing voice and the voice has the 'singer's formant', that is, a cluster of high overtones that result in an amplitude or 'ring' which allows the voice to stand out and be heard over a full symphony orchestra or in a large hall.

Sister Mary Leo herself, when questioned about her method of teaching, denied that she had one, saying it was her own personality: 'My system is myself,' she said in 1959.[1] At the end of her career she was still giving the same answer. When interviewed in 1983 she said, 'It's my own personality… I felt it came from myself.'[2] This was a reflection of her personal brilliance as an empirical teacher; it also reflects the empirical tradition of bel canto teaching which she had inherited. She knew the sound she wanted, and using an experimental approach she would try various ways to get it. If one idea didn't work she would discard it and try something different. Her conception of what constituted a beautiful tone was her benchmark, and the basis of everything she did. She was guided by her own training, her aesthetic sense, her aural tonal concept, and her innate artistry. She was also guided by her knowledge of the music and text and their requirements for convincing performance and, most importantly, her ability to fire the imagination of a pupil by suggesting thoughts and imagery to attain a free, pure, vibrant and resonant tone.

The training that Sister Mary Leo received as a singer places her firmly in the tradition of the Italian school of bel canto singing. Indeed, a line of succession can be traced from Sister Mary Leo back to the famous Spanish tenor, actor, teacher and composer Manuel Garcia (1775–1832), who trained singers in the traditional Italian method at his Ecole Garcia in Paris. One of his most successful pupils was his son, also Manuel Garcia (1805–1906), a baritone and singing teacher who became professor at the Paris Conservatoire from 1847 to 1850 and at the Royal Academy of Music in London from 1848 to 1895. While working as an administrator in military hospitals in France, Manuel Garcia the younger studied the physiological aspects of the voice, and in 1840 he wrote *Memoire sur la voix humaine*. This and his *Traite complet de l'art du chant* were standard works for many years.

Mathilde Marchesi (born Graumann), 1821–1913, was a German mezzo-soprano and singing teacher, a pupil of the younger Garcia, who based her singing method on his and was seen as a teacher of the classical Italian school. Marchesi published numerous vocal exercises, mostly under the title *L'art du chant*, and her method (*Ecole Marchesi: methode de chant theorique et pratique*) in 1886.

When the young Nellie Armstrong (later Nellie Melba) went from Melbourne to Europe in 1886 to try and make her way as a singer, it was Madame Marchesi who recognised her talent and took her into her Ecole Marchesi in Paris. Fourteen months later Nellie Melba made her debut in Brussels as Gilda in *Rigoletto*, going on to become the leading diva of her day. It is also worth noting that Melba's very first singing teacher in Melbourne was Madame Christian, a Sister of Charity and former pupil of Manuel Garcia. Madame Christian later established the Garcia School of Music at Potts Point, Sydney, in 1911. An interesting speculation, though it cannot be confirmed, is that Kathleen Niccol may have had some lessons from Madame Christian when she made her reputed visit to Sydney in the early 1920s.

As has already been noted, Nellie Melba took the young New Zealand contralto Ivy Ainsley (who changed her name to Irene Ainsley) under her wing when Ainsley arrived in Europe in 1904. Melba not only gave Ainsley lessons, she also arranged for her to have lessons from Madame Marchesi, and presided over her debut at the Bechstein Hall, London, on 10 July 1906, even acting as her accompanist. It can thus be seen that when Sister Mary Leo received singing lessons from Madame Irene Ainsley in Auckland in the early 1920s, she was benefiting from a tradition of empirical teaching which stretched back to the classical Italian schools.

Sister Mary Leo achieved her brilliant results without being able to describe what she was doing, or why her techniques worked. While she had some understanding of the physiology of the voice, she did not possess a terminology sufficient to allow her to describe her method or what she did to achieve her pupils' vocal results. She did not talk in terms of vibrations or acoustics. A comment she made in 1976 is revealing of her lack of knowledge:

> ...*no one knows how tone is produced except the Lord himself. We're all working in the dark. I don't know whether it's produced by the vocal chords or the sinuses, but I take the sinus method because I think I've had more success that way.*[3]

Research into the science of the voice was embryonic in the early years of Sister Mary Leo's teaching career, and the books that she would have read on teaching singing were empirically based. While the comment above indicates that Sister Mary Leo did not keep abreast of the most recent research as she got older, it does not seem to have been a problem for her. She still achieved the results!

The first landmark book of the scientific study of singing, William Vennard's *Singing: The Mechanism and the Technique*, was published in 1967. Since then many other voice researchers have studied and published their works on the science of voice production, and some have used their knowledge to explain why the methods and techniques used by the old masters were successful. The 'secrets' of the maestri are secret no more.

With the benefit of the great advances that have been made in the science of voice production since the 1960s it is possible to look back and describe Sister Mary Leo's teaching methods with an understanding and a terminology that she herself did not have. In achieving the bel canto sound Sister Mary Leo used what we now describe as the 'appoggio' technique. Appoggio, which literally means to lean upon, support and sustain, is a concept of the interdependence of breath management and tone. As described by Richard Miller, a leading voice researcher and teacher:

> ...*Appoggio is a system for combining and balancing muscles and organs of the trunk and neck, controlling their relationships to the supraglottal resonators, so that no exaggerated function of any one of them upsets the whole...*[4]

To achieve this lovely balance between body and the sound of the voice it is necessary to have what is known as 'the noble posture'. This is an axial alignment of the body, with head, neck and torso in line with the pelvic and hip regions, and the legs and feet. The bel canto sound is based on the technique of appoggio. It also involves the principle of 'agguistamento', the modification of vowel sounds, in order to retain tonal quality while articulating at various pitch levels.

When this biography was being prepared, former pupils of Sister Mary Leo were asked to describe her teaching method. They came up with a range of answers, many of which fit into the descriptions of bel canto, appoggio and agguistamento given above. When their comments are looked at as a whole, a number of common themes emerge. They are set down here not as a scientific analysis of the way Sister Mary Leo taught, but as an anecdotal record, in combination with comments she herself made when interviewed about her teaching methods.

A very important part of Sister Mary Leo's philosophy was that every pupil should be treated as an individual. She adapted her method of teaching to the needs of each student, and made up exercises to suit their different personalities. She saw her 'psychological approach' as possibly the unique feature of her teaching. She believed she had to understand what was going on in a pupil's mind, so that she would know how the pupil was 'assessing and assimilating' her teaching, and stressed the importance of really getting to know her students, in order to 'gain their respect and confidence'.[5]

Sister Mary Leo once said that while she also enjoyed teaching the violin, cello and piano, it was her love of acting that led her into teaching singing. She certainly had a great gift for interpretation. Her pupils were introduced to a wide range of songs, and each type of song had to be sung in the appropriate way, whether it be a folk song or an operatic aria. She taught her pupils 'to think of the meaning in the words of a song before thinking of how to produce a note… And to sing from the heart. Attitude is all important.'[6]

She implored her students to feel what they sing:

> …*the words of a song must have meaning and her students must understand and convey that meaning… An artist can convey sorrow from her heart, but she must do it without tears — the tears should come from the audience.*

Dame Joan Sutherland, the great Australian coloratura soprano, is reported to have told Sister Mary Leo: 'I can always tell your students; when they sing there is such a strong soul quality that one knows they mean the words they are singing.'[7]

Sister Mary Leo distinguished between an artist: 'She is one who touches the heart,' and a singer: 'She can convey a tune, but that isn't communication.'[8] She believed that a singer had to sing with her soul, and said there was no point in singing the notes if the audience were left 'cold as a stone'. 'The eyes are the mirror of the soul,' she would say. 'Use your soul and let it come out in your eyes.'[9] Similarly, hand actions were pointless unless they were the expression of true feeling. 'You can express your soul through your hands,' she said. 'Express yourself right through to your fingertips.'[10]

'I can never make a singer — I can develop the voice,' was one of her sayings. 'The singer must come from within.' When listening to singers at the competitions she would pick out students with a beautiful tone but no heart in their singing, and she would say that unless they felt from their heart they would never make a singer. A good voice was not enough. 'You must have soul, feeling. You must be able to move people.'[11]

Another important feature of Sister Mary Leo's teaching was her

Sister Mary Leo taking a singing lesson in the 1950s.

(Hill Thomas Ltd/Auckland Sisters of Mercy Archives)

'quick ear', or one could say 'acute aural musical sense', which had undoubtedly been enhanced by her playing and teaching of the violin. A singing teacher had to possess an exceptional ear, she said, in order to 'discriminate unerringly between a really beautiful sound and one that is just not quite right'.[12] She believed that a teacher had to 'hear beauty quickly', and if she heard an ugly sound she would correct and prompt to achieve the sound she wanted. Learning a stringed instrument was essential for singers, she said, because they learned 'to use their ears when tuning the strings'.[13]

She had a conceptual method of teaching rather than an analytical one, using pictures in the mind rather than technical suggestions. Instead of talking about the voice mechanism she would ask her pupils to imagine certain things happening: to get greater body support to an ascending passage she might suggest that the pupil imagine fingers running down her spine. Other imagery she used was, 'Imagine you've got a plum in your mouth,' or 'Imagine your mouth is full of marbles.' This imagery caused a lifting of the velum (soft palate), helping an

Rehearsing with a string group, about 1956.

(Hill Thomas Ltd/Auckland Sisters of Mercy Archives)

appropriate mix of partials to develop a focused sound, or a sound with a ringing quality. She used a similar approach with instrumental pupils and would make up words and verses for runs or phrases in the music which excited the pupil's imagination and improved their playing.

Sister Mary Leo also used movement to help elicit a focused bel canto tone, such as putting a finger on the bridge of the nose and imagining the sound floating out above it or from between the eyes. At times she would suggest bending over and down to feel the sound ringing in the head. Another technique, used to achieve resonance, was telling the pupil to imagine she was singing down into a deep well. If a student was having trouble with a top note she might throw a pencil at their feet just as they were coming to the note, and tell them to bend down and pick it up. This took the pupil's attention away from the top note and helped her to (seemingly) toss it off the top of her head.

'Thought notes' were a very basic principle in Sister Mary Leo's teaching method, probably the one she stressed equally with breathing and support. These were notes that were sung with little effort. As explained by Sister Mary Leo the 'thought note' idea came from the thought of singing in the frontal sinuses of the head. By merely thinking the sound and willing it, it would happen. The thought notes idea was used to help a pupil find head tone, which is the legitimate, healthy, upper register of the female voice. It is recognised by a pure, clear, effortless ringing sound. She would ask her pupils to sing a sustained note softly for as long as possible without wobbles and using a head tone. Starting on E flat 5, she would ask them to work down the chromatic scale. Starting with 'a very light tone — conceived in the mind', she would gradually increase the tone, and always worked from the principle of starting with a small voice and building it up, rather than starting with a big sound and gradually refining it down. Anyone, she said, 'could screech a high D or E flat': her pupils were not allowed to sing notes in the high registers unless they could sing them softly first.

A 'thought note', if rightly placed, would carry, and to test this she would send her pupils out of the building or along the corridor to sing from a distance. She used the same technique when judging the quality of a violin, because she saw the voice and the violin as being very similar. 'A well-produced voice will travel — it's like a violin,' she said.[14] Putting a finger on the forehead between the eyes to think 'thought notes' was another important part of her teaching. She also developed a concept called a 'cat sound', in an attempt to get resonance. After telling a pupil to sing a 'thought note' she would tell her to 'connect up with the air' in the sides of her face and sing a cat sound, a proper sound: 'Sing into the nose with the nose closed. Then when you open the nose you get the correct thing; what you're aiming at.'[15]

In Sister Mary Leo's words, she used her 'sinus teaching' to get a 'head tone' which gave a youthful tone or ring to the voice that was not achieved by singing 'down here in the vocal chords'. She gave her pupils a lot of exercises aimed at developing their head tone, including imagining the voice exiting through the forehead, or thinking of the notes floating in the head. She also asked them to imagine the sound coming from the top of the head, down the nose and pulling the sound down to 'hit the floor'. It was singing with the head tone which produced the pure, floating, bell-like, almost disembodied kind of quality in the upper register that was evident in many of her students' voices.

Another technique she used was to ask the pupil to raise her hand and draw it towards her face with a circular movement, coming back towards the nose and face, saying 'Draw it in, draw it in.' This gave the effect of singing in a very contained way, with a more focused and concentrated tone and appropriate breath energy. Another technique was to tell her pupils to imagine a string going from their forehead to the far wall, and a series of stars on the string. As they sang they had to draw the stars in towards them. She would also tell them to place a hand on the bridge of the nose and draw the sound in, letting it 'ring' in front of the eyes.

In order to achieve purity of tone Sister Mary Leo placed great emphasis on evenness of the voice and absence of the sound of breath. Muscular support for the throat and no tension in the upper body was also emphasised. She would tell students to sing something and then fall forward from the neck, in order to loosen up the neck. She also taught the placement of the voice (the 'impostazione della voce'), telling her pupils to use their smiling muscles so that the singer's voice would be placed high and forward in the mask.

Exercises included single-note sustained exercises going right through all the vowels trying to match up the quality of the singer's best vowel. For most singers, Sister Mary Leo used to say, the best vowel was /i/. Once the vowel sounds were mastered, consonants would be added.

Sister Mary Leo used a very simple technique to teach her pupils to breathe from the diaphragm, simply telling them to place their hands on their stomach and watch their hands move as they breathed in and out in three stages. At times she would measure their chest expansion to demonstrate progress. Another breathing exercise recalled by some pupils consisted of lying on one's back on the floor with the heavy piano stool and reel-to-reel tape recorder sitting on top of the stomach. Using her diaphragmatic breathing the pupil would have to push these heavy objects up and down.

To teach 'breath support', the controlled management of the inhalation and exhalation of breath, for the necessary flow of air on which to

The reel-to-reel tape recorder, in use here for a singing lesson with pupil Pettine-Ann Croul in 1960, was also used by Sister Mary Leo for breathing exercises.

(New Zealand Magazines Archive)

create sound and to feel the accompanying muscular action in the trunk, Sister Mary Leo would tell her pupils to pull up their lower abdomen until it felt as if it were touching their backbone. Or she would say, 'Place your hand on your chest and lean into your chest. At the same time lift your chest out against the pressure of your hand.' Another approach was to put her hands round the student's waist and say, 'Use your body, come on, use your body.' To encourage greater control of the exhalation of the breath she borrowed an old idea from the Italianate school which involved placing a lighted candle in front of her pupils, and asking them to sing a passage without the candle flickering too much. She also told them to practise their breathing as they walked to work; breathing in to one lamp post, then making the breath last to three lamp posts down the road.

Coloratura singing, the ability to sing with agility and flexibility, was a feature of many of Sister Mary Leo's pupils. She encouraged agility and purity of tone, and made sure her pupils, even those with heavier voices, could negotiate trills and turns. She taught that relaxation of the tongue and jaw were important to help produce a more natural sound. She also taught 'messa di voce', that is the effortless singing of a crescendo and a decrescendo, while retaining the quality of sound throughout. Her technique allowed for versatility and singing in several styles.

The connection between speaking and singing is an important one. Sister Mary Leo used this idea to elicit a more forward and focused tone. As she said in 1981:

If I asked you your name you wouldn't have to take a deep breath and get all ready for it. You'd just answer Mary Jane or whatever it is. You wouldn't go to a lot of fuss. Well, singing is as easy as that ... no difference between singing and speaking. Perhaps you might say singing is speaking on a tune.[16]

She taught her pupils to regard singing, like talking, as communication. Instead of saying 'Good morning' to her classes, she would often sing 'Good morning girls,' and they would respond in song, 'Good morning Sister.'[17]

Sister Mary Leo taught scales, arpeggios, and intervals. The three vocal exercise books which she requested her pupils buy — at least those of the late 1950s — were Roland Foster's *Vocal Success*, Vaccai's *Practical Method of Italian Singing* and Diack's *Vocal Exercises on Tone Placing and Enunciation*. Diack and Foster would be used for lessons on topics like how to sing dipthongs, while Vaccai was used to assist singing of Italian and to help develop purity of vowel sounds and 'legato' (smooth) singing from note to note, or syllable to syllable. She would also use songs such as Mozart's 'Alleluia' from *Exultate Jubilate* for the same reason.

The repertoire she taught included English folk songs, arias, oratorios and art songs. Once a pupil was singing well in the English language, Sister Mary Leo would lead them on to singing in Italian, German and French, the pronunciation and diction of which she

A line-up of Sister Mary Leo's students who gained their singing diplomas (ATCL or LTCL) in 1964. From left to right: Kiri Te Kanawa, Rae Chapman, Catherine Harrop, Alison Boak, Malvina Major, Lyndsay Kearns and Fiona Wright. Absent are Lynne Cantlon and Laurette Gibb.

(Auckland Sisters of Mercy Archives)

taught phonetically. She taught the Italian repertoire, German lieder, some French and some Spanish folk songs, teaching at the level that the student was capable of achieving, and introducing new repertoire very slowly. Her 'girls' might learn just six songs each year but each one was learnt to performance standard.

Sister Mary Leo was pushed in the direction of teaching operatic arias because these were demanded by the aria competitions, although she personally felt that art songs and lieder were harder to perform, and were more revealing of the real artist. She felt that with opera 'you can perhaps get away with things'.[18] Sister Mary Leo and Sister Francis Xavier did not like modern pop music, always preferring music that was melodic and harmonious. Sister Mary Leo's favourite piece of music was said to be 'The Swan', by Saint-Saëns.

Part of Sister Mary Leo's approach was to insist that individual singing pupils also had to attend one of her singing classes and sing in her choir. Pupils generally began learning from her in a class, and as they improved they would graduate to a shared lesson, first in fours and then in twos. The first lessons in class were on stagecraft, and consisted of the girls walking across the stage from one side to the other while Sister corrected their posture, telling them to 'stand tall, don't slouch'. This would be followed by a lesson in bowing. The girls were told to put one foot behind the other, bow to their audience and wait for the applause. The rest of the class duly clapped. The girls were taught always to respond to their audience and acknowledge it, and to walk off with the same poise with which they had walked on. 'No slouching on and off stage.'[19]

After the lessons in stage manners came exercises in breathing, and then finally some singing exercises and song studies. Pupils in her singing classes had to sing before each other and learn to criticise themselves and one another.[20] They were promoted to private lessons with Sister when their voice was considered mature enough, for most girls around the age of 16.

Some pupils were asked to sing to the girl who came to the next lesson because, as Sister said, 'You learn by listening.' She also used a tape recorder so her pupils could 'hear their own voices and detect their own errors'.[21] This also gave them the opportunity of practising projecting themselves to an unseen audience.

Having sung to her singing class, a student would then be encouraged to go out and perform the song at a concert or recital, in a competition or for an exam. As part of preparing for performance Sister Mary Leo placed great emphasis on clear enunciation, phrasing and interpretation. She coordinated the technique of singing with communication with the audience. A good beginning and stirring end was paramount, and she always worked hard for a good finale.

All of Sister Mary Leo's former pupils comment on the attention she paid to deportment, stagecraft and presentation. She stressed deportment, telling her pupils to keep their bodies straight, tall and relaxed, and liked to tell the story of the gentleman who had told her that Heather Begg had only to walk on to the stage and make a bow for him to feel he had got his money's worth because her presence was so regal. Sister Mary Leo was very conscious of grooming and would often tell her pupils that one-third of their success was achieved before they opened their mouths. She taught a sense of style, a 'certain polish of presentation', and taught her pupils to take pride in their appearance. They became known for carrying themselves with poise

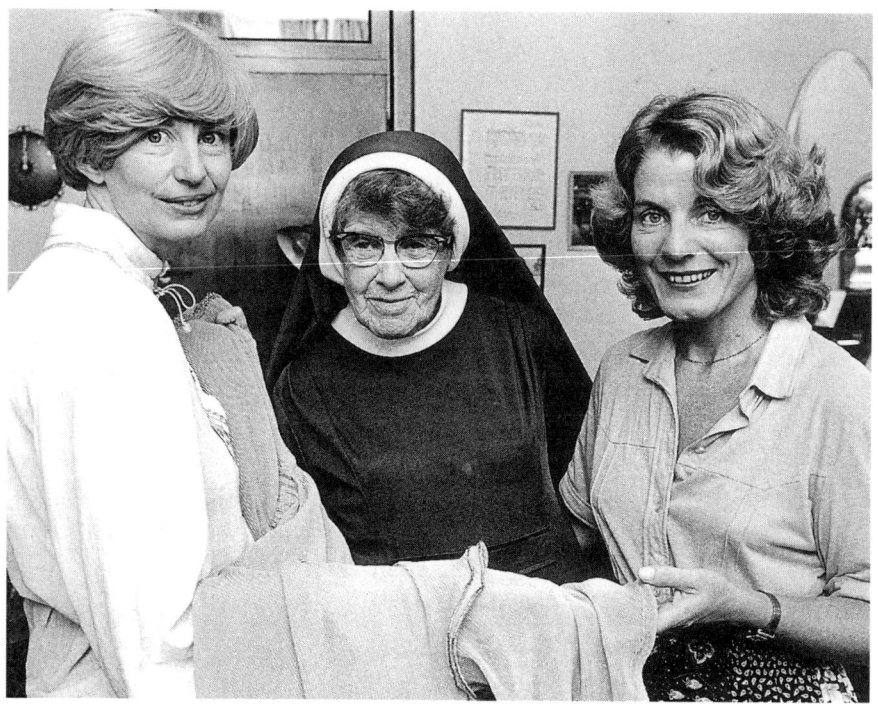

Sister Mary Leo placed great importance on presentation and liked to check out her pupils' evening dress before any performance. Here she looks at the costume worn by Lyndsay Freer (right) in a 1980 production of Gluck's Orpheus and Eurydice. *The director of the production, Janette Heffernan, is on the left.*

(Lyndsay Freer)

and majesty, and it was said that Sister Mary Leo's students were recognisable not only by their voice training but by their appearance.

When it was time for her pupils to make their debut in public, Sister would ask them to call in at the convent with their evening dress to make sure they were presentable, and they would also have to report back on the performance the next day. She insisted they sing in long dresses, and that their shoes should not be seen by the audience. She said it wasn't much use having a lovely voice if you didn't look the part, and she never allowed her pupils to wear trousers on stage. The acting and stagecraft necessary for singing operatic arias was also taught by Sister Mary Leo, and several pupils recall her hitching up her habit and doing a demonstration of the habanera from *Carmen*.

One of her sayings was that it was pride, not nerves, that made people nervous of singing in public. She did not even allow her pupils to talk about nerves:

> *When they come to audition if they say they're nervous I say, that's the worst thing you could say if you want me to take you. You better keep that quiet. I don't like nervous people ... it's not nerves, it's pride. You're thinking of what people think of you and ... therefore you're saying you're nervous ... when they said 'I could have sung that better if I hadn't been so nervous — so proud', they correct themselves you see because I won't let them. I said, 'Nerves is a swear word in this studio. Please don't use it.'*[22]

Techniques that she developed to help her pupils get over their self-consciousness included getting four of them to compose a little song and then sing a line each — ending with an appropriate cadence. This helped take their minds off the technique of singing and relieved the tension. She believed her pupils needed 'to apply patience and perseverence to ridding themselves of shyness'.[23] To be great, 'singers must lose their sense of self and immerse themselves in their music. This dedication is designed to make them humble, which is "the sign of a really great artist".'[24] Pupils were taught to 'forget themselves, forget their audiences, and give their heart and soul to their voices'.[25]

Sister Mary Leo had a holistic approach to teaching, and said that she saw herself as training a person and a personality, not just a singer. Part of her training included instructing her pupils in a selfless attitude towards their art. She told them to sing for two reasons only: 'Firstly for the glory of God and secondly for the pleasure of others.' Their voices were 'gifts to be shared' and they were not to sing for self-glorification. Pupils were trained to think of each other; '…the success of one is the success of all. If one is jealous of another then something has gone wrong with her interior fugue,' she said.[26] She treated her 'girls' in a motherly fashion: she was strict but she did not want them to be frightened of her. She believed that '…the real spiritual quality of a voice does not appear unless there is peace and happiness in the soul',[27] and she encouraged her pupils to come and discuss their troubles with her. 'Each pupil I have … I give my full attention. I teach her as if she were my own child.'[28]

When interviewed in later life she talked about teaching by kindness and only using 'force' when kindness failed. One example she gave was the occasion she shouted 'Stare!' at a girl who would not use her eyes when she was singing. Another was when she told a girl she would not teach her any more because the girl kept making the same silly little mistake:

> I had to be very angry with her, and she got such a shock, she'd never seen me in that mood before. I wasn't really in a rage but I pretended I was and she fell on the chair and she broke into tears. 'I'm sorry Sister, I'm sorry I caused you all that.' I said, 'I'm sorry to treat you like that M… but you drove me to it'.[29]

Sister Mary Leo was considered somewhat unorthodox in her attitude towards the age at which she would start teaching singing students. Most of her pupils began in their teens because she believed 14 and even younger was not too young for girls to learn to use natural voices correctly. As long as the voice was not forced she believed the fundamentals could be taught, and built upon, while real voice production could be left until later. Sister Mary Leo used her own judgement as to whether a voice was ready to sing certain roles, surprising critics by allowing young voices to sing difficult roles on some occasions, but at the same time holding other voices back. In her view it depended on the maturity of the voice and whether or not the singer had the necessary technique. She never forced a voice, and did not let pupils sing beyond their ability.

According to Malvina Major, who sat in on many auditions, Sister Mary Leo 'had a tremendous ability to hear something below the murk and say that's the voice and that's what I want to train'.[30] Sister Mary Leo herself said she looked for 'quality of tone, personality, a good ear and a certain amount of musical background' in prospective pupils.[31] Asked if she could tell the potential of a pupil at a first audition she replied not always, because pupils were embarrassed at their first audition and never did themselves justice. Sometimes she would 'give them a term to try out'. Some of her pupils took a long time to blossom, she said; 'You just have to have patience.'[32] There was a sense of excitement when you discovered a new voice, she said. 'Seeing a voice coming on is a great joy to any teacher.'[33]

Above all Sister Mary Leo would keep things simple and achievable for her students, often teaching them things without them being aware of what they were learning. She achieved a brilliant simplicity in her approach.

Naturally her style of teaching did not entirely suit everyone. Her conceptual approach worked very well with pupils who responded readily to imagery, but was less successful with pupils who liked to understand and analyse the vocal processes, who liked to know the how and why of what they were being asked to do. Pupils who were tense or inhibited did not always appreciate the Saturday class when criticism of their performance had to be endured and where inhibitions tended to increase. Some students found that they had not developed good breathing techniques under her tuition, possibly because they were not relaxed or uninhibited enough. Another criticism that has been made of Sister Mary Leo is that she found it difficult to work with a singer who had a big range. Allied to this was the way she sometimes failed to correctly classify her pupils' voices. For example Ann Gordon had a vocal range of three and a half octaves but was trained by Sister Mary Leo as a mezzo-soprano. After going to study at the London Opera Centre at the age of 23 Ann quickly moved from being a mezzo-soprano to a coloratura soprano singing 'Queen of the Night'. Similarly, Kiri Te Kanawa was described by Sister Mary Leo in 1965 as a 'heavy lyric with a mezzo quality: her range is approximately from low G to high C, or D flat'.[34] She too moved to singing soprano in her early years in London.

Sister Mary Leo gave little attention to the use of a fuller tone for big voices or the breathing and support required to carry a larger sound. She did not cope as well with singers with low voices. Generally speaking she avoided the chest voice register and encouraged all her pupils to sing in their head tone, through E flat 4 and below.

So what happened when Sister Mary Leo's pupils went overseas and learned from other teachers? Looking back did they feel she had given them a good grounding or did they have to 'unlearn' things she had taught them? The answer to this question is probably personal to every pupil, but there is consensus that Sister Mary Leo's teaching built on and enhanced the natural voice, developing the head tone par excellence, and never damaging a voice. This statement alone is a great compliment. Pupils who went overseas and learned from other teachers certainly continued to develop and in some cases changed their technique, but this can be seen as a natural process; as her voice matures a singer will often need to develop new approaches and techniques.

Perhaps the greatest compliment ever paid to Sister Mary Leo's teaching was made by Joan Sutherland in 1972. Anne Rasmussen, at the time a soloist at the Bern Opera House in Switzerland, had written to Joan Sutherland asking whether she would consider teaching her. Joan Sutherland replied that because of their busy schedule neither she nor her husband were able to take pupils, and added: 'I frankly cannot imagine that there is a voice teacher anywhere in the world better than Sister Mary Leo with whom you have had the good fortune to study for so many years...'[35]

Chapter Eight

A National Icon

1973–1979

In June 1973 Sister Mary Leo was created a Dame Commander of the Order of the British Empire in the Queen's Birthday Honours List, for her 'unique contribution to the service of her country as the leading women's vocal teacher in New Zealand and a recognised leader among the singing teachers of the world'.[1] News of the honour resulted in an outpouring of congratulatory messages. *Zealandia* described how when the news came through Sister Mary Leo was in the hall at St Mary's Convent teaching her usual Saturday morning singing class. As often happened she didn't have time for morning tea, but at lunchtime found she was in demand for newspaper photographs. The rest of the day was taken up with phone calls, telegrams, visitors, radio, television and newspaper reporters all arriving. The Post Office gave up delivering the telegrams individually, and began sending them round in bundles. That night the nuns at St Mary's Convent put on a celebration tea and entertainment, leading Sister Mary Leo to comment that it was a change for her to be on the receiving end of a concert because, 'usually I'm asked to do the entertaining'.

By the following Tuesday she had received so many letters and messages of congratulation that she had not had time to read them all. News of the honour was widely reported, in one case with an unexpected accompanying photograph. The *Sunday News* published an article with the banner headline 'NUNS PUT ON TEA THEY'RE SO HAPPY!', placing it alongside the newspaper's regular 'Sunday Male' feature. This caused some concern to Sister Mary Leo and the

Dame Sister Mary Leo with the acting Mother General of the Sisters of Mercy, Mother Carmel, reading telegrams after she was created a Dame Commander of the British Empire, June 1973.

(Zealandia Archives)

newspaper later apologised for the mistake, assuring her that the placement was entirely unintentional and had come about through 'pressure of deadlines'.[2]

It was at this point in her life that Sister Mary Leo's family name, Kathleen Niccol, came to public attention. Parliamentary officials told Sister Mary Leo that protocol demanded she should be known as Dame Kathleen Niccol. She argued against this, saying everyone knew her by her religious name. *Zealandia* made the point by asking:

Have you ever heard of Kathleen Niccol? No? Well, that's precisely why the internationally renowned music teacher, Sister Mary Leo ... didn't want to be known by her secular name when the Queen created her a Dame Commander of the Order of the British Empire in the Queen's Birthday Honours List.[3]

It was finally agreed that she could be known as Dame Sister Mary Leo.

Among the letters of congratulation that Sister Mary Leo received at this time was one from Kiri Te Kanawa, who added that following Sister Mary Leo's visit the previous October she had discovered her spectacles on the piano. Of far greater significance, however, was the fact that Kiri had been awarded the OBE at the same time.

'Double pleasure will be felt in the harmonious coincidence that places Sister Mary Leo and one of her most successful pupils Miss Kiri Te Kanawa (Mrs Park), on the same list,' commented the *New Zealand Herald*.

When her investiture took place in Wellington in November 1973 Sister Mary Leo was accompanied by her sister Jessie O'Sullivan and her niece, Margaret O'Sullivan.

The damehood prompted letters from both the English *Who's Who* and *Debrett*, the first inviting Dame Sister Mary Leo to provide an entry, while *Debrett* informed her that she would be included in the 1974 edition. It also prompted Collins publishers to approach the Sisters of Mercy about having a biography of Sister Mary Leo written. Sister Veronica Delany, an outstanding English scholar and teacher who had written the centenary history of the Auckland Sisters of Mercy and in the late 1960s spent two years at Oxford University studying for a Bachelor of Literature, agreed to write the biography.

After interviewing Sister Mary Leo's sister Jessie O'Sullivan Sister Veronica wrote the early chapters of the biography, but despite an optimistic forecast, made in August 1975, that Collins would be releasing the biography later that year, it remained unfinished. This was probably due to Sister Veronica's very heavy workload, but it is also more likely to have appeared if Sister Mary Leo herself had wanted the book published. A colleague has suggested that to have a biography appear in her lifetime would have been most unusual and quite untraditional. The fact that work on the book was still officially 'in progress', however, enabled Sister Mary Leo to put off other would-be biographers. As late as March 1979 reference was still being made to the 'official biography of Dame Leo being written by Sister Veronica...'[4]

A television documentary begun in 1975 seems to have been similarly used by Sister Mary Leo to discourage other prospective filmmakers. She was not keen on the documentary idea, saying: 'I've put it off and put it off. First they wanted to do it when Kiri was successful overseas. Then, when I got the title, they were after me again. Now, perhaps this will keep them away.'[5] But while the college *Annual* later reported that the fourteen-strong choral group was joined by Mina Foley as soloist for the filming, the documentary was never completed, probably due to a lack of funding.

None of this prevented other published tributes from appearing, however. She was first listed in the New Zealand *Who's Who* in 1978, and in 1979 appeared, with photograph, in *Notable New Zealanders*, the first pictorial edition of the *Who's Who*. In the same year a short biography of Sister Mary Leo was included in Jane Wordsworth's *Leading Ladies*, a book which featured 23 outstanding New Zealand women. (Kiri Te Kanawa was also included.)

Her entry in *Notable New Zealanders* is interesting because her year of birth is given correctly as 1895. On several previous occasions it had been given as 1896, probably due to the fact that even family members were not sure of the date. Jessie O'Sullivan, when questioned by Sister Veronica Delany, said 'I don't know her proper age. I think the third of the fourth 1896.' That Sister Mary Leo herself knew her year of birth is shown by its entry in the Convent register, yet her sensitivity about its publication extended up until 1973 when the citation written by Sister Veronica Delany as part of her nomination for the DBE began by noting that Sister Mary Leo had 'always requested that her age or date of birth should not be given in material published'.

But misinformation about Sister Mary Leo's education had not been corrected, and *Notable New Zealanders* repeated the *Who's Who* entry describing her as educated at Convent, Auckland Teachers' College and Auckland University.[6] Given the non-appearance of her name in the registers of Auckland Teachers' College and Auckland University, these entries are curious, particularly as Sister Mary Leo had been sent a telegram in June 1979 from the managing editor of the Paul Hamlyn Group asking her to check the entry for *Notable New Zealanders*.

Was Sister Mary Leo embarrassed by her lack of tertiary education, or did she genuinely believe that attendance at the occasional lecture given at the university gave her grounds for saying she had been educated there? Similarly, she could well have attended weekend classes at the Teachers' Training College during her year as a pupil-teacher at Richmond Road School, and may have thought this gave her a claim to having been educated there. These questions can never be answered and were not an issue for the general public who, universally it seemed, revered and respected Sister Mary Leo.

She had become a national icon, and people were keen to pay tribute. One of the more unusual was the naming of a racehorse after her. By 'Music Teacher', out of 'Splendid', 'Dame Mary Leo' won its first start as a three-year-old, but was later sold and put out to stud after several less successful races. More conventional honours were the numerous invitations to royal and vice-regal occasions including, in January 1974, an invitation to attend an evening reception on the Royal yacht *Britannia* during a visit of the Queen to Auckland. Sister Mary Leo loved these occasions, often taking a pupil as her partner and enjoying a small glass of sherry. Another honour was an award — a plaque of embossed copper — presented by NEBOA (the New Zealand Entertainment and Ballroom Operators' Association) for her outstanding services in the entertainment field of the arts. The award was presented at a dinner at Trillo's Downtown, Auckland, which was attended by about a thousand people. She also joined Robina Reardon in cutting the cake at the 80th anniversary of the founding of the Navy League; at the invitation of Mrs Reardon, Sister Mary Leo's pupils had supplied musical numbers for the Navy League for many years.

Whereas in the 1960s Sister Mary Leo had begun travelling to Australia to support her pupils in the aria competitions, now she received invitations in her own right. In October 1973, shortly before receiving her DBE, she was an honoured guest at the opening of the Sydney Opera House. In 1976 she went as a guest of the Australian Opera Company to hear Joan Sutherland, Heather Begg and Kiri Te Kanawa performing in the Sydney Opera House; Kiri Te Kanawa in *Simon Boccanegra* and *La Bohème*, and Heather Begg in *Der Rosenkavalier*. Travelling with her were two former St Mary's pupils, Katie

Sister Mary Leo and Robina Reardon cut the cake at the Navy League's 80th birthday celebration. Sister Mary Leo's pupils had supplied the music for Navy League occasions for many years.

(New Zealand Herald)

Loomb and Penelope Chambers. Once again there is a note of childlike pride in the letter she wrote home to Sister Joan Hopkinson after seeing *Simon Boccanegra*. Kiri had sung superbly and was the only member of the cast to have flowers thrown to her from all parts of the opera house, Sister Mary Leo reported. During this five-week visit to Sydney she also attended the Sydney Eisteddfod and the New South Wales State Conservatorium 60th anniversary celebrations. As well, she caught up with old pupils; 'I have so many ex-pupils over here ... it is hard to cope with them all — the phone is very busy,' she wrote home.

Kiri Te Kanawa and Sister Mary Leo were once again linked in the media in 1978 when a photograph of Dame Sister Mary Leo appeared in the *New Zealand Woman's Weekly* with the caption, 'She had to fly to Australia to hear her most famous pupil (Kiri Te Kanawa) sing.' The same article highlighted the frustration of New Zealand's young singers who had to go overseas to find work. Kiri Te Kanawa was quoted pleading for the establishment of a New Zealand opera house, a call backed by Sister Mary Leo when she said, 'We've got the talent and ability to stage opera. The Grand Opera society has been a wonderful supporter of young singers over the years ... but we need an opera house here.'[7] This is perhaps the closest Sister Mary Leo ever came to publicly making a political statement.

On this occasion Sister Mary Leo had flown to Sydney to see *La Traviata* at a special performance for New Zealanders in the Sydney Opera House. The star and her former teacher met after the performance and had their photograph taken, but they did not have much time to talk. 'So many people kept stopping me and telling me how proud I should feel, that we hardly had time to speak,' Sister Mary Leo was reported as saying. She still found the trip very worthwhile:

The evening went off beautifully... The people went mad and they would not let Kiri leave the stage.

Nobody could find any fault at all. The hall was packed and we all enjoyed it immensely.[8]

The linking of Sister Mary Leo with 'her most famous pupil' at this time appears to have had the effect of enhancing the reputation of both women. Sister Mary Leo gained credit from Kiri's outstanding success (even though Kiri had not had lessons from her since 1965), while Kiri's popularity was increased by her connection with the spiritual and personal qualities embodied in Sister Mary Leo.

In November 1979 Sister Mary Leo was named the recipient of an award chosen from nominations made by readers of the *Woman's Weekly*, who had to describe in no more than 75 words the woman who had made the most visible difference to her community. Mrs Josephine Higgins, who wrote the winning nomination for this 'New Zealand Woman's Weekly-Elizabeth Arden Visible Difference Award', said of Sister Mary Leo: 'She is known in music circles for her wonderful talent which she has passed on to her grateful pupils. They in their turn — aided by her patience and dedication — have reached their goals all over the world.' At a ceremony in Auckland Sister Mary Leo, now aged 84 and described at this time as 'tiny' and 'frail-looking', was presented with $250 and a specially designed trophy.[9]

If further evidence were needed of Sister Mary Leo's popularity it comes from her inclusion in a list of the seven most respected Kiwis, chosen in a nationwide competition organised by Rotary in 1982. Entrants were asked to name the seven living New Zealanders they most respected. Sister Mary Leo appeared in sixth place on the list in the company of mountaineer Sir Edmund Hillary, Prime Minister Robert Muldoon, former Prime Minister Sir John Marshall, heart surgeon Sir Brian Barratt-Boyes and High Court Judge Peter Mahon; the only other woman on the list was Dame Kiri Te Kanawa, who appeared in second place. Once again the teacher and former pupil were coupled together in the public mind.

When she was asked to comment on her inclusion in the list Sister Mary Leo said she was honoured and very pleased the proceeds were going to such a good cause (medical aid in the South Pacific Islands). Typically, she also drew attention away from herself and towards her pupils by saying she was 'very pleased to have my past pupil listed with me'.[10]

Where did her popularity come from? Why was a religious sister who spent her life in a music teaching room so widely loved? In attempting to answer this question account must be taken of Sister Mary Leo's religious vocation. In a talk she gave at an ecumenical gathering in 1974 she described how the vow of celibacy freed the religious to offer 'pure and warm affection — a sort of spiritual motherhood, if you like — to all she serves, and even all she meets'.[11]

This 'spiritual motherhood' was evident in the large number of friends and former pupils she kept in touch with: her Christmas mail in 1975, from all parts of the world, amounted well into three figures. But the impact of her personality was also felt on people who met her only briefly. Josephine Higgins, for example, who nominated her for the *Woman's Weekly* award, said she had met Dame Sister Mary Leo and was impressed by her as 'a quiet and unassuming person'.

Throughout her life Sister Mary Leo maintained her daily religious devotions. As she said in 1965, 'Religious exercises come first in our life. They occupy from two to three hours a day and equip us for the work to come.'[12] On another occasion she said her spiritual exercises were 'far more important to her than any of her pupils — or all of

Sister Mary Leo seated at the piano in her teaching room in Stella Maris shortly before the building was removed in August 1975. 'I shall be very sad to leave here,' she is quoted as saying at this time. 'It is one of those things for progress and it has to be done.' The photographs on the piano show, from left to right: Heather Begg, Patricia House, Lyndsay Freer, Malvina Major, Hannah Tatana, Marie Robinson, Lynne Cantlon and Kiri Te Kanawa.

(New Zealand Herald)

them put together'.[13] The importance of her religion can also be seen in the answer she gave when asked: 'If you could have your life all over again would you choose again to be a singing teacher?'

'I'd choose again to enter religion,' she replied. 'I don't know about the singing teacher.'[14]

The impact of Sister Mary Leo's religious devotion has been felt by many of her pupils. The Rev. Roy Bowden, for example, who in the 1960s trained as a Methodist minister, later said that his first experience of the presence of God came 'in the tranquil yet strengthening atmosphere of St Mary's music school', where as an eight-year-old he had begun singing lessons with Sister Mary Leo. 'It was there as a child that I found what serving God meant. For my singing teacher, Sister Mary Leo, was a great example of a devoted servant of Christ.'[15] Dame Kiri Te Kanawa, looking back from a perspective of thirty years, has said that her most vivid memory of Sister Mary Leo was her great devotion to religion, and that the deep sense of religion Sister Mary Leo gave her still remained. Another pupil, Irene Tirbutt, felt that the special quality of singing in Sister Mary Leo's pupils came from her inner serenity; she said she felt at peace, never unhappy or on edge when she was with Sister Mary Leo. 'It's a genuine love. It's her expression of God I think.'[16]

Pianist Joy Crabtree, who accompanied many of Sister Mary Leo's singers between 1971 and 1975, was received into the Catholic church during this time and had many long conversations with Sister Mary Leo about her faith. Sister Mary Leo was the first real influence in her journey to Catholicism, Joy said, and a close relationship developed between them. Yet Sister Mary Leo did not put religious pressure on any of her pupils. Malvina Major has recalled that when she had been with Sister Mary Leo for just a few months she told her she would like to become a nun. 'Oh darling, just wait till you're 21 and we'll talk about this again,' said Sister Mary Leo.[17]

Like other Catholics of the time Sister Mary Leo held orthodox beliefs in God, the Trinity, the Virgin Mary and Jesus Christ, the son of God. She believed that every Christian was called to a holiness, that is, a daily life of 'loving union with God our Father, through Christ his Son, and in the Spirit'. The particular way of holiness which she had chosen was as a Sister of Mercy, and her apostolate was as a specialist music teacher. She saw the gift of music as a gift from God:

> *The talent of a lovely voice is an endowment from Him, a pathway that should lead singer and listeners to the truth and beauty that is God Himself. My students are always taught to realise this, and thus there is no fear or need for them to become conceited about their successes. My own talent — which is perhaps best described as a gift for creative training of voices — is also something I hold from God. I am humbly grateful to Him for it, without any undue personal pride.*[18]

On another occasion she said:

I am thankful that my work brings me into contact with a wider circle than my immediate pupils: with their families and relatives, with professional colleagues, with former students, and with friends and acquaintances in many spheres of life. With them I can share in due measure something of the love, peace and joy that my life consecrated to God brings to me.[19]

Asked what she strived to show her students and her audiences, she replied: 'I want people to be uplifted through the medium of song, so that they will be transported from the mundane things of life to the realms of soul fulfilment.'[20] Her widespread popularity would indicate that she achieved this aim. People did feel uplifted by her pupils' singing, and they felt warmth, affection and respect for her as a result.

Reporters who interviewed Sister Mary Leo had often written about the special 'spiritual' quality evident in her pupils' singing. An *Auckland Star* reporter in 1959 concluded that this 'spiritual' quality proved that 'the soul of the teacher can have a profound and lasting influence on the pupil'. It came from the way Sister Mary Leo kept her pupils humble. 'God has blessed you with a voice,' she would tell them. 'You will lose that voice if you become conceited about it… Real art is humble.'[21]

In 1960 the *St Mary's College Annual* commented:

Sister Mary Leo's secret is not only her great musical skill and her unrivalled ability as a teacher. It lies deeper, in her great love of God, and her love of others for His sake, that infuse into all her work a wonderful quality of spiritual charm and purity.[22]

In another interview Sister Mary Leo spoke of the way she helped the girls 'to rid themselves of tension by developing an inner tranquillity. You'll find it, I hope, in our stars.'[23] Other interviewers noted the selflessness of her motivation: '…her life now is centred around poverty and selflessness. And it is this selflessness that has, perhaps, been the springboard to her ability as a music teacher.'[24] It was also noted that she was not teaching for a living. As she commented in 1965, 'The money doesn't mean a thing to me. It all goes to the Order. As far as I, personally, am concerned, they could be having their tuition for nothing.'[25]

Even the most pragmatic commentator would have to agree that being a Sister of Mercy played a part in Sister Mary Leo's success as a teacher. As has already been noted, the communal way of life liberated her from any mundane domestic concerns and enabled her to work with total dedication as a teacher for almost twelve hours a day. Her teaching load of about 60 pupils a week was heavy by any teachers' standards, and that alone must account for some of her success. With so many pupils passing through her hands, it is only to be expected that a certain proportion would be high achievers.

Most observers would also agree that there is some truth in the claim that the training in personal values and attitudes given by Sister Mary Leo improved her pupils' well-being and hence their performances.

One example of the impact that her singers had on listeners is found in a letter she received from a prisoner in Mt Eden jail. For a number of years Sister Mary Leo took a choir of nuns to Mt Eden to sing the Christmas mass, with some of the prisoners joining in with their guitars or singing. At Christmas 1967 for the first time she took her senior girls' choir to the prison to sing first in the main block and then in the high-security wing. Some of the choir members remember feeling quite uncomfortable in the prison, in contrast to Sister Mary Leo who was quite unconcerned and smiled and waved to the inmates. She befriended some who later presented her with gifts: a little interwoven tray made of used matches, a carved wooden tray, and in one case her own portrait, painted from a photograph, by convicted murderer Ronald Jorgensen. After the Christmas 1967 performance a prisoner who was detained in the high-security wing sat down and wrote a letter to Sister Mary Leo, describing the way his bitterness, feelings of isolation and rejection had been overcome by the singing of the choir, giving him new hope:

> *From the moment the Sisters began to sing ... I no longer felt lonely, confined or unhappy. I am certain that I have never before heard any*

sound so beautiful, so clear or so full of compassion and the spirit of Christmas than the voices of the Sisters in song. It evoked in me an emotion so strong that I realised I was not as I had previously believed devoid of any feelings whatsoever.

Sister Veronica Delany believed this Christmas morning performance, and the response it evoked, revealed a great deal about Sister Mary Leo. Standing in the prison corridor, heard only by a few prisoners whom she could not see, Sister Mary Leo still conducted her choir with all the artistry, finesse and power that she would have put into a choir filling a town hall or opera house. She was a supreme artist, said Sister Veronica, who could 'do nothing slovenly'. She was also deeply compassionate, and from her feeling for the isolation and bitterness of the prisoners, she offered them all the pleasure and consolation that lay in her power.

Sister Veronica reminds us that Sister Mary Leo was also:

...a woman consecrated to God. This dedication imparted to her work a spiritual dimension which is impalpable, indefinable, but indisputedly present in everything she does. This quality in herself, finds expression in the voices she trains, moulds and blends.

And it was this quality, Sister Veronica believes, that would have so moved the prisoner who responded with this letter.[26]

When writing about Sister Mary Leo's life as a teacher, with its annual round of examinations, competitions and performances, it is easy to forget the religious cycles which continually formed part of the fabric of her life. As well as the regular annual religious festivals there were the special occasions, such as the 125th anniversary of the arrival of the Sisters of Mercy in Auckland. Sister Mary Leo, aged 80 by this time, trained a choir of sisters to lead the singing in the Mass of Thanksgiving held in St Patrick's Cathedral on 12 April 1975. A festal celebration held afterwards at the Mandalay Reception Centre concluded with the choir singing the Latin anthem 'In Aeternum Jubilantes'. A group photograph of more than 200 sisters, all members of the Auckland community, was taken at St Mary's in the afternoon.

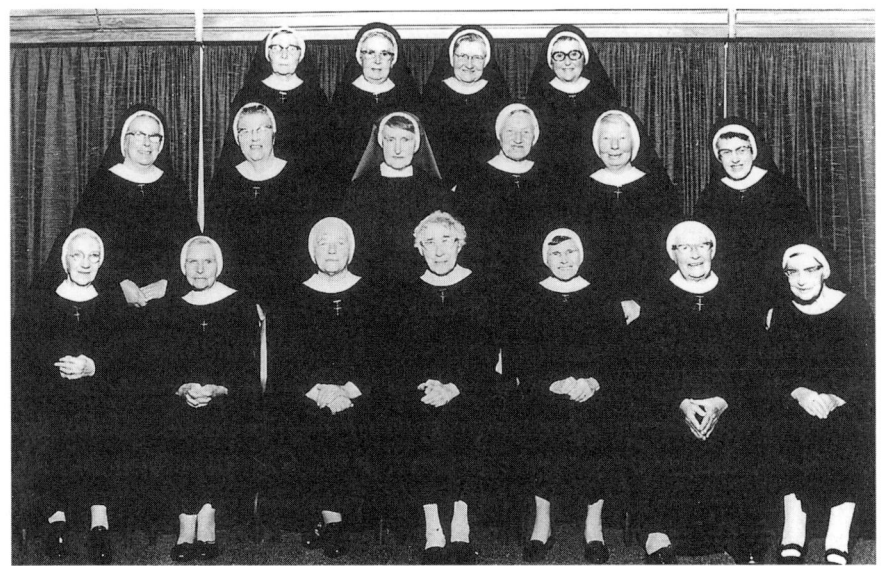

Sister Mary Leo and her profession group celebrate their golden jubilee in 1976. Front row, from left: Sr Mary Isodore, Sr Mary Fabian, Sr Mary Anita, Sr Mary Michael, Sr Mary Immaculata, Sr Mary Rita, Sr Mary Acquinas. Second row: Sr Mary Rosaria, Sr Mary Jerome, Sr Mary Leonard, Sr Mary Anastasia, Sr Mary Perpetua, Sr Mary Leo. Third row: Sr Mary Joseph, Sr Mary Clement, Sr Mary Damian, Sr Mary Kieran.

(Zealandia Archives)

An event of greater personal significance to Sister Mary Leo was the golden jubilee in 1976 of her religious profession. Seventeen of the original 25 sisters gathered among a congregation of nearly 200 sisters at St Mary's for a special mass of thanksgiving. Present at the mass was Archbishop Liston, who fifty years earlier had received the sisters' first vows in the Church of the Assumption, Onehunga. Altogether the seventeen sisters had completed a total of 850 years as Sisters of Mercy.

'Words are inadequate to express the riches of these seventeen lives in the history of the diocese of Auckland,' said Bishop Mackey, speaking at the mass...

seventeen lives that for half a century have given witness to the ideals of religious life: poverty in material things, yet full of the riches of grace; chastity, the purifying of love so that it is centred only on God, and then pours itself out on God's creation; and obedience, the following of Christ, who lived only to fulfil his Father's will.[27]

In honour of the occasion past and present pupils clubbed together to buy Sister Mary Leo a travelling case and music bag. About 25 singers gathered in her music room to give her the presents and to sing 'Auld Lang Syne'.

Meanwhile, Sister Mary Leo continued with her work at St Mary's School of Music well into her eighties: her classes, her individual pupils, the ceaseless round of preparation for competitions, examinations and performances. Pupils continued to win prizes. When the John Court Memorial Aria at the Auckland Competitions was replaced by the Lady Doig Aria, the winner in 1970 was Sister Mary Leo's pupil Doreen Donnell. Doreen also won the Classical Aria, the Oratorio and Soprano test, and the Desford Women's Vocal Championship. Two years later Louise Malloy won the Lady Doig Grand Aria, also winning the Lewis Eady Vocal Scholarship, and both the New Zealand Composer Vocal Solo and Folk Song classes; in 1973 she won the *New Zealand Herald* Aria (which had replaced the Lady Doig Aria). The Higginbotham operatic solo prize was won by Patricia House, who also gained third place in the Auckland Aria, and second place in the Sydney *Sun* Aria and the Melbourne *Sun* Aria. The following year (1974) Irene Tirbutt was the winner of the $1000 *New Zealand Herald* Aria, while Linda Shearer was placed second. Linda's turn to win came in 1975.

The 1970s saw new and different vocal competitions appearing. The old pattern of the sixties, when pupils won the John Court aria, the Mobil Song Quest and then one of the Australian arias, had gone. When Patricia-Anne Shaw won the $2000 *Times* Newspaper Aria at Hamilton in 1972, the competition was said to be the largest in Australasia. The same year Patricia-Anne won the Australian Under-25 Mozart Aria contest, and came second in the Mobil Song Quest. By 1975 there was a New Zealand-wide operatic aria, held that year in Dunedin. Sister Mary Leo's pupil Fay Hadden won first place, with Donna Awatere runner-up. In 1977 a fifth former at St Mary's and pupil of Sister Mary Leo, Sharon Tuapawa, won the talent quest 'Opportunity Knocks' run by TV2.

Pupils who came to Sister Mary Leo later in her career found her a lovable and sympathetic friend. When Anne Young (later Anne Marabini Young) arrived in Auckland from Christchurch in 1976 Sister Mary Leo took a whole afternoon off teaching to help her buy a piano. Sister later wrote a letter of introduction to Richard Bonynge, who auditioned Anne and gave her a scholarship to the Australian Opera which began her operatic career. Similarly, Sister Mary Leo helped Australian soprano Irene Tirbutt to settle into Auckland by telephoning her in the evenings or sending other people to talk to her. Irene found herself having long chats with Sister Mary Leo, often quite late in the evening, about houses or fashion or any other topic, including personal problems. Irene also enjoyed Sister Mary Leo's sense of fun, which came out on occasions like a farewell dinner with a small group of friends who were in Sydney for the opening of the Opera House in 1973. Going down in the lift after dinner they all began to sing 'Auld Lang Syne', Irene deliberately singing out of key. 'Don't sing like that! Don't sing like that Irene! You know it's not good,' said Sister Mary Leo, giggling all the time. On another occasion Irene, accompanist Joy Crabtree and Sister Mary Leo were driving home in Joy's car after the aria finals in Auckland. 'We're going for a drink,' said Sister Mary Leo as they pulled up in front of a Herne Bay milk bar. 'Three chocolate milkshakes,' she ordered. 'No, make that four, I'll take one home for Sister Francis Xavier.'

For many years Sister Mary Leo and Sister Francis Xavier had rooms next to each other, and no matter how late she came home Sister Mary Leo always said good night to Francis Xavier. 'If she's asleep I'll wake her up,' she would say.

The companionship that the two sisters had enjoyed for so long ended without warning. In June 1977 Sister Mary Francis Xavier McGarry died suddenly overnight. She had worked in the St Mary's music school with Sister Mary Leo for a period of 40 years, and was described after her death as: 'A performer of rare artistry, and equal modesty, and an accompanist of delicate sensitivity...' By her friends, colleagues and pupils, she was remembered more for her personal qualities: kindliness, loyalty, warmth, '...and the dedication of her life of prayer and service'.[28] In strong contrast to Sister Mary Leo she remained relatively unknown to the outside world, and there are few photographs of her. But her significant contribution to the world of music is well known to anyone who had contact with her at St Mary's music school.

Sister Mary Leo's reaction to Sister Francis Xavier's death reflected her strong religious faith. Lyndsay Freer, who called on Sister Mary Leo to offer her condolences, was taken into the chapel. In a very matter of fact way Sister Mary Leo touched Sister Xavier on the forehead, the hair, the hands, saying as she did so, 'Look at those hands, just think of all the music those hands have made. Feel her hands dear.' Rather than a sense of loss Sister Mary Leo seemed to feel only a great confidence that Sister Francis Xavier was all right, and in a better place than this world. In the weeks that followed Sister Mary Leo talked about Sister Francis Xavier quite openly and frequently.

Sister Mary Leo continued with her work, with Val Hungerford now primarily acting as accompanist for her singing students, but there are indications that her teaching had lost some of its earlier vigour. Her teaching day was now a more usual eight and a half hours, and the number of pupils had dropped from 60 down to about 40. It was still a remarkable workload for a woman in her eighties.

Increasingly the news of the School of Music in the college annuals concerned former rather than current pupils. In fact, the immediate falling off in news from the music school which followed the death of Sister Francis Xavier in 1977 suggests that with her death the heart had gone out of it. Her death probably affected Sister Mary Leo more than she allowed to show. In contrast to her great liveliness of earlier years pupils would sometimes arrive at lessons to find her sitting in a chair with her feet on a footstool. 'What's the first item on the concert programme today?' she would ask. She even dozed off occasionally while a pupil was singing.

In March 1979 Mina Foley returned to the stage after an eighteen-year absence. During the long period when Mina had been out of public life, Sister Mary Leo had remained a constant friend. Mina had been having lessons from Sister Mary Leo since 1975, and although Sister told a reporter she had no one favourite pupil, she did admit to preferring Mina Foley's voice above any other she had trained, saying, 'She has a phenomenal voice and a remarkable range.'[29] In November 1975 Mina had caused considerable interest by singing from the rear gallery of St Patrick's Cathedral in a St Cecilia's Day concert. The *Auckland Star* reviewer noted that she 'displayed her well-remembered qualities of a rich middle register (overlaid with a strong vibrato) and an upper register (to a top F) of remarkable agility and clarity. Hers remains a striking and thoroughly individual voice.'[30]

After the March 1979 concert, the *New Zealand Herald* said of Mina:

She sang 16 songs and arias and brought a ball-room of damp-eyed opera buffs to their feet in ovation.

If the reaction was part-admiration for a woman who bravely tackled a hard road back to self-confidence, impartial critics declared that the magical high notes of Dame Sister Mary Leo's most brilliant pupil trilled and thrilled anew.[31]

The *Star* reviewer said:

The lyric coloratura, trained by Dame Sister Mary Leo who has recently been giving her refresher lessons, tackled some of the most testing pieces in the repertoire, and showed that the brilliant range, particularly the crystal-clear, bell-like top, was still there.[32]

In a major feature article which appeared at this time Sister Mary Leo was quoted as saying:

Given the health and strength vital for an operatic career, Mina Foley's voice could have taken her to the very top... [Her voice had] matured with age, naturally. But she's still unique in her sound. Retraining was difficult at first because she had to regain her confidence, but with gentle handling, she is getting back to where she used to be.[33]

After eight months of further training from Sister Mary Leo, Mina performed in a second concert in November 1979. All 400 tickets to the Museum auditorium were sold more than a week before the concert and Robina Reardon was quoted as saying, 'We could have sold the hall 10 times over... We should have taken the Town Hall.'[34]

There is a particular poignancy about Mina Foley's return to the stage at this time: she had first become a pupil of Sister Mary Leo in 1944, and had been her first star. Now, when Sister Mary Leo's energy as a teacher was beginning to wane, the two women were once again working closely together. Although there are mixed opinions about the quality of Mina's singing at this time, for Sister Mary Leo she was still, and would always be, her favourite and most gifted pupil.

Chapter Nine

Fame and Frailty

1980–1989

The fame that a teacher achieves comes from the success of her pupils. In the 1980s, Sister Mary Leo's two 'golden' girls of the 1960s were on a rising wave of popularity. Malvina Major, who for a number of years had given priority to her family life, began a return to the New Zealand operatic stage in 1983 and in 1986 embarked on a successful come-back as an international singer. Kiri Te Kanawa's rise to international stardom had continued since her 1971 Covent Garden performance as the Countess in *Le Nozze di Figaro*, and reached a high point when she was invited to sing at the wedding of the Prince of Wales and Lady Diana Spencer in 1981.

While Kiri's decision not to sing opera in New Zealand until there was a suitable venue had caused some criticism in this country, her return in 1983 to sing at fundraising concerts for Auckland's Aotea Centre restored her as a public favourite. Once again the links between Kiri Te Kanawa and Sister Mary Leo were reinforced, when Sister was presented with two complimentary tickets to Kiri's fundraising recital by the Mayor of Auckland, Colin Kay.

The increasing popularity of Kiri Te Kanawa and Malvina Major had the effect of enhancing Sister Mary Leo's stature and reputation at a time when her own physical strength was diminishing. More and more, news of Sister Mary Leo in the last nine years of her life concerns problems with her health. These years were a time of contrast, with moments of glory punctuated by trips to hospital.

Sister Mary Leo continued to teach from the new music school —

four rooms in the former Novitiate, which was now called 'Coolock' (after the home of the founder of the Sisters of Mercy, Catherine McAuley) — but her hours of work were decreasing. By 1982 she was teaching from 8.30 to 5 p.m. and she was no longer conducting her choir. As she spent less time teaching, she spent more time praying in the chapel of St Mary's Convent.

Despite her frailty talented pupils continued to seek her out, and they scored some notable successes. Rhonda Bryers recorded her fourth album, 'Favourite Arias and Sacred Songs', with Dame Sister Mary Leo as producer, in May 1980. In the same year Patricia Wright was given a grant of $20,000 by an anonymous Australian donor to enable her to go to Europe for further training. Lynn Anderson won the *New Zealand Herald* Aria in 1981; Tracey King went to London to learn from the renowned teacher Vera Rosza and to attend the Guildhall School of Music, while Nicola Waite, who won the Marianne Mathy Scholarship in Sydney in 1982, went to Milan for training with Rina Malatrasi.

But among her friends was a recognition that Sister Mary Leo's life was drawing to a close, and efforts were made to ensure that tribute was paid before it became too late. One such occasion was a 'glittering musical evening' staged in her honour by past and present pupils in 1981, in the ballroom of the Intercontinental Hotel. Ballads, folk songs, operatic arias and items from stage shows were sung by present and former pupils including Mina Foley, Rhonda Bryers, Sharon Tuapawa, Lynn Anderson and Tracey King.

Moves were also taken to ensure that her name would live on after her. Ironically, one memorial to Sister Mary Leo which should have lasted for ever — it was literally set in concrete — has now been lost. When Queen Elizabeth Square was opened in February 1980 at the foot of Auckland's Queen Street, Dame Sister Mary Leo and the city's long-serving mayor, Sir Dove-Myer Robinson, were invited to leave imprints of their hands and feet in a block of wet concrete. The intention was to add those of other famous Aucklanders and to mount them 'in a dignified fashion' outside the Downtown building. The concept was not continued with, however, and by 1996 the impressions could not be seen anywhere in Queen Elizabeth Square.

Another memorial was more longlasting. The Dame Sister Mary Leo Scholarship Foundation was established under the auspices of the Auckland Grand Opera Society with the aim of acknowledging and commemorating Sister Mary Leo's contribution to the artistic success of many singers in Auckland, in New Zealand and on the international opera scene, and to provide a fund from which scholarship awards could be made to young New Zealand singers. Within a month of announcing the establishment of the scholarship in 1980, $1000 had been donated, and a series of fundraising events were in train. These included a 'Grand Concert' at the Founders Theatre in Hamilton in July 1980 where Mina Foley made a rare appearance, a concert in the auditorium of the Auckland Museum in the same month with Patricia Wright as the principal soloist, and a gala concert in Auckland.

The gala concert, held in a packed Auckland Town Hall on 7 October 1980, was a nostalgic evening on which Sister Mary Leo's first star pupil, Mina Foley, joined forces with many other successful former pupils to perform a programme of music redolent of the School of Music's concerts of the sixties. Malvina Major sang 'as superbly as ever, the voice full and true, with the creamy texture which makes it a delight to the ear', said reviewer Desmond Mahoney, while Mina Foley received a standing ovation even before she opened her mouth to sing:

> *And more than a quarter of a century after her first timid but electrifying appearances in the Town Hall, Mina Foley demonstrated her uncanny ability to produce perfectly rounded, liquid-sounding coloratura notes absolutely true in pitch with a quality that is unique.*[1]

This reviewer went on to say that it was difficult to tell whether the greater wave of affection from the packed auditorium went out to Dame Sister Mary Leo or to Mina Foley. The *New Zealand Herald* review by Lin Saunders described the long concert, which ran into a fourth hour, as 'a real feast of operatic music [which] could well be rated the outstanding event of its kind in at least the last decade'.[2] Tickets were highly priced, but the performers all gave their services free and financially the concert was a great success, raising nearly $20,000 for the scholarship fund. To top off the evening the St Mary's School of Music choir reassembled for the occasion, singing Verdi's 'La Vergine degli Angeli' with Mina Foley as soloist, and 'The Nuns' Chorus' with Malvina Major taking the solo part. The choir of 58 voices was made up of present pupils singing alongside many of Sister Mary Leo's experienced and successful past pupils. 'Auckland has no lovlier [sic] sound of women's voices,' Lin Saunders noted.

It was a big night for Sister Mary Leo, who not only conducted the choir, but was also presented with an engraved tribute by the mayor, Sir Dove-Myer Robinson, on behalf of the Grand Opera Society. The tribute expressed the Society's recognition, gratitude and affection, commenting that Sister Mary Leo's 'achievements as a music teacher outstanding in creative brilliance have singularly enhanced New Zealand's musical reputation and guided many New Zealand singers to adorn the opera houses and concert halls of the world'.[3] Sister Mary Leo, in 'the shortest speech on record', thanked everyone, and said she felt very humble that God had given her a gift and that she did her best with it — and now could they get on with the concert![4]

The first competitions for the Dame Sister Mary Leo Scholarship were held in March 1982, with several former pupils involved as either administrators or judges. Anthony Hollows arranged for the preliminaries during the week preceding the final on March 22 to be judged by Pettine-Ann Croul and conductor Juan Matteucci. For the finals they were joined by Heather Begg and Donald McIntyre. Not long before the first scholarship competition a fundraising auction was held which raised about $4500. Items donated for the auction included a soccer shirt autographed by Elton John, a traditional Tibetan scarf from the Dalai Lama, a baton used by Juan Matteucci, Donald McIntyre's first violin, a cosmetic bag from Vanessa Redgrave, running shoes from John Walker, paintings from and by Shona McFarlane, Lance Cairns' cricket bat autographed by the New Zealand cricket team, a jockey's whip from Norm Holland, and records from Rod McKuen. At the end of 1982 a fundraising recital was held in the Auckland Museum auditorium, featuring soprano Nicola Waite.

Sister Mary Leo continued to take an interest in the Scholarship competition, the continuing story of which is followed up in the afterword. In 1982 and 1983 she attended the finals and was photographed congratulating the winners, Glenese Metcalfe in 1982, and a former pupil, Rhona Fraser, in 1983. When Christchurch bass Ted Rhodes won the scholarship in 1986, Dame Sister Mary Leo was warmly welcomed to the competition final, just days after an article had appeared in the *Herald* headed 'Real Star May Not Be There':

> *Dame Sister Mary Leo, the Auckland music teacher behind many of New Zealand's operatic successes, may not be able to attend this year's final of the opera contest that bears her name.*
>
> *The 90-year-old nun, who taught music well into her eighties, is now confined to a wheelchair and whether she is able to attend either the opera grand final at the Auckland Town Hall on Friday night or the Pope's Mass on Saturday will depend on how she feels on the day.*[5]

In fact she managed to attend both events, although the Pope's visit to the Auckland Domain was disappointing; a colleague described how the motorcade moved so quickly and security was so tight that they hardly saw him.

Even at this late stage in her career Sister Mary Leo was still receiving media attention. Yet there is a difference between getting publicity for one's cause and becoming conceited about achievements, and Sister Mary Leo seems to have managed to keep this distinction intact. Her former colleagues all insist that she remained humble and modest despite her success, and say her sympathetic and loving nature was apparent in the way she never forgot the elderly and sick sisters in the convent. She herself stressed the importance of not becoming proud: 'I'm terrified of being proud or stuck up, because that destroys the whole thing, destroys the beauty of art. I'm not like that, thank God,' she told a *New Zealand Times* reporter in 1982. She went on to say:

> *I've had a lot of success. I must admit that. But I'm not one that gets very excited about these things. I've had so much of it over the years I've got used to it.*

I'm not a naturally proud character — perhaps not enough so for what I've achieved. I take things too much for granted.[6]

Evidence of Sister Mary Leo's stature in Auckland in these later years of her life is shown in the way her condition was noted and reported on in the daily newspapers. In August 1981 she was reported as being in a satisfactory condition in Mater Hospital after what was described as 'minor surgery', possibly the removal of a gangrenous toe. Even from her hospital bed she was busy organising concerts, and she was also well enough to attend a concert entitled 'A Night at the Opera' (which included items by Mina Foley) held at the Symphonia Theatre on 15 September 1981.

Her health was not sufficiently good, however, to allow her to fly to London in 1981 to take part in Kiri Te Kanawa's 'This Is Your Life' programme, screened by Thames Television on Christmas Day. She did send a filmed message and later received letters from several people involved in the programme expressing their disappointment that she had not been present (as she was 'a vital part of the story') and appreciation of what she had done.

'It was a great disappointment that you were not well enough to travel for the occasion, which you would certainly have enjoyed. Your own contribution came over very well indeed,' said James Robertson,[7] whose connections with Sister Mary Leo went back to the 1950s when he had conducted performances of the New Zealand Opera Company in which her pupils were singing. Thames Television's Eamonn Andrews said he was charmed by her affectionate greeting to Kiri, while Maurice Leonard wrote expressing thanks for her enormously helpful contribution and said how thoroughly professional she had been in front of the camera.[8]

By this time Sister Mary Leo was receiving on-going personal assistance from her colleagues. Sister Veronica Delany helped by attending to correspondence when she was prevented from writing by poor circulation in her hands, while Sister Joan Hopkinson increasingly took on the role of caring for Sister Mary Leo. From 1981 Sister Joan made Sister Mary Leo's bed in the morning, cleaned her room, accompanied her from the convent to the music room each morning, and generally

'Good wishes overwhelm nun.' Sister Mary Leo surrounded by cards and letters in her hospital room, January 1984.

(News Media: Auckland Star Collection)

kept an eye on her, a role she continued to play until Sister Mary Leo's death. There came a time when Sister Mary Leo needed to be leaning on an arm to go anywhere, and Sister Joan provided that arm. Sister Mary Leo responded by affectionately calling Joan 'Matron'. A card which she sent to Sister Joan on her feast day in 1983 was inscribed:

> *To My very dearest Matron with deepest love and sincere gratitude for the kindnesses of all kinds which you are always so willing to bestow on me. God bless you ever and spare you to me for many years to come. Sincerely yours in J.C., The Old Dame.*

Poor circulation was a continuing problem for Sister Mary Leo. Pupils recall her wearing gloves and 'her poor blue hands' in winter. The circulatory problem also contributed to difficulties with her salivary glands which caused her to suffer from a very dry mouth, and her speech at times became quite thick.

In October 1983 Sister Mary Leo was admitted to the Mary Agnes Ward at the Mater Misericordiae Hospital; according to the *New Zealand Herald* she was suffering from a respiratory ailment and general fatigue. After six weeks in hospital she was reported to be aiming to be home for Christmas. She was 'eager to return to St Mary's Convent in Ponsonby, so she could continue her teaching', and was sorry she was not well enough to attend a performance of *The Mikado* in which two of her pupils, Tracey King and Sunny Morete, were playing leading roles. Cards and flowers from friends and pupils all over the world filled her room.[9] On Christmas Eve she was reported to be still in the Mater Hospital, in good spirits, and expected to return to St Mary's Convent by mid January. The newspapers continued to document the progress of her illness; under the heading 'Cards Pay Own Tribute' a report in the *Herald* said 'Dame Sister Mary Leo will have to leave the Mater Misericordiae Hospital in Epsom soon — her room there is not big enough to take many more cards and gifts from well-wishers and former pupils.' She spoke brightly of 'returning to her work in a couple of weeks'.[10] In an article headed 'Good Wishes Overwhelm Nun', Sister Mary Leo was pictured surrounded by cards and letters, and it was reported that she had put an advertisement in the paper thanking all the people who had written to her, because she did not have time to reply to them all.[11] By mid January it was reported that she was back at St Mary's in Ponsonby, and would be back to work teaching soon.

This long period in hospital was probably due to a mastectomy that Sister Mary Leo is known to have had after breast cancer was diagnosed. But despite such setbacks to her health, friends and visitors never heard a complaint. She showed no sign of frustration at her reduced mobility but was always cheerful, showing warmth and interest in her visitors. Even when she was in great discomfort questions about her health would be deflected. Sister Mary Leo would simply not answer but begin talking about something else. Even in hospital she could still be her old autocratic self, and there is a story that on the day after her mastectomy she insisted on having a bath, despite all the drips and drains and tubes that were still attached to her.

By July 1984 Sister Mary Leo was well enough to travel to Sydney

Sister Mary Leo and Sister Mary Joan Hopkinson in 'Coolock', 1985 — the last photograph of Sister Leo taken in the music room.

(Auckland Sisters of Mercy Archives)

as guest of honour at the annual Australian Singing Competition, which included the $15,000 Mathy Scholarship. This was her first trip away since February 1981 when she had travelled to Sydney with Robina Reardon and Sister Joan Hopkinson to see Heather Begg in *The Beggar's Opera*, and it was to be her last trip away from Auckland.

Her presence in Sydney was noted in the local papers and an interview appeared in *The Australian* under the heading 'The Dame Behind Dame Kiri'. She was still 'alert and opinionated' and had 'lost none of the spark that drove her most famous pupil', *The Australian* reported. The question she had been asked so many times before about her teaching methods drew the same reply. She would give nothing away but said, 'I'm really just a psychologist… If you can get inside the person and bring out the best in their character, you also bring out the best in their voices.' She was still teaching, she said, but regretted she had to turn some young hopefuls away. At one point her natural garrulity got away from her and she let slip some criticism of Dame Kiri Te Kanawa's performance at the royal wedding. She hadn't liked the frock Kiri was wearing, and thought she had sung a little too quickly. The reporter described how: 'Dame Mary then spent the next 10 minutes obviously wishing she hadn't said that, stressing she was very proud of Dame Kiri and that it was a great honour that she had been asked to sing at the wedding.'[12]

At Christmas 1984 some forty former pupils, accompanists and Robina Reardon once again gathered to pay tribute with a surprise party where they sang 'The Nuns' Chorus' and 'La Vergine degli Angeli'. In a letter to Heather Fryer, a former student, Sister Joan Hopkinson described it as a truly magic evening when the girls were in tears of joy. Sister Mary Leo's version of the occasion was:

My pupils past and present sprang a pleasant surprise on me and came to the convent with Christmas gifts and they sang some choruses of bygone days… The whole evening was a delightful one… I must close as my eyes have been giving me trouble recently and I find it hard to see the lines.[13]

In July 1985, less than a year after her last trip to Sydney, Sister Mary Leo fell and broke a pelvic bone and was admitted to the orthopaedic ward of Middlemore Hospital. The injury meant that for the first time she was not able to attend the final of the Dame Sister Mary Leo Scholarship, which was held in the same week. It also led to the eventual cancellation of the proposed 'This Is Your Life' programme which Television New Zealand were planning, with the help of Sister Joan Hopkinson. Filming had been scheduled to take place one week after Sister Mary Leo's fall.

The fall led to a long period in traction in the Mater Misericordiae Hospital, and from this time until her death Sister Mary Leo lived mainly at the Mater, later called the Mercy Hospital. The pupils she had been preparing for competitions were taken over by a former pupil, now a singing teacher, Marie Morris (née O'Leary). Sister Mary Leo went home to St Mary's Convent for Christmas 1985 but because she required night care she later returned to the Mater. When she and

Heather Begg visits Sister Mary Leo in 1987.

(New Zealand Herald)

ten colleagues celebrated the diamond jubilee of their religious profession in January 1986 with a Mass of Thanksgiving at St Mary's Convent, the photograph of this occasion shows Sister Mary Leo looking rather frail and bent, sitting in a wheelchair. In March 1987 Sister Mary Joan Hopkinson reported that Sister Mary Leo was good in herself though her toes were sore and she was not able to exercise them to keep the circulation moving. The nurses took her for a daily run round the block in the wheelchair, which Sister thoroughly enjoyed, but she was by now very frail.

Heather Begg, who last saw Dame Sister Mary Leo in November 1987, found it hard to see her strength failing, her speech and eyesight blurred, and age and sickness taking their toll:

> ...it really wrung my heart to see her pathetic and frail condition. She drifted in and out of knowing me and not knowing me, hanging on to me at times with a little strength in her painfully thin, dear hands, and her gaze one moment steady, meaningful and loving, the next

shifting out of focus in sheer physical tiredness. It was very painful for me, but in a way I felt some comfort to know that my visit had brought her some joy.

I prefer to remember her as that strong willed, feisty dedicated woman of old — ('she who must be obeyed'!) in her hey-day, when her many successes made her famous, and a Dame, and a real force to be reckoned with.

As so often happened, a reporter and photographer were on hand to record the visit and a large photograph appeared on the front page of the *New Zealand Herald* the following day with the heading 'Visit from Pupil A Real Tonic'. The reporter described how Dame Sister Mary Leo had offered to give the noted mezzo-soprano a singing lesson, and went on to say that some of the energy that she had put into her tutoring was still evident in her voice as she ordered the nurses to 'come on, come on' and get her back to bed.[14]

Friends who visited Sister Mary Leo in her final years often found a large ginger cat sleeping on her lap. After years of not being allowed a cat in the convent, she welcomed the opportunity of adopting the hospital's ward cat. A photograph which appeared in the newspaper in 1987 showed Sister Mary Leo, the cat 'Topaz' on her knee, with her most famous pupil, Dame Kiri Te Kanawa, who was back in New Zealand to judge the Mobil Song Quest.

Patricia-Anne Shaw and her husband, tenor Ken Cornish, were among the friends who visited Sister Mary Leo in hospital and sang to her. Ken relates how, even lying in bed in a fluffy pink bedjacket, she was still her old, imperious self. 'Sing to me,' she would command, and as Ken began to sing nurse aids, staff and visitors would come to the door of the room and listen. He recalls one occasion when he asked her what she would like to hear: 'Girls Were Made to Love and Kiss,' came the reply, so Ken sat on the commode by her bed, held her hand, and sang to her. An apple-cheeked nun in the neighbouring bed thought she would put in a request too. 'Sing something Irish,' she said, but Sister Mary Leo was not impressed and more or less told the other nun that this was *her* concert — it was not for anyone else to make requests.

Sister Mary Leo was not well enough to attend her sister Jessie's

90th birthday party in Huntly in 1988, but a former pupil, Rita Baars, sang solos at the Mass of Thanksgiving and a colleague and former pupil, Sister Muriel Shallue, played the organ. At Christmas 1988 Patricia-Anne Shaw organised a small concert for Sister Mary Leo in the St Joseph's hospice where she was then staying.

Her death occurred on 5 May 1989 at the Mercy Hospital.

After her death it was reported that she had remained 'alert and cheerful' to the end despite her frailness, and 'almost never mentioned herself'.[15] In a tribute written after her death, Lyndsay Freer described what it was like to visit Sister Mary Leo in her latter days:

> *While recently in hospital she was weak and frail. But the moment a visitor entered her room her face became animated with the familiar crooked smile. She would joke about her condition, observing that she was still here because the Lord wasn't quite ready for her...*
>
> *She was not at all concerned with her health and well-being. She lived in the constant presence of the Lord, quite unafraid of what the future might hold, knowing where she was going, and trusting Him to lead her there as and when He would.*[16]

A Vigil Mass was held in the chapel of St Mary's Convent on 7 May, and a Requiem Mass in the Catholic Cathedral, Auckland, on 8 May. The congregation of about 1000 people began arriving from 8.30 a.m. for the 10.30 a.m. service. Over the weekend before the service about 60 former pupils formed a choir to sing at the funeral, while Lyndsay Freer sang the only solo, 'Tota Pulchra Es'. A choir from the Sisters of Mercy also sang a motet. The *New Zealand Herald* noted that 'Tears flowed freely in the choir loft of St Patrick's Cathedral, Auckland yesterday...'

The celebrant for the mass was the Bishop of Auckland, the Most Reverend Denis Browne, who said of Sister Leo:

> *While she demanded high standards, she did not allow the tension of competition to overcome the sheer thrill of enjoying the beauty of music.*[17]

The main eulogy was given by Sister Judith Leydon, the Superior of the Sisters of Mercy, who summed up the main characteristics of Sister Mary Leo's life well:

> *The motivating force behind all that she did was her faith in God; she had total trust in Him, recognising that her gifts came from Him, and being utterly wholehearted in using them in His service. She was a woman of prayer, always faithful to our community prayer, to personal prayer, frequently being the last person in the chapel at night, snatching short moments during her busy day, for a brief time with the Lord, and placing her care and joys under the intercession and protection of Mary, the Mother of God.*
>
> *She could be a hard taskmaster. She demanded that those around her give always of their best, nothing less would do, and she practised this herself. There was nothing 'small' nor grudging about her. She was a woman of great maturity and compassion; she understood human frailty, and gave of herself to each person she met. She lived life to the full enjoying everything, from the concert halls of the great to the more mundane pleasures of a beach holiday at Waiheke Island with the Sisters.*
>
> *Sister Mary Leo was a woman of joy, a delightful companion, a faithful friend, and dedicated teacher, a loving and loved family member, and a cherished part of our religious community. For more than sixty-five years she was a Sister of Mercy. She will be greatly missed. Today we thank God for the gift that He gave to us in her, and we celebrate her life with us. We give her back to Him, gladly as she would wish, commending her to his eternal love and care.*
>
> *May the angels lead her into paradise where she will make sure there is heavenly singing and dancing.*[18]

Ann Stott spoke on behalf of all the students who had studied with Dame Sister Mary Leo, ending her tribute with the words:

> *Dame Sister Mary Leo has laid an exceptional foundation for us all to build upon. Wherever our music schools are formed or an opera stage completed or the Dame Sister Mary Leo Scholarship contended it will*

be done for many years to come by folk who took a little inspiration from this great lady. Sister Mary Leo was our mentor, but so like a friend and mother. May God bless her and hold her always in his hands.

Afterword

The Dame Sister Mary Leo Scholarship

The story of the Dame Sister Mary Leo Scholarship, established in 1980 under the auspices of the Auckland Grand Opera Society (see chapter 9), is bound up with that of the Sydney-based Marianne Mathy Scholarship. This competition, held for the first time in 1982, is funded from a bequest by Marianne Mathy, one of Australia's great singing teachers. After Nicola Waite, a New Zealand singer (and former pupil of Dame Sister Mary Leo), won the first Marianne Mathy competition, it was decided that the two scholarship trust foundations should work together.

This happened for the first time in 1983, when 21 singers competed for the Dame Sister Mary Leo Scholarship, with 6 finalists competing in the Auckland Town Hall on 12 March. The first prize was $15,000, with the runner-up receiving $1000 plus preferential entry into the Marianne Mathy scholarship. Lynne Cantlon and Elisabeth Hellawell, both former students of Sister Mary Leo, were on the judging panel, while Frances Wilson, a former pupil of Sister Frances Xavier, accompanied the singers in the first half of the programme. The winner, mezzo-soprano Rhona Fraser, was another singer who had formerly studied with Sister Mary Leo. A guest artist at the final was Mina Foley, who as Lin Saunders noted in the *Herald* the next day, 'swells any audience'.

When the runner-up in the 1983 competition, Wayne Morris, was not able to compete in the Marianne Mathy competition, Philippa Reade (another former pupil of Sister Mary Leo) was accepted as a substitute, and competed in the contest at semi-final level. Although she did not reach the finals, she was offered a year's scholarship to the Queensland State Conservatorium of Music. The Scholarship Trust Foundation was further benefited in July 1983 when pianist Michael Houstoun gave an all-Beethoven recital in Auckland, while Dame Kiri Te Kanawa offered cash grants and professional help to the 1983 and 1984 winners. By 1983 the Dame Sister Mary Leo Scholarship seemed established as New Zealand's premier singing award.

The winner of the $15,000 scholarship in 1984 was Australian mezzo-soprano Deborah Riedel, while another Australian singer, soprano Fiona Maconaghie, won the 1985 event. In 1986, for the first time, a male singer, Christchurch bass Ted Rhodes, won the scholarship.

But in 1986 the scholarship entered on troubled times when a decision was made to cancel all links between the Dame Sister Mary Leo Scholarship and the Marianne Mathy Scholarship. This decision caused great concern to Robina Reardon, who made sure that Dame Sister Mary Leo's personal views (she was in favour of retaining links with the Australian scholarship) were made known to the Grand Opera Society. The question of whether Australian singers should be able to compete for the Dame Sister Mary Leo Scholarship, combined with administrative difficulties, meant that no further contests were held during Dame Sister Mary Leo's lifetime. It was not until December 1990 that members of the Society resolved to pass over the administration of the scholarship to an independent board. The board, when appointed, organised its first scholarship competition for August 1992. The winner of the $15,000 scholarship this year was Philippa Reade, a former pupil of Dame Sister Mary Leo, with another former pupil, Carmel Carroll, taking third place. On the stage of the concert chamber at the final was a large portrait of Dame Sister Mary Leo. As accompanist Joy Crabtree played the piano that night she was certain that Sister was there with them. 'It was just as though we were back in the music room and we were having a rehearsal ... she wasn't there in person, but she was certainly there in spirit...'

After the 1992 competition there was a further lapse of five years before the Dame Sister Mary Leo Foundation once again organised a competition in 1997, with a first prize of $10,000. The winner this year was bass singer Jonathan Lemalu from Dunedin.

Future competitions organised by the Dame Sister Mary Leo Foundation will ensure that her name is not forgotten. But the spirit of this great teacher also lives on through those who knew her. In the lives and work of her former students, as they perform, teach and pass on her training, there is a lasting memorial to Sister Mary Leo which will continue for generations to come. As a former pupil said at her funeral service — 'there's a little bit of Sister in all of us'.

Appendix

Winners of the John Court Memorial Aria who were pupils of Sister Mary Leo

1950	Mina Foley
1952	Maureen Fletcher (later Gordon)
1953	Elisabeth Hellawell
1954	Ivy Rodan
1955	Judith Edwards
1957	Marie Robinson
1958	Mary O'Brien
1959	Joan Cochrane
1962	Lynne Cantlon
1963	Cheryll Hewitt
1964	Kiri Te Kanawa
1965	Joan Kennaway
1966	Jacqueline Chapman
1967	Marie-Thérèse Laurijssen
1969	Donna Awatere

Placegetters in the Mobil Song Quest who were pupils of Sister Mary Leo

1956	Joan Cochrane, third.
1959	Mary O'Brien, first; Angela Shaw, second.
1961	Patricia Price, first; Hannah Tatana, second.
1963	Malvina Major, first; Kiri Te Kanawa, second.
1965	Kiri Te Kanawa, first.
1967	Anne Rasmussen, first.
1970	Patricia House, first.
1972	Patricia-Anne Shaw, second.
1974	Patricia Wright, third.
1977	Nicola Waite, third.
1979	Gillian Trott, third.
1989	Tracey King, first.

Acknowledgements

Writing the biography of Dame Sister Mary Leo was a fascinating and challenging experience. Coming from a non-Catholic background, and with no personal experience as a singer, I had much to learn. I attempted to write a book that would be enjoyed both by readers like me, who have no background in the Catholic or singing worlds, but also by the students who knew Sister Mary Leo so well. This was not easy. Each student seems to have felt she had a 'special' relationship with her teacher, and to write about the very special person experienced by each of her friends and pupils was simply impossible. Instead I have tried to present a picture of the whole woman and to offer an explanation as to why she was as she was. My sources were reported interviews with Sister Mary Leo herself, comments made by her former pupils, and interviews with her sister Jessie, former friends and colleagues. While attempting to remain faithful to the information that was given to me, I have also aimed to present an interpretation of Sister Mary Leo's complex personality. I hope that, like me, readers will find some inspiration in this story of a vital, highly talented and devoted religious woman.

I would like to thank Luisa Shannahan (formerly Lois Clausen) for her constant support and encouragement throughout the period that I was working on the book. Her expert knowledge and experience as a former pupil of Sister Mary Leo, and now as a singing teacher, has informed the whole book. She also made a major contribution to the writing of chapter 7, dealing with Sister Mary Leo's teaching methods. I would also like to gratefully acknowledge the help I received from Sister Marcienne Kirk, Archivist for the Auckland Sisters of Mercy. She welcomed me to St Mary's on my trips to Auckland, made the Sisters of Mercy Archives freely available to me, and patiently answered my queries. In Whangarei I was helped greatly by Mrs Noreen Birchall, whose extensive knowledge of the Onerahi district proved invaluable. In Hawke's Bay Molly Paterson and Buster Harker provided generous assistance. Sr Colleen Dempsey, Archivist for the

Sisters of St Joseph in Auckland, and staff of the music reference section of the Auckland Public Library gave help beyond the call of duty for which I am grateful.

My research costs were met largely by a grant of $5000 from the New Zealand History Research Trust Fund. I am also extremely grateful for grants of $1000 from the Auckland Sisters of Mercy, $935 from the Federation of University Women Harriette Jenkins Award, and $300 from Peter and Alana Cooke which also helped meet costs. For help with the writing process I would particularly like to thank Luisa Shannahan, Sr Pauline O'Regan, Sr Patricia Graham, Sr Marcienne Kirk and Lyndsay Freer, who read and commented on my draft manuscript, although finally the responsibility for selection and interpretation of the material in the book lies with me. I would also like to sincerely thank the people listed below who have assisted me by providing information. Without their help this book could not have been written.

Interviews

Inness Anderson née Lovett, Joan Aronsten, Sr Margaret Browne, Sr Eileen Burrell, Patricia-Anne Cornish née Shaw and Ken Cornish, Max Cryer, Sr Veronica Delany, Tania Dyett, Sr Pauline Engel, Lyndsay Freer née Kearns, Mary Furness, Bobs (Marjory) Gardner, Alison Glass née McGregor, Maureen Gordon née Fletcher, Vivienne Gordon née Adams, Angela Gorton née Shaw, Sr Patricia Graham, Buster Harker, Elisabeth Hellawell, Sr Joan Hopkinson, Fr David Jillett, Kathleen Karl, Clive Littin, Janice Lunn, Sr Kathleen Markham, Zita Outtrim née Austin, Cecilia Parkes née Connelly, Molly Paterson née Wilson, Sr Majella Patterson, Sr Mary Vianney Park, Sr Claver Schollum, Kathryn Schollum, Sr Muriel Shallue, Eileen Walker née Tootill, Sr Raphael Watt.

Interviews conducted by Lois Clausen

Patricia-Anne Cornish née Shaw, Joy Crabtree, Sr Veronica Delany, Doreen Donnell née McNabb, Mina Foley, Lyndsay Freer née Kearns,

Ann (later Alexandra) Gordon, Elisabeth Hellawell, Anthony Hollows, Sr Joan Hopkinson, Sr Fidelma Kearney, Joan Kennaway née Choat, Hazel Millar-Boyd, Jessie O'Sullivan and Kathleen Karl, Robina Reardon, Ann Stott, Patrick Towsey.

Written replies to a questionnaire devised by Lois Clausen were received from the following former pupils of Sister Mary Leo

Julianne Adamo née Picot, Inness Anderson née Lovett, Heather Begg, Raewyn Blade, Roy Bowden, Hazel Millar Boyd, Carmel Carroll, Alana Bolton Cooke, Patricia-Anne Cornish née Shaw, Elizabeth Edwards née Loomb, Heather Fryer, Rita Geraghty, Joan Glen née Negus, Fay Hadden, Christine Hallett née Treseder, Elisabeth Hellawell, Anthony Hollows, Val Hungerford, Kathleen Johnson, Margot Lloyd, Marianne Mackie née Bowden, Dame Malvina Major, Leonie McRae, Marie Morris née O'Leary, Mary O'Brien, Patricia Price, Phillipa Reade, Collene Roche, Jacqueline Shone née Chapman, Susan Steele, Ann Stott, Gillian Trott née Redstone, Frances Wilson, Patricia Wright, Anne Marabini Young.

The following responded to requests for information

Joan Aronsten (Sydney), Auckland City Council, Auckland College of Education, Auckland Grammar School, Auckland Performing Arts Society Inc., Auckland Public Library, Auckland University Registry, Heather Begg, Noreen Birchall, Diana Cable, Catholic Diocese of Auckland Archives, Rita Chalmers, Fr Walter Cooke (Waipukurau), Joan Crompton née Harker (Melbourne), Sr Colleen Dempsey, Elizabeth Edwards, Paul Gleeson for Dame Kiri Te Kanawa, Professor Peter Godfrey, Hawke's Bay Museum, Kathleen Karl, Ron Kirkwood, Mailee Lee (Sydney), Lynne Lennan née Cantlon, James McNeish, Ministry of Education (Wellington), Napier Public Library, National Archives (Wellington), National Archives (Auckland), Malcolm Niccol, North Shore Performing Arts

Competitions Society, Cecilia Parkes née Connelly, Molly Paterson née Wilson, Richmond Road School (Auckland), St Joseph's School (Grey Lynn), Sisters of St Joseph Archives (Sydney), Sisters of the Good Shepherd (Sydney), State Library of New South Wales, Sydney Conservatorium of Music, Trinity College (London), Whangarei Public Library.

Notes

Chapter 1
1. Ted Reynolds, 'Dame Sister Mary Leo: The Enigma of a Famous Nun', *New Zealand Herald*, 6 May 1989.
2. Undated article re Malcolm Niccol in 'Main Scrapbook', vol. 13, pp. 216–7, Auckland Institute and Museum.
3. Obituary, *The Evening Post*, 29 July 1925.
4. Undated [poss. 1899] article re Malcolm Niccol in 'Main Scrapbook', vol. 13, pp. 216–7, Auckland Institute and Museum.
5. [Item re the biennial meeting of the Grand Lodge of NZ Masons], *New Zealand Free Lance*, 3 May 1902.
6. Obituary, *The Evening Post*, 29 July 1925.
7. Jessie O'Sullivan interviewed by Sr Veronica Delany [1974], Auckland Sisters of Mercy Archives.
8. Robert Gilmore, 'Convent Quiet — and a Chorus of Great Voices', *Auckland Star*, 23 October 1965.
9. Jessie O'Sullivan interviewed by Sr Veronica Delany [1974], Auckland Sisters of Mercy Archives.
10. 'Jessie's reminiscences', Auckland Sisters of Mercy Archives.
11. Jessie O'Sullivan interviewed by Sr Veronica Delany [1974], Auckland Sisters of Mercy Archives.
12. Jessie O'Sullivan interviewed by Lois Clausen, 1993.
13. Jessie O'Sullivan interviewed by Lois Clausen, 1993.
14. Jessie O'Sullivan interviewed by Lois Clausen, 1993.
15. Letter from Helen Evans, Administration Assistant, Auckland College of Education, 7 August 1995; also the magazine of the Auckland Training College, *The Manuka*, for the years 1907–1914.
16. AJHR 1913–1915; Supplement to the *NZ Gazette*, 1913–1916.
17. *Northern Advocate*, 20 August 1915 and 3 November 1916.
18. *A History of Onerahi District & School 1893–1993*, Whangarei, 1993.
19. *Northern Advocate*, 7 March 1916.
20. *Northern Advocate*, 21 December 1915.
21. *Northern Advocate*, 11 November 1916.
22. *Northern Advocate*, 22 December 1916.
23. *Northern Advocate*, 21 March 1919.
24. Onerahi Public School Inspection Report, 1918, National Archives Auckland.
25. *Northern Advocate*, 5 October 1915; 5 December 1916; 13 February 1917.

26. *Waipukurau Press*, 13 June 1921.
27. *Waipukurau Press*, 7 October 1921.
28. *Waipukurau Press*, 16 December 1921.
29. Robert Gilmore, 'Convent Quiet — and a Chorus of Great Voices', *Auckland Star*, 23 October, 1965; Sr Mary Leo interviewed by Bill McCarthy for TVNZ, Radio New Zealand Sound Archives, 1981.
30. 'Talk Given by Sister M. Leo at Baptist Tabernacle', 1 May 1974, Auckland Sisters of Mercy Archives.
31. Jessie O'Sullivan interviewed by Sr Veronica Delany [1974], Auckland Sisters of Mercy Archives; Jessie O'Sullivan interviewed by Lois Clausen, 1993.
32. Alastair Morrison, 'Dame Sister Mary Leo — Teacher', *New Zealand Times*, 26 December 1982.
33. Jessie O'Sullivan interviewed by Sr Veronica Delany [1974], Auckland Sisters of Mercy Archives.
34. 'Aspirations to become an opera singer died when Mary Leo entered the convent...', Alastair Morrison, 'Dame Sister Mary Leo — Teacher', *New Zealand Times*, 26 December 1982.
35. Jessie O'Sullivan interviewed by Sr Veronica Delany [1974], Auckland Sisters of Mercy Archives.
36. Jessie O'Sullivan interviewed by Sr Veronica Delany [1974], Auckland Sisters of Mercy Archives.

Chapter 2
1. Jessie O'Sullivan interviewed by Clive Littin [1974], Auckland Sisters of Mercy Archives.
2. 'Talk Given by Sister M. Leo at Baptist Tabernacle', 1 May 1974, Auckland Sisters of Mercy Archives.
3. Letter to Dearest Mother from Sr M. Leo, Auckland Sisters of Mercy Archives.
4. 'Record Profession', *The Month*, 16 February 1926.
5. Poem dated 19 January 1926, Auckland Sisters of Mercy Archives.
6. 'Talk Given by Sister M. Leo at Baptist Tabernacle', 1 May 1974, Auckland Sisters of Mercy Archives.
7. Poem dated 19 January 1926, Auckland Sisters of Mercy Archives.
8. Letter to 'My dearest' from Sr M. Leo, Auckland Sisters of Mercy Archives.
9. Sr Mary Leo, 'A Celebration of Faith', 1979, Auckland Sisters of Mercy Archives.
10. Sr Mary Leo, 'A Celebration of Faith', 1979, Auckland Sisters of Mercy Archives.
11. Sr Mary Leo interviewed by Bill McCarthy for TVNZ, Radio New Zealand Sound Archives, 1981.

Chapter 3
1. *St Mary's College Annual*, 1958, p. 34.
2. Jenny Wheeler, 'An Investment with Very Slow Returns', *New Zealand Woman's Weekly*, 23 October, 1978, p. 4.
3. *St Mary's College Annual*, 1941, p. 87.
4. *St Mary's College Annual*, 1940, p. 31.
5. *St Mary's College Annual*, 1936, p. 45.
6. Jessie O'Sullivan interviewed by Sr Veronica Delany [1974], Auckland Sisters of Mercy Archives.
7. Concert programme, 'Centenary of the Sisters of Mercy, Auckland Festival Concert', Auckland Sisters of Mercy Archives.
8. Quoted in *St Mary's College Annual*, 1950, p. 24.
9. *St Mary's College Annual*, 1950, pp. 44–46.
10. *St Mary's College Annual*, 1950, pp. 42–43.

Chapter 4
1. *St Mary's College Annual*, 1950, p. 43.
2. 'Miss Foley Going to Australia', *Auckland Star*, 6 September 1950; 'Mina Foley Leaving for Australia', *Auckland Star*, 21 September 1950.
3. *St Mary's College Annual*, 1950, p. 43.
4. 'Has Always Wanted to Sing Opera', *Auckland Star*, 16 October 1950.
5. *St Mary's College Annual*, 1951, pp. 49–50.
6. 'Italian Scholarship for Mina Foley', *New Zealand Herald*, 8 August 1951.
7. 'Visitors Hear "One of Voices of the Century" ', *Auckland Star*, 5 September 1952.
8. 'St Mary's College Concert Packs Town Hall', *Auckland Star*, 23 October 1952.
9. 'Mina Foley Triumphs in Wellington', *Auckland Star*, 29 January 1953.
10. 'Mina Foley on Crest of Popular Wave', *New Zealand Herald*, 22 August 1955.
11. Phyllis Brusey, *Ring Down the Curtain*, p. 106, quoting review by J.J.C. in the *Evening Post*.
12. *St Mary's College Annual*, 1955, pp. 44–45.
13. Tribute to Dame Sister Mary Leo, written by Heather Begg for the *New Zealand Herald*, 6 May 1989.
14. 'Teacher of Song Makes Talent Bloom', *New Zealand Weekly News*, 1 December 1965.
15. Alana Bolton Cooke, 'Stand Tall, Don't Slouch — Sing!', *New Zealand Woman's Weekly*, 25 October 1993, p. 44.
16. Letter from Paul Gleeson, International Management Group, quoting Dame Kiri Te Kanawa, 13 August 1996.
17. 'Her Voice Is Young Yet', *Auckland Star*, 11 September 1963.

18. Malvina Major quoted in Adrienne Simpson and Peter Downes, *Southern Voices: International Opera Singers of New Zealand*, Auckland, 1992, p. 206.

Chapter 5
1. *St Mary's College Annual*, 1956, p. 58.
2. *St Mary's College Annual*, 1959, pp. 48–49.
3. 'Customs in Use', Auckland Sisters of Mercy Archives.
4. Robert Gilmore, 'Convent Quiet — and a Chorus of Great Voices', *Auckland Star*, 23 October 1965, p. 15.
5. Robert Gilmore, 'Convent Quiet — and a Chorus of Great Voices', *Auckland Star*, 23 October 1965, p. 15.
6. Ella Lee to Sister Mary Leo, 30 July 1964, Auckland Sisters of Mercy Archives.
7. Terry Snow, 'Her Famous Pupils Don't Forget', *Auckland Star*, 27 March 1979.
8. 'Major Awards to St Mary's Music School', [1963] article in Sr Laurentia's Scrapbook, Auckland Sisters of Mercy Archives.
9. Sr Mary Leo interviewed by Bill McCarthy for TVNZ, Radio New Sound Archives, 1981.
10. *St Mary's College Annual*, 1960, p. 27.
11. Quoted in *St Mary's College Annual*, 1961, p. 41.
12. Quoted in *St Mary's College Annual*, 1962, pp. 24–25.
13. *St Mary's College Annual*, 1963, p. 19.
14. *St Mary's College Annual*, 1963, p. 19.
15. 'Sister Mary Leo Proud of Girls', *New Zealand Herald*, 29 September 1964; 'Clue to Nun's Success As Music Teacher', *New Zealand Herald*, 30 October 1964.
16. Jo Noble, 'The Nun with a Gift for Teaching Music', *New Zealand Woman's Weekly*, 8 March 1965, pp. 8–11.
17. 'Teacher of Song Makes Talent Bloom', *New Zealand Weekly News*, 1 December 1965, p. 3.
18. Ernest R. Hilgard, *Introduction to Psychology*, New York, 1990.
19. Elizabeth Dunn, 'The World of Sister Mary Leo', *New Zealand Woman's Weekly*, 5 February, 1973, pp. 4–5.
20. Malvina Major speaking on 'Holmes' show, 5 May 1989, New Zealand Television Archive.
21. Louise Malloy speaking on 'This Day', 13 September 1972, New Zealand Television Archive.
22. Sr Mary Leo interviewed by Bill McCarthy for TVNZ, Radio New Zealand Sound Archives, 1981.
23. Sister Mary Leo speaking on 'This Day', 13 September 1972, New Zealand Television Archive.

24. Lynne Cantlon interviewed by Sr Veronica Delany [1976], Auckland Sisters of Mercy Archives.
25. Alastair Morrison, 'Dame Sister Mary Leo — Teacher', *New Zealand Times*, 26 December 1982.
26. Jo Noble, 'The Nun with a Gift for Teaching Music', *New Zealand Woman's Weekly*, 8 March 1965, pp. 8–11.

Chapter 6
1. 'Sister Mary Leo Proud of Girls', *New Zealand Herald*, 29 September 1964.
2. David Jillett, *Malvina: A Biography of Dame Malvina Major*, Auckland, 1995, p. 73.
3. Dame Malvina Major, fax to publisher, 23 July 1998.
4. David Fingleton, *Kiri Te Kanawa: A Biography*, London, 1982, p. 39.
5. *New Zealand Herald*, 26 September 1966.
6. David Jillett, *Malvina: A Biography of Dame Malvina Major*, Auckland, 1995, p. 65.
7. Walter M. Abbot (ed.), *The Documents of Vatican II*, New York, 1966, p. 478.
8. [Heading obscured], *Auckland Star*, 15 May 1968.
9. L.C.M. Saunders, 'Undiminished Impact of Junior Choir', *New Zealand Herald*, 27 May 1968.
10. 'Big Crowd Expected to Hear Top Voices', undated unsourced article; 'Sister Mary Leo to Conduct Her Choir', undated unsourced article.
11. 'Promising Voices in Concert; Star Pupil at Town Hall', *New Zealand Herald*, 10 November 1969.
12. Letter to Dearest Mother from Sr M. Leo [1972], from Westown Motor Hotel, Auckland Sisters of Mercy Archives.
13. 'Choirs Pay Tribute To Teacher', *New Zealand Herald*, 29 October 1971.
14. Undated unsourced article, Auckland Sisters of Mercy Archives.
15. 'Trip for Sister Mary Leo with Grant Aid', *Zealandia*, 23 July, 1972.

Chapter 7
1. 'Sister Leo's "Girls" Have a Special Quality in Their Voices', *Auckland Star*, 6 November 1959.
2. Sister Mary Leo speaking on 'Top Half', 24 November 1983, New Zealand Television Archive.
3. 'Sister Mary Leo Talks About Her Teaching', Radio New Zealand Sound Archives, 1976.
4. Richard Miller, *The Structure of Singing: System and Art in Vocal Technique*, New York, 1986, p. 23.
5. Jo Noble, 'The Nun with a Gift for Teaching Music', *New Zealand Woman's Weekly*, 8 March 1965, pp. 8–11.
6. Robert Gilmore, 'Convent Quiet — and a Chorus of Great Voices', *Auckland*

Star, 23 October 1965, p. 15.
7. Elizabeth Dunn, 'The World of Sister Mary Leo', *New Zealand Woman's Weekly*, 5 February 1973, pp. 4–5.
8. Elizabeth Dunn, 'The World of Sister Mary Leo', *New Zealand Woman's Weekly*, 5 February 1973, pp. 4–5.
9. Sr Mary Leo interviewed by Bill McCarthy for TVNZ, Radio New Zealand Sound Archives, 1981.
10. 'How Important Are Your Hands?' *New Zealand Herald*, 7 October 1967.
11. Alastair Morrison, 'Dame Sister Mary Leo — Teacher', *New Zealand Times*, 26 December 1982.
12. Robert Gilmore, 'Convent Quiet — and a Chorus of Great Voices', *Auckland Star*, 23 October 1965, p. 15.
13. 'Stars Come Out to Honour Dame Sister Leo', *New Zealand Tablet*, 9 December 1981.
14. Sr Mary Leo interviewed by Bill McCarthy for TVNZ, Radio New Zealand Sound Archives, 1981.
15. 'Sister Mary Leo Talks About Her Teaching', Radio New Zealand Sound Archives, 1976.
16. Sr Mary Leo interviewed by Bill McCarthy for TVNZ, Radio New Zealand Sound Archives, 1981.
17. Robert Gilmore, 'Convent Quiet — and a Chorus of Great Voices', *Auckland Star*, 23 October 1965, p. 15.
18. 'Sister Mary Leo Talks to Owen Jensen', Radio New Zealand Sound Archives, 1972.
19. Alana Bolton Cooke, 'Stand Tall, Don't Slouch — Sing!', *New Zealand Woman's Weekly*, 25 October 1993, p. 45.
20. 'Sister Leo's "Girls" Have a Special Quality in Their Voices', *Auckland Star*, 6 November 1959.
21. Robert Gilmore, 'Convent Quiet — and a Chorus of Great Voices', *Auckland Star*, 23 October 1965, p. 15.
22. Sr Mary Leo interviewed by Bill McCarthy for TVNZ, Radio New Zealand Sound Archives, 1981.
23. Robert Gilmore, 'Convent Quiet — and a Chorus of Great Voices', *Auckland Star*, 23 October 1965, p. 15.
24. Elizabeth Dunn, 'The World of Sister Mary Leo', *New Zealand Woman's Weekly*, 5 February 1973, pp. 4–5.
25. 'Sister Leo's "Girls" Have a Special Quality in Their Voices', *Auckland Star*, 6 November 1959.
26. 'Sister Leo's "Girls" Have a Special Quality in Their Voices', *Auckland Star*, 6 November 1959.
27. Sr Mary Leo interviewed by Bill McCarthy for TVNZ, Radio New Zealand Sound Archives, 1981.

28. 'Sister Leo's "Girls" Have a Special Quality in Their Voices', *Auckland Star*, 6 November 1959.
29. Sr Mary Leo interviewed by Bill McCarthy for TVNZ, Radio New Zealand Sound Archives, 1981.
30. Malvina Major speaking on 'Holmes' show, 5 May 1989, New Zealand Television Archive.
31. 'Well Deserved Honour For Sister Leo', *Zealandia*, 10 January 1963.
32. 'Sister Mary Leo Talks to Owen Jensen', Radio New Zealand Sound Archives, 1972.
33. Alastair Morrison, 'Dame Sister Mary Leo — Teacher', *New Zealand Times*, 26 December 1982.
34. David Fingleton, *Kiri Te Kanawa: A Biography*, London, 1982, p. 39.
35. Letter to Anne Rasmussen from Joan Sutherland Bonynge, quoted in the *St Mary's College Annual*, 1972, pp. 26–27.

Chapter 8

1. Citation prepared by Sister Mary Veronica Delany, and submitted by Sister Mary Carmel O'Sullivan, the Acting Superior General of the Sisters of Mercy, Auckland, at the request of the New Zealand Government, Auckland Sisters of Mercy Archives.
2. 'Nuns Put On Tea They're So Happy', *Sunday News*, 3 June 1973; 'We Do Our Penance', *Sunday News*, 10 June 1973.
3. Rod Pascoe, 'The Dame of St Mary's', *Zealandia*, 17 June 1973, p. 20.
4. Terry Snow, 'Her Famous Pupils Don't Forget', *Auckland Star*, 27 March 1979.
5. Roz Pulley, 'Fame Hounds the Shy Nun', *Manawatu Evening Standard*, 30 August 1975.
6. *Who's Who in New Zealand*, 11th edition, Wellington, 1978; *Notable New Zealanders: The Pictorial Who's Who*, 1st edition, Wellington, 1979.
7. Jenny Wheeler, 'An Investment with Very Slow Returns', *New Zealand Woman's Weekly*, 23 October 1978, pp. 4–6.
8. 'Kiri "Perfect" for Reunion Night', *New Zealand Herald*, 12 September 1978.
9. 'For Dame Sister Mary Leo, an Award with a Visible Difference', *New Zealand Woman's Weekly*, 19 November 1979, pp. 59–60, 'Dame Sister Mary Leo … Surely a Sound Choice', unsourced undated article, Auckland Sisters of Mercy Archives.
10. 'Here Are the Seven Most Liked Kiwis', *Auckland Star*, 15 June 1982.
11. 'Talk Given by Sister M. Leo at Baptist Tabernacle', 1 May 1974, Auckland Sisters of Mercy Archives.
12. Robert Gilmore, 'Convent Quiet — and a Chorus of Great Voices', *Auckland Star*, 23 October 1965, p. 15.
13. Jo Noble, 'The Nun with a Gift for Teaching Music', *New Zealand Woman's*

Weekly, 8 March 1965, pp. 8–11.
14. Sister Mary Leo speaking on 'This Day', 13 September 1972, New Zealand Television Archive.
15. Robert Gilmore, 'Convent Quiet — and a Chorus of Great Voices', *Auckland Star*, 23 October, 1965, p. 15.
16. Irene Tirbutt interviewed by Sr Veronica Delany [1976], Auckland Sisters of Mercy Archives.
17. Malvina Major talking on 'Holmes' show, 5 May 1989, New Zealand Television Archive.
18. 'Talk Given by Sister M. Leo at Baptist Tabernacle', 1 May 1974, Auckland Sisters of Mercy Archives.
19. Sr Mary Leo, 'A Celebration of Faith', 1979, Auckland Sisters of Mercy Archives.
20. Elizabeth Dunn, 'The World of Sister Mary Leo', *New Zealand Woman's Weekly*, 5 February, 1973, pp. 4–5.
21. 'Sister Leo's "Girls" Have a Special Quality in Their Voices', *Auckland Star*, 6 November 1959; Terry Snow, 'Her Famous Pupils Don't Forget', *Auckland Star*, 27 March 1979.
22. *St Mary's College Annual*, 1960, p. 27.
23. Robert Gilmore, 'Convent Quiet — and a Chorus of Great Voices', *Auckland Star*, 23 October 1965, p. 15.
24. 'Teacher of Song Makes Talent Bloom', *New Zealand Weekly News*, 1 December 1965, pp. 3–4.
25. Jo Noble, 'The Nun with a Gift for Teaching Music', *New Zealand Woman's Weekly*, 8 March 1965, pp. 8–11.
26. Sr Veronica Delany, 'Dame Sister Mary Leo; a personal record', pp. 2–3, Auckland Sisters of Mercy Archives.
27. *St Mary's College Annual*, 1976, p. 103.
28. *St Mary's College Annual*, 1977, p. 98.
29. Roz Pulley, 'Fame Hounds the Shy Nun', *Manawatu Evening Standard*, 30 August 1975.
30. Roger Harris, 'Excellent Music for St Cecilia', *Auckland Star*, 24 November 1975.
31. Susan Maxwell, 'Magic Voice of Mina Foley Is Heard Again', *New Zealand Herald Weekend Magazine*, 17 November 1979.
32. ' "Special Guest" Gets a Standing Ovation', *Auckland Star*, 26 March 1979.
33. Susan Maxwell, 'Magic Voice of Mina Foley Is Heard Again', *New Zealand Herald Weekend Magazine*, 17 November 1979.
34. 'Soprano Returns', *Auckland Star*, 6 November, 1979; 'Foley Sell-out', *Auckland Star*, 16 November 1979.

Chapter 9

1. Robin Bailey, 'Tribute to a Legend', *Auckland Star*, 8 October 1980.
2. 'Singers Galaxy in Outstanding Operatic Feast', *New Zealand Herald*, 8 October 1980.
3. Copy of tribute, Auckland Sisters of Mercy Archives.
4. 'Dame Sister Mary Leo — Scholarship Foundation', Newsletter of the Sisters of Mercy, New Zealand 1980.
5. 'Real Star May Not Be There', *New Zealand Herald*, 18 November 1986.
6. Alastair Morrison, 'Dame Sister Mary Leo — Teacher', *New Zealand Times*, 26 December 1982.
7. Letter to Sister Mary Leo from James Robertson, 29 October 1981, Auckland Sisters of Mercy Archives.
8. Letters to Sister Mary Leo from Maurice Leonard of Thames Television Ltd, 27 October 1981 and 9 November 1981; letter to Sister Mary Leo from Eamonn Andrews of Thames Television Ltd, 10 November 1981; Auckland Sisters of Mercy Archives.
9. 'A Christmas Prayer', *Auckland Star*, 17 November 1983.
10. 'Cards Pay Own Tribute', *New Zealand Herald*, 4 January 1984.
11. 'Good Wishes Overwhelm Nun', *Auckland Star*, 4 January 1984.
12. David Brearley, 'The Dame Behind Dame Kiri', *The Australian*, 27 July 1984.
13. Letter to Lois Clausen from Sister Mary Leo, 28 November 1984.
14. Janine Ogier, 'Visit From Pupil a Real Tonic', *New Zealand Herald*, 12 November 1987.
15. Ted Reynolds, 'Dame Sister Mary Leo: The Enigma of a Famous Nun', *New Zealand Herald*, 6 May 1989.
16. Lyndsay Freer, 'A Loving, Warm and Gifted Woman', *The Tablet*, 17 May 1989.
17. Quoted in *The Tablet*, 17 May 1989, p. 2.
18. Eulogy by Sister Judith Leydon, Auckland Sisters of Mercy Archives.

SELECT BIBLIOGRAPHY

A. Primary sources

Auckland Sisters of Mercy Archives
Auckland Public Library, New Zealand Room and Music Reference Section
Auckland Institute and Museum Library
National Archives, Auckland
Sisters of St Joseph of the Sacred Heart Archives, Auckland

Newspapers and periodicals
St Mary's College Annual 1931–1979
The Northern Advocate 1915–1919
The Waipukurau Press 1920–1923

Articles (selected)
'Record Profession', *The Month*, 16 February 1926.
'St Mary's College Concert Packs Town Hall', *Auckland Star*, 23 October 1952.
'Sister Leo's "Girls" Have a Special Quality in Their Voices', *Auckland Star*, 6 November 1959.
'Sister Mary Leo Director St Mary's College of Music Auckland', *Woman's Viewpoint*, December 1962, p.12.
'Well Deserved Honour For Sister Leo', *Zealandia*, 10 January 1963.
'Sister Mary Leo Proud of Girls', *New Zealand Herald*, 29 September 1964.
'Sister Leo Is Welcomed With Cheers', *New Zealand Herald*, 20 October 1964.
'Clue to Nun's Success As Music Teacher', *New Zealand Herald*, 30 October, 1964.
Noble, Jo, 'The Nun with a Gift for Teaching Music', *New Zealand Woman's Weekly*, 8 March 1965, pp. 8–11.
Gilmore, Robert, 'Convent Quiet — and a Chorus of Great Voices', *Auckland Star*, 23 October, 1965, p.15.
'Teacher of Song Makes Talent Bloom', *New Zealand Weekly News*, 1 December 1965, p. 3.
'How Important Are Your Hands?' *New Zealand Herald*, 7 October 1967.
'Iron Bars Do Not Stop Nun', *New Zealand Herald*, 16 May 1968.
'Cream of Pupils', unsourced, 18 May 1968.
Saunders, L.C.M., 'Undiminished Impact of Junior Choir', *New Zealand Herald*, 27 May 1968.

'Choirs Pay Tribute To Teacher', *New Zealand Herald*, 29 October 1971.
'Trip for Sister Mary Leo with Grant Aid', *Zealandia*, 23 July 1972.
'Pupils Stand To Benefit By Her Tour', *New Zealand Herald*, 27 December 1972.
'Opera Teacher Back After World Tour', *Auckland Star*, 27 December 1972.
Pascoe, Rod, 'New Shows Did Not Impress Sr. M. Leo', *Zealandia*, 28 January 1973.
Dunn, Elizabeth, 'The World of Sister Mary Leo', *New Zealand Woman's Weekly*, 5 February, 1973, pp. 4–5.
Pascoe, Rod, 'The Dame of St Mary's', *Zealandia*, 17 June 1973, p. 20.
'Singing Now More Popular', *Auckland Star*, 26 January 1974.
Pulley, Roz, 'Fame Hounds the Shy Nun', *Manawatu Evening Standard*, 30 August 1975.
'Laurels Reaped By Teacher and Star', *New Zealand Herald*, 9 February 1976.
'Kiri "Perfect" for Reunion Night', *New Zealand Herald*, 12 September 1978.
Wheeler, Jenny, 'An Investment with Very Slow Returns', *New Zealand Woman's Weekly*, 23 October 1978, p. 4.
Snow, Terry, 'Her Famous Pupils Don't Forget', *Auckland Star*, 27 March 1979.
'For Dame Sister Mary Leo, An Award With a Visible Difference', *New Zealand Woman's Weekly*, 19 November 1979, pp. 59–60.
'Famous Footprints for City Landmark', *New Zealand Herald*, 19 February 1980.
'Singers Galaxy in Outstanding Operatic Feast', *New Zealand Herald*, 8 October 1980.
Bailey, Robin, 'Tribute to a Legend', *Auckland Star*, 8 October 1980.
'Stars' Teacher in Hospital', *New Zealand Herald*, 18 August 1981.
Saunders, L.C.M., 'Special Night at the Opera', *New Zealand Herald*, 16 September 1981.
'Singers Pay Tribute', *New Zealand Herald*, 2 November 1981.
'Stars Come Out to Honour Dame Sister Leo', *New Zealand Tablet*, 9 December 1981.
Shaw, Owen, ' "Singers' Friend" Initiated Scholarship', *New Zealand Herald*, 13 March 1982.
'Here Are the Seven Most Liked Kiwis', *Auckland Star*, 15 June 1982.
Morrison, Alastair, 'Dame Sister Mary Leo — Teacher', *New Zealand Times*, 26 December 1982.
'A Christmas Prayer', *Auckland Star*, 17 November 1983.
'On Road to Recovery', *New Zealand Herald*, 24 December 1983.
Brown, Cyril, 'The Magic of Mobil Song', Mobil Song Quest Programme, 1983.
'Cards Pay Own Tribute', *New Zealand Herald*, 4 January 1984.
'Good Wishes Overwhelm Nun', *Auckland Star*, 4 January 1984.
Brearley, David, 'The Dame Behind Dame Kiri', *The Australian*, 27 July 1984.
'Real Star May Not Be There', *New Zealand Herald*, 18 November 1986.
Ogier, Janine, 'Visit From Pupil a Real Tonic', *New Zealand Herald*, 12

November 1987.
Rapson, Bevan, 'Tributes Flow for a "Tough Teacher" ', *New Zealand Herald*, 6 May 1989.
Reynolds, Ted, 'Dame Sister Mary Leo: The Enigma of a Famous Nun', *New Zealand Herald*, 6 May 1989.
Freer, Lyndsay, 'A Loving, Warm and Gifted Woman', *The Tablet*, 17 May 1989, p. 2.
Clausen, Lois, 'Dame Sister Mary Leo, DBE 1895–1989', *Institute of Registered Music Teachers of New Zealand Journal*, No. 23, June 1989, p. 29.
'Unspoilt by Success', *New Zealandia*, July 1989, pp. 30–32.
Cooke, Alana Bolton, 'Stand Tall, Don't Slouch — Sing!', *New Zealand Woman's Weekly*, 25 October 1993, pp. 44–45.

Tapes and videos

'Sister Mary Leo Talks to Owen Jensen', 1972, T902, Radio New Zealand Sound Archives.
'Sister Mary Leo Talks About Her Teaching', 1976, T1006, Radio New Zealand Sound Archives.
'Sr Mary Leo interviewed by Bill McCarthy for TVNZ', December 1981, T2678-2681, Radio New Zealand Sound Archives.
Reminiscences, Anthony Hollows.
Requiem Mass, Catholic Cathedral Auckland, 8 May 1989.
'Nothing Less Than One's Best', Radio New Zealand, 16 June 1989.
Items from the New Zealand Television Archive: 'This Day', 13 September 1972; 'Kaleidoscope', 1 April 1977; 'Top Half', 24 November 1983; 'Top Half', 8 July 1985; 'Holmes', 5 May 1989; 'Top Half', 5 May 1989; 'Network News', 5 May 1989; 'Network News', 8 May 1989.

Unpublished

Clausen, Lois, *An overview of religious women of the Federation of the Sisters of Mercy and their work as music educators in the four congregations of Auckland, Wellington, Christchurch and Dunedin from 1850 to 1980*, Research Essay, University of Canterbury, 1989.
Daily Attendance Registers, Onerahi School.
Scrapbooks of Angela Gorton née Shaw.
Scrapbooks of Patricia-Anne Cornish née Shaw.

B. Secondary sources: books

Abbott, Walter M. (ed), *The Documents of Vatican II*, New York, 1966.
A History of Onerahi District & School 1893–1993, Whangarei, 1993.
Attwater, Donald (ed.), *The Penguin Dictionary of Saints*, Harmondsworth, 1965.

SELECT BIBLIOGRAPHY 223

Ball, Ann, *A Litany of Mary*, Indiana, 1988.
Barr, J., *The City of Auckland New Zealand 1840–1920*, Auckland, 1922.
BNZ Waipukurau, A Century of Service, 1878–1978, Wellington, 1978.
Bolster, Angela M., *Catherine McAuley: Venerable for Mercy*, Dublin, 1990.
Brusey, Phyllis, *Ring Down the Curtain*, Wellington, 1973.
Bryder, Linda, *Below the Magic Mountain: A Social History of Tuberculosis in Twentieth Century Britain*, Oxford, 1988.
Catholic Encyclopedia, Vol. 9, New York, 1910.
de Joux, Oswald, *St Leo's Convent School, Devonport*, Auckland, 1989.
Delany, Veronica, *Gracious is the Time*, Auckland, 1950.
Doscher, Barbara M., *The Functional Unity of the Singing Voice*, New York, 1988.
Fatima in Lucia's Own Words, Postulation Centre, Fatima, Portugal, 1989.
Fingleton, David, *Kiri Te Kanawa: A Biography*, London, 1982.
Gray, Margaret, *Abbott's Ford: A History of Waipawa*, Waipawa, 1989.
Harris, Norman & Te Kanawa, Kiri, *Music and a Maori Girl*, Wellington, 1966.
Hetherington, John, *Melba: A Biography*, London, 1967.
Hilgard, Ernest R., *Introduction to Psychology*, New York, 1990.
Huata, Awatere, Donna, *My Journey*, Seaview Press, 1996.
Jillett, David, *Malvina, A Biography of Dame Malvina Major*, Auckland, 1995.
Manén, Lucie, *Bel Canto: The Teaching of the Classical Italian Song-Schools, Its Decline and Restoration*, Oxford, 1987.
Marchesi, Blanche, *Singer's Pilgrimage*, New York, 1978.
Miller, Richard, *The Structure of Singing: System and Art in Vocal Technique*, New York, 1986.
Munro, Jessie, *The Story of Suzanne Aubert*, Auckland, 1996.
Murphy, Agnes G., *Melba: A Biography*, New York, 1977.
Musgrove, S. (ed.), *The Hundred of Devonport: A Centennial History*, Devonport, 1986.
Notable New Zealanders: The Pictorial Who's Who, Auckland, 1979.
O'Brien, Ven. Richard Baptist, *Life of Catherine McAuley*, New York, [1862].
O'Regan, Pauline, *A Changing Order*, Wellington, 1986.
Power, Sister Anne Marie, *Sisters of St Joseph of the Sacred Heart: New Zealand Story, 1883–1983*, Auckland, 1983.
Proust, A.J. (ed.), *History of Tuberculosis in Australia, New Zealand and Papua New Guinea*, Canberra, 1991.
Reed, A.W., *Auckland City of the Seas*, Wellington, 1955.
Sadie, Stanley (ed.), *The New Grove Dictionary of Music & Musicians*, Vol. 7, London, 1980.
Sadie, Stanley (ed.), *The New Grove Dictionary of Opera*, Vol. 3, London, 1992.
St Andrew's Parish Centennial Souvenir Booklet 1865–1965, Waipukurau St Andrew's Parish, [1965].
St Joseph's Convent School Grey Lynn Centennial 1984.

The Seventy-fifth Anniversary of the Landing in New Zealand of the Sisters of Mercy 1850–1925, Auckland, [1925].

Simpson, Adrienne, *Opera's Farthest Frontier: A History of Professional Opera in New Zealand*, Auckland, 1996.

Simpson, Adrienne & Downes, Peter, *Southern Voices: International Opera Singers of New Zealand*, Auckland, 1992.

Smith, F.B., *The Retreat of Tuberculosis 1850–1950*, London, 1988.

Stanley, A.O. (ed.), *Waipukurau District High School, 1866–1956, Jubilee Souvenir*, [Waipukurau, 1956].

Tolerton, Jane, *Convent Girls*, Auckland, 1994.

Vennard, William, *Singing: The Mechanism and the Technique*, New York, 1967.

Waipukurau Hospital Centennial Souvenir Booklet 1879–1979, [Waipukurau, 1979].

Walsh, Thomas, *An Illustrated Story of Devonport and the Old North Shore from 1841–1924*, Auckland, 1974.

Walsh, William Thomas, *Our Lady of Fatima*, New York, 1954.

Who's Who in New Zealand, Wellington, 1978.

Wordsworth, Jane, *Leading Ladies*, Wellington, 1979.

Index

Page numbers in italics indicate illustrations.

Acquinas, Sister Mary *182*
Adamo, Julianne, née Picot 122
Ainsley, (Madame) Irene (Ivy) 62, 63, 152, *153*
Alcock, Marie 66
Alderson, C. *139*
Anastasia, Sister Mary *182*
Anderson, Inness, *see also* Lovett, Inness 79
Anderson, Lynn 189
Anita, Sister Mary *182*
Appleby, J. *139*
Armstrong, Florrie, née Ormiston *30*
Armstrong, Nellie, *see* Melba, Nellie 152
Aronsten, Joan and Max 128
Auckland competitions 71, 84-86, 88, 90, 93, 131 183
Auckland Grand Opera Society 123, 145, 175, 190, 191, 203, 204
Auckland Light Opera Company 92, 94
Austin, Mother 72
Austin, Zita, later Outtrim, Zita 71, 73, 78, 80, 81
Awatere, Donna 132, 184, 206

Baars, Rita 200
Barker, Mr R. 86
Battersby, M. *139*
Begg, Heather 96, 102, 126, 130, *132*, 133, 141, 146, 164, 173, *177*, 191, 196, 198
Bender, L. *139*
Beren, S. *139*
Black, D. *139*
Blade, Raewyn *119*, 146
Boak, Alison *162*
Bolton, Alana, *see also* Cooke, Alana *119*
Bosworth, Ina 62, 73
Bowden, Roy 97, 177
Boylan, Alice, née Cannell 15, 20, 42
Braidwood, Antonia 66, 82, 84, 94
Briggs, Betty 66
Brodeur, S. *139*
Browne, Bishop Denis 200
Browne, Sister Margaret, formerly Sister Mary de Porres 145-150
Burns, Sister Mary Peter 43
Butt-Rumford, Clara 64
Bryers, Rhonda 189
Byers, Sister Mary Natalie 102
Cannell, Agnes, *see also* Niccol, Agnes 15
Cannell, Alice, *see also* Boylan, Alice 15

Cannell, Catherine, *see also* Cunningham, Catherine 15
Cannell, Florence 15
Cannell, Genevieve Cecilia, later Sister Mary Wilfred 15, 43
Cannell, Frances, *see also* Howard, Frances 15
Cannell, Mary Ann, née Gorrod 14, 15
Cannell, William Thomas 15
Cantlon, Lynne 112, 113, 115, *119*, *121*, 124, 130, *132*, 133, 147, *162*, *177*, 203, 206
Carmel, Mother 170
Carroll, Carmel 204
Carroll, Marie 70
Carter, Winifred 73
Cavalier, Sister Cecilia 23
Chambers, Pauline *119*
Chambers, Penelope 174
Chapman, Jacqueline *119*, *142*, 206
Chapman, Rae *119*, *162*
Churchill, M. *139*
Clement, Sister Mary *182*
Cochrane, Joan 94, 96, 206
Cole, Arthur 66
Cooke, Alana, *see also* Bolton, Alana 99
Cooke, Winifrede 82
Cornish, Ken 122, 199
Cornish, Patricia-Anne, *see* Shaw, Patricia-Anne
Crabtree, Joy 178, 184, 204
Croul, Pettine-Ann 113, 126-128, 130, *132*, 133, *160*, 191
Cryer, Max 141
Cumming, Rev. John *98*
Cunningham, Catherine née Cannell 15

dal Monte, Toti 90
Dalley, Beryl 94, *132*
Dallow, Ailsa 66
Dame Sister Mary Leo Scholarship 190-192, 197, 201, 203-205
Damian, Sister Mary *182*
Davis, Adrienne *119*, *121*, 150
Davis, Noeline 66
Dawe, Colleen *121*
de los Angeles, Victoria 105-107
Delany, Sister Veronica 63, *106*, 112, 171, 172, 181, 193
Demyan, Sherry 146
di Stefano, Guiseppe 108
Ding, S. *139*

Dobbs, Mattiwilda 108
Doig, Christopher 134
Donnell, Doreen 183
Doran, Colleen 82, 94
Drummond family *30*
Drysdale, Janet *70*
Dunn, Elizabeth 118
Dunn, L. *139*
Dwyer, Sister Mary Philomena 65

Eddleston, P. *139*
Edwards, Betty *70*
Edwards, Judith 96, 102, 206

Fabian, Sister Mary *182*
Farquhar, David 115
Farry, J. *139*
Finlinson, Maureen 69, 80
Fischer, Madame 62
Fletcher, Maureen, later Gordon, Maureen 69, 80, 82, 84, 94, 206
Foley, Mary *70*
Foley, Mina 11, 69, 71, 80, 82, 84-92, 94-96, 107, 109, 112, 126, 132, 172, 185-187, 189-191, 193, 203, 206
Fraser, Rhona 192, 203
Freer, Lyndsay, *see also* Kearns, Lyndsay *121*, 122, *142*, *164*, *177*, 185, 200
Fryer, Heather *139*, 197

Garcia, Manuel (1775-1832) 152
Garcia, Manuel (1805-1906) 152
Geraghty, Rita 120, 147
Germain, John *93*
Gibb, Laurette *119*, *142*, *162*
Gordon, Ann (Alexandra) 108, *119*, *121*, 131, 133, 167
Gordon, Maureen, *see also* Fletcher, Maureen 74, 78
Gordon Vivienne, née Adams 101
Gorrod, Mary Ann, *see* Cannell, Mary Ann
Graham, Sister Mary Patricia (formerly Sister Mary Philomena) 72, 118
Grey Lynn Convent School, *see* St Joseph's School 32

Hadden, Fay 183
Hall, Carmel *66*
Hall, Maureen *66*
Hall, Maurice *66*
Hallett, Christine, née Treseder 141
Hannaford, Freda *66*
Hannaford, Patricia *66*
Hannaford, Shirley 82
Harker, Eileen 37
Harker, Joan, later Crompton, Joan 36-39
Harker, Leslie 37, 39
Harker, Marjory (Bobs) 37, 39

Harker, Peter 37
Harper, Valerie 80
Harrop, Catherine *119*, *162*
Hawkes, Betty, later Pullman, Betty 25
Heald, Anna 94
Heffernan, Janette *164*
Hellawell, Elisabeth 80, 82, 94, 95, 112, *121*, 126, *132*, 133, 203, 206
Hempleman, Margaret *121*
Henson, Mother Mary Benignus 46, 48, 49
Herbert, John *66*
Hewitt, Cheryll 206
Hickey, Carmel *66*
Higgins, Josephine 175, 176
Hodgetts, Ann *142*
Hoko, A. *139*
Hollows, Anthony 94, 97, 98, 118, 191
Hopkinson, Sister Mary Joan 118, 174, 193, 194, 196-198
Hotchin, Sister Mary Dora 102
House, Patricia 134, *177*, 183, 206
Houston, Michael 204
Howard, Frances, née Cannell 15
Hughes, Sister Mary Catherine 65
Hungerford, Val 185

Immaculata, Sister Mary *182*
Isbister, Val *121*
Isodore, Sister Mary *182*

Jackson, A. *139*
James, Audrey *70*
Jerome, Sister Mary *182*
John Court Memorial Aria 85, 86, 92, 93, 130, 131, 134, 183, 206
Johnson, Kathleen *94*, 120
Joseph, Sister Mary *182*

Karoly, Professor C. Moor 62
Kearney, Sister Fidelma 102
Kearns, Lyndsay, *see also* Freer, Lyndsay *119*, *162*
Kennaway, Joan 130, 206
Kenny, Mother Mary Josephine 46, 60
Kieran, Sister Mary *182*
King, Tracey 189, 195, 206
Knight, Daphne 67
Kraus, Lili 73, 107

Ladley, Sister Gabrielle Mary *106*
Laine, Cleo 141
Laurijssen, Marie Thérèse 146, 147, 206
Lee, Ella 107, 108, 130
Lemalu, Jonathan 205
Leo, (Dame) Sister Mary Leo, *see also* Niccol, Kathleen Agnes 11, 74, 90, 92-95, 113, 114, 169-175, 188-205; as a religious 12, 19, 20, 41-60, 89, 97, 103-106, 136, 137, 144, 145,

147, 176-182, 185; as teacher 11, 12, 18-20, 23, 25-31, 33-38, 59-65, 67-73, 75-81, 83-89, 96-112, 115-117, 120-124, 126-129, 131-134, 138-140, 142, 151-168, 179, 180, 181, 183-189, 196; personal attributes 12, 77, 78, 116-119, 125, 130, 134, 135, 141, 143, 145-150, 176, 192, 195
Leonard, Sister Mary 182
Leydon, Sister Judith 201
Liston, Bishop J.M. 54, 89, 182
Loomb, Elizabeth *119*, *121*
Loomb, Katie 174
Lovett, Inness, later Anderson, Inness 66, 69, 80, 84
Lunn, Janice *119*
Lynch, B. *139*

McAuley, Sister Mary Catherine 44, 189
McGarry, Sister Mary Xaveria, see also Xavier, Sister Francis 63, *64*
McIntyre, Donald 191
McKenzie, Frances 70
Mackie, Marianne, née Bowden 123, 124
McLeod, S. *139*
Maconaghie, Fiona 204
McRae, Leonie 99
Maher, Mother Cecilia 44, 55, 61, 83
Major, (Dame) Malvina 11, 100, *119*, 121, 126-135, 141, *162*, 167, *177*, 178, 188, 190, 191, 206
Malatrasi, Rina 189
Malloy, Louise 122, 134, *142*, 183
Marchesi, Mathilde 62, 152, 153
Marianne Mathy Scholarship 189, 203, 204
Marinovich, T. *139*
Markham, Kathleen, later Sister Kathleen 70
Marrayat, L. *139*
Mathy, Marianne, see Marianne Mathy Scholarship
Matteucci, Juan 191
Meima, I. *139*
Melba, (Dame) Nellie 62, 64, 152
Melbourne *Sun* Aria 11, 85, 127-131, 133, 183
Menehira, M. *139*
Metcalfe, Glenese 192
Michael, Sister Mary 182
Millar, Hazel, later Millar-Boyd, Hazel 113, *119*
Miller, Richard 154
Mobil Song Quest 11, 95, 96, 131, 134, 183, 199, 206
Morete, Sunny 195
Morris, Marie, see also O'Leary, Marie 121, 197
Munro, Donald 90

Negus, Joan 66, 69, 71, 73, 80
New Zealand Opera Company 94, 105, 107, 120

Niccol, Agnes, née Cannell 15, 16-18, 20, 22, 23, 29, 46, 58, 59, 74, *75*, 109
Niccol, Annie, née Atkins 14
Niccol, Henry 12, 13
Niccol, Henry Malcolm 14, 16, 21, 22, 29, 47-49, 74
Niccol, Jessie Sarita, see also O'Sullivan, Jessie 12, 16, 17, 19, 20, 21, 23, *24*, 32, 40-43, 46, 48, 54, 58, 74
Niccol, John Henry (Jack) 16, 19, 22, 24, 31, 32, 43, 58
Niccol, Kathleen Agnes, see also Leo, (Dame) Sister Mary 12-51, 146, 152, 170
Niccol, Malcolm 13, 14, 49, 97
Niccol, Ysabel Alice (Belle) 16, 19, 20, *24*, 32, 41, 43, 46, 58, 59, 74
Noble, Jo 126

O'Brien, Mary 92, *93*, 96, 107, 108, 113, 115, *121*, 126, 206
Ockelford, K. *139*
O'Donnell, Mother Mary Genevieve 62
O'Leary, G. *139*
O'Leary, Marie, see also Morris, Marie *119*, *121*
Ormiston, Edward 25, 31
Ormiston, Florence 25
Ormiston, Mrs 30
Ormiston, Chris 30
O'Sullivan, James Bruce 74
O'Sullivan, Jessie 39
O'Sullivan, Jessie Sarita, née Niccol 12, 14, 19, 40, 42, 47, 48, 54, 58, 60, 61, 63, 68, 74, 75, 171, 172, 199, 200
O'Sullivan, Kathleen 74
O'Sullivan, Margaret 74, 171
O'Sullivan, Marie 74

Palmai, Monique *121*
Park, Desmond 137, 148
Park, Sister Mary Vianney 63
Parkes, Cecilia, née Connelly 29, 32
Paterson, Molly, see Wilson, Molly 38
Paterson, Sister Mary Majella 72, 103, *106*
Payne, Daphne *121*
Pearson, L. *139*
Perpetua, Sister Mary 182
Peterwood, George 29
Picot, Mary 122
Pompallier, Bishop Jean Baptiste 45
Price, Patricia 66, 82, 113, *119*, *121*, *132*, 134, *142*, 206

Rasmussen, Anne *103*, 113, 134, *135*, 147, 168, 206
Raymond, Cuthbert 38
Raymond, John 38
Reade, Philippa 203, 204
Reardon, Kathleen 66, 132

Reardon, Robina 123, 125, 173, *174*, 187, 196, 197, 204
Redstone, Gillian, *see also* Trott, Gillian 119, *121*, 133, *135*
Reed, Barbara 38
Reed, Dr James Lewis 38
Rhodes, Ted 192, 204
Riedel, Deborah 204
Rita, Sister Mary *182*
Robertson, James 131, 193
Robinson, Marie 94, 107, 146, 147, *177*, 206
Robinson, (Sir) Dove-Myer 144, 189, 191
Roche, Collene, née Dawe 120
Rodan, Ivy 206
Rogers, L. *139*
Rosaria, Sister Mary *182*
Rosza, Vera 189
Rowe, L. *139*
Rush, Sally *119*
Rutland, Harold 112

St Joseph's School, Grey Lynn, also known as Surrey Hills Convent School 22, 32, 58
St Leo's Convent School, Devonport 17-19, 50
St Mary's Convent, Auckland 43-46, 51, 53, 54, 63, 64, 75, 81, 83, 89, 115, 129, 142, 145, 169, 189, 195, 197, 198, 200
St Mary's College, Auckland 45, 46, 62, 64-73, 76-84, 86, 87, 88, 92, 94, 95, 96, 99, 105, 107, 109, 110, 111-113, 114, 127, 129, 130, 132, 133, 138, 143, 144, 172, 179, 184; choir 67, 68, 80, 82, 84, 90, 91, 99, 102, 112, 113, 119, 138-144, 180, 181
St Mary's School of Music 69, 71-73, 78, 80, 81, 83, 88, 90, 91, 98-101, 105, 112, 113, 118, 120, 130, 132, 137, 138, 141, 143, 144, 177, 183-185, 190, 191
Saunders, L.C.M. (Lin) 112, 138, 190, 191, 203
Schipa, Tito 85
Schwarzkopf, Elizabeth 108, 130
Seagar, Beatrice *70*
Shallue, Sister Muriel, formerly Patrick, Sister Mary 72, 103, 200
Shannahan, Lois *113*
Shaw, Angela 94, 96, 107, 126, 206
Shaw, Patricia-Anne 122, 124, 125, *142*, 183, 199, 200, 206
Shearer, Linda 183
Shewan, L. *139*
Short, Gordon 90
Simm, Margaret *70*, 80
Sisters of Mercy 12, 18, 19, 44, 50, 55, 57, 60-62, 77, 92, 97, 147
Sisters of Mercy, Auckland 32, 43-46, 49-51, 53, 55, 56, 61, 72, 75, 77, 81-83, 89, 105, 106, 117, 125, 135-137, 144, 171, 180-182, 200
Smith, Janice *121*

Smith, Susan *142*
Smythe, Sister Laurencia 22
Souzay, Gerard 107
Stanfield, A. *139*
Stauber, Madame Greta 92
Stead, R. *139*
Stone, Wynne *70*
Stott, Ann 97, *98*, 124, 201
Stott, Len *98*
Streich, Rita 108, 134
Sutherland, (Dame) Joan 146, 155, 168, 173
Sydney *Sun* Aria 97, 127, 128, 130, 131, 133, 183

Tamihere, R. *139*
Tatana, Hannah 113, *119*, *121*, 126-129, *132*, 133-134, *177*, 206
Te Kanawa, (Dame) Kiri 11, 99, *119*, *121*, *129*, 130-134, 137, 142, 146, 148, *162*, 168, 171-178, 188, 193, 196, 197, 199, 204, 206
Theresa, Sister 61
Thurlow, J. *139*
Tirbutt, Irene 178, 183, 184
Trott, Gillian, née Redstone 206
Tuapawa, Sharon 184, 189
Turnock, T. *139*
Twohill, Margaret *70*

Vennard, William 153
von Dadelszen, Gretchen *35*

Waite, Nicola 189, 191, 203, 206
Walker, Eileen, née Toothill 72
Walsh, Rev. Ernie *98*
Waugh, June *66*
Weber, K. *139*
Welesten, Else 150
Whelch, Edna 35
Whelch, Eileen 35
White, Doris 69, *70*
White, Patricia 71
Wilbraham, Leah *121*
Wilson, Eva 32, 36
Wilson, Frances 94, *119*, 203
Wilson, Leslie 32, 35, 36,
Wilson, Molly, later Paterson, Molly 33, 35, 38
Wilson, Nancy 33-35
Winterburn, Diane *119*, 132
Wright, Fiona *121*, *162*
Wright, Patricia 125, 126, *139*, 189, 190, 206

Xaveria, Sister Mary, later Xavier, Sister Francis McGarry 46, 58, 61, 63-64, 67, 72, 74-76, 87, *93*, *95*, *106*, 110, 111, *121*, 125, 133, *162*, 184, 185, 203

Young, Anne Marabini 184